FRONTPAGE 2000

in easy steps

MICHAEL PRICE

COMPUTER STEP

In easy steps is an imprint of Computer Step
Southfield Road . Southam
Warwickshire CV47 0FB . England

http://www.ineasysteps.com

Copyright © 1999–2001 by Computer Step. All rights reserved. No part of this book may be reproduced or transmitted in any form or by any means, electronic or mechanical, including photocopying, recording, or by any information storage or retrieval system, without prior written permission from the publisher.

Notice of Liability
Every effort has been made to ensure that this book contains accurate and current information. However, Computer Step and the author shall not be liable for any loss or damage suffered by readers as a result of any information contained herein.

Trademarks
Microsoft® and Windows® are registered trademarks of Microsoft Corporation. All other trademarks are acknowledged as belonging to their respective companies.

Printed and bound in the United Kingdom

ISBN 1-84078-042-8

Table Of Contents

1 Introducing FrontPage 2000   7

The Internet	8
Internet access	9
Web space	10
Your Web site address	12
FrontPage 2000	13
FrontPage packages	14
Requirements	15
Features of FrontPage	16
FrontPage Webs	18
Building your Web site	19
FrontPage views	20
Installing FrontPage 2000	21

2 Using FrontPage 2000   23

Starting out	24
The FrontPage tutorial	25
Creating your first Web site	26
Make a FrontPage Web	27
Navigation view	28
Page titles and names	29
Building the home page	30
Adding a link	32
Adding an animated picture	33
Arranging the items	34
Viewing the page	35
Previewing the page	36
Closing down	37

3 Adding to your Web   39

Inserting plain text	40
Adding formatted text	42
Adding files to your Web	44
Wrapping up images	46
A page of photographs	48

Display timings	49
Thumbnail images	50
Useful links	51
Creating text hyperlinks	52
Verified hyperlinks	54

4 Enhancing the Web — 55

Formatting headings	56
Connecting pages	58
Bookmarks	60
Shared borders	61
Navigation bars	62
Graphical themes	64
Customising the theme	66
Arranging files and folders	68
Adding a new page	70

5 Finalise the Web — 71

Requesting feedback	72
View page	74
Which browser?	75
View the Web	76
Modify text	78
Check spelling	80
Completing tasks	82
Web reports	84
Backup	86

6 Publishing the Web — 87

Ways to publish	88
ISP and FTP	89
Try the form	91
Select a WPP	92
ISP with WPP and HTTP	93
Using Hypermart	94
Form results	96
Using banners	97
Full function WPP	99
Selective publishing	100

7 Promoting the Web — 101

Will you be seen?	102
Your ISP or WPP	103
Announcement	104
Be listed by search sites	105
Register your site	106
Meta-variables tags	108
Registration services	110
Search sites	112
Rating your Web site	113
Apply the rating	114

8 Bells and whistles — 115

Counting on success	116
Add a time stamp	118
Horizontal lines	120
Background sound	121
List effects	122
Display form results	124
Using colour	126
Print a page	128
Temporary files	130

9 Upgrading Webs — 131

Import the Web	132
Analyse the Web	134
Upgrade the Web	136
Frames page	138
The main page	140
No frames	142
Guest book	143

10 Web designs — 145

Web page size	146
Web structures	148
Create the parent	149
Create subwebs	150
Set up the parent Web	151

Preview the Webs	152
Publish the Webs	153
Visiting subwebs	154
Edit the Web server	156
Switching sites	158

11 Tables, images and forms — 159

Creating tables	160
Draw a table	162
Convert text to table	163
Tables within tables	164
Image maps	165
Hotspots	166
Set up a discussion group	168
Discussion group Web	170
Web conversations	172

12 Sources of help — 173

Local help	174
Web help	175
The Download Catalogue	176
Install an add-in	177
Using J-Bots	178
More info from MS	179
FrontPage Bulletin	180
FrontPage Frenzy.	182
Design guides	183
VBA macros	184
Web Workshop	186

Index — 187

Introducing FrontPage 2000

FrontPage 2000 allows you to create and manage Web sites for personal or business use. This chapter will introduce the use of Web space, discuss the features of FrontPage 2000 that help you build and use Web sites and show you how to install the software.

Covers

The Internet | 8

Internet access | 9

Web space | 10

Your Web site address | 12

FrontPage 2000 | 13

FrontPage packages | 14

Requirements | 15

Features of FrontPage | 16

FrontPage Webs | 18

Building your Web site | 19

FrontPage views | 20

Installing FrontPage 2000 | 21

Chapter One

The Internet

> **HOT TIP:** Send and receive documents, e-mails, data, device drivers, images or sounds, to a Web server or to another user.

You can use the Internet in many different ways. At its simplest, it is a mechanism for exchanging mail with anyone else who has direct or indirect access to the Internet.

> **HOT TIP:** A Web page is defined using the HTML markup language. The page can contain many elements, including text, pictures, sound and video.

To make this easier, the Internet has evolved a format for publishing information, known as the Web page. The Internet provides access to millions of Web pages, stored on thousands of computers (Web servers). The Web pages are linked together in groups known as Web sites. Each Web site has a unique address (Universal Resource Locator or URL) that allows you to access the primary home or welcome page for the site. Web pages usually refer to other Web pages with relevant, related contents.

> **DON'T FORGET:** Use the search engines on the Internet to look for Web sites and Web pages by content, then follow links to other pages and other sites.

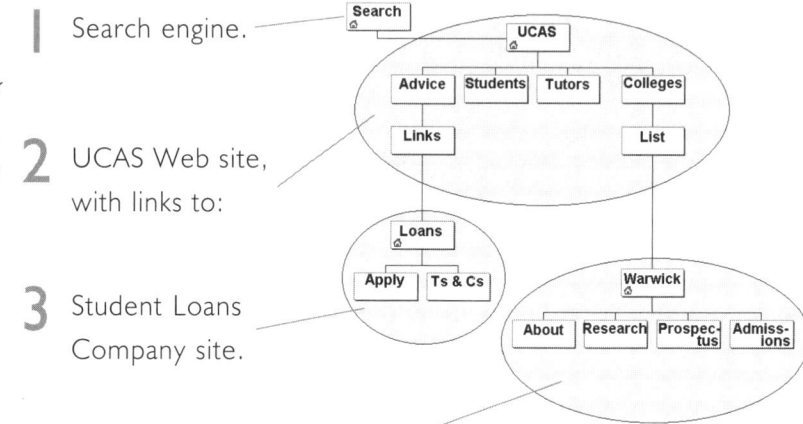

1. Search engine.

2. UCAS Web site, with links to:

3. Student Loans Company site.

4. University of Warwick.

Internet access

To surf the Internet, you need an account with an Internet service provider (ISP) and the hardware and software to connect to the Internet.

You can create a dialup connection between your PC and the Internet, using a modem and a telephone line. You make the connection when you need to transfer mail or to access information. The connection exists just for the period of the Internet session. The link is made to the Web server belonging to your ISP, but once you have dialled in, you can run Internet navigation software, such as Netscape or Internet Explorer, to view documents.

This is the most economical method for less frequent usage, since the set up costs for the modem and the telephone line rental are relatively low, and you pay only for the times when your connection is active. The telephone line is available for other purposes such as fax or voice when you are not using the Internet. You can minimise the time you spend connected, if you increase the capacity of the dialup connection by choosing a higher speed modem (up to 56 Kbps), or by switching to the digital ISDN type of connection (for 64 Kbps or 128 Kbps).

The best choice of connection depends on the way you use the Internet, but it is usually dialup for home and small offices, or leased line for businesses.

Telephone system

User PC

Modem or Router

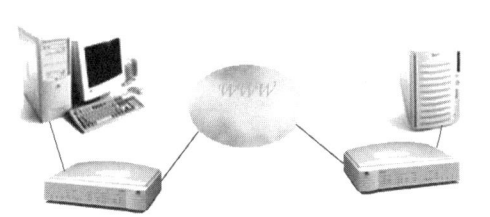

ISP Web server

Dialup or Leased line

For higher rates, or when you want to make your data directly accessible from the Internet, you need a leased line. This provides a dedicated connection that is permanently available. The capacity of the line (the bandwidth) can be chosen, and ranges from 64 Kbps to 2 Mbps or more. The leased line can be rented on a fixed fee, based on the capacity, or charged by usage – the amount of data sent over the line.

ASDL is now becoming available, as a high speed alternative to ISDN or leased line connections.

Web space

You can create and manage your own Web site, and be part of the information resource provided on the Internet.

You don't need a Web site to browse the Internet and search for information, but having your own Web site does allow you to make your own contribution to the Internet. You may want a personal Home page, where you can store links to other Web sites and Web pages that you often want to visit. You can add information to this page or add additional pages, to share with other users on the Internet.

If you have programs, pictures or other data that you would like to share, you can also add these. Soon your Home page will develop into a Web site in its own right, that other users will enjoy visiting.

Personal Web space is often used to gain experience with the Internet, but it can also be used to support your business or service.

You can include more features such as a hit counter to record visits and a guest book to record comments. If you are in business of any type, you can use your Web site to inform others about your goods and services, and give them the opportunity to define their requirements and place their orders.

A typical home page will contain:

You may also find adverts, banners and popup windows – to qualify the site for "free" Web resources.

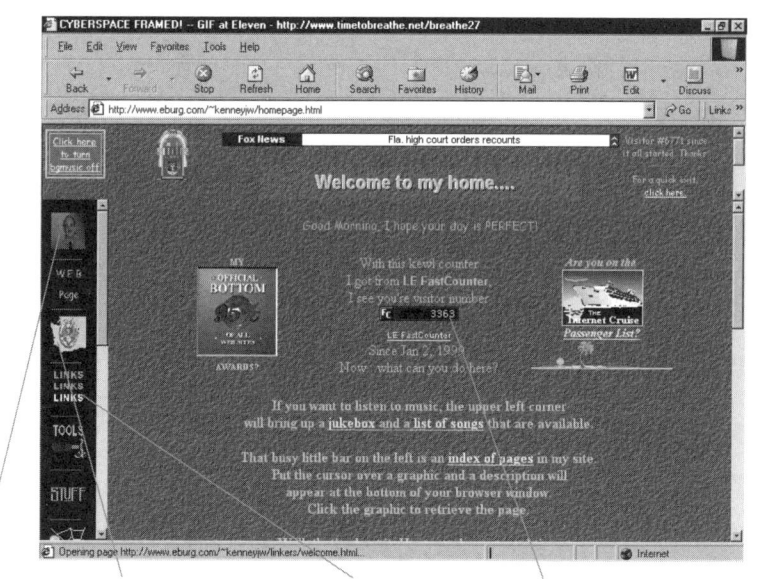

Data about the author   Information about the area   Links to other Web sites   Visits Counter

...cont'd

> **HOT TIP**
> You can find extra free Web space, but using this means that your Web site must carry various types of adverts and banners.

The disk storage or Web space occupied by the Web site on the server may be provided by the Internet Service Provider. Most ISPs include 5 MB or 10 MB of Web space free, when you subscribe to their Internet connection service. This is sufficient for personal use, but the bigger or more complex your Web site, the more Web space you will require, so you may need to purchase additional capacity.

For individuals and smaller businesses starting out on the Internet, the ISP Web servers provide all the necessary functions.

If your ISP does not provide space, or if you have a larger business need, you may choose one of the Web hosting services with Web space and connection functions. There are also Web Presence Providers (WPPs), who specialise in Web hosting. The actual connection is provided by your ISP.

Microsoft provides lists of Internet service providers, for personal, small business and corporate users. You can find the latest versions of the lists at:

http://www.microsoft.com/uk/NEXTSTEPS/isp.htm

> **HOT TIP**
> For more advanced corporate Web sites requiring larger space, dedicated servers may be required. These will be managed at a data centre, with direct highspeed access to the Internet.

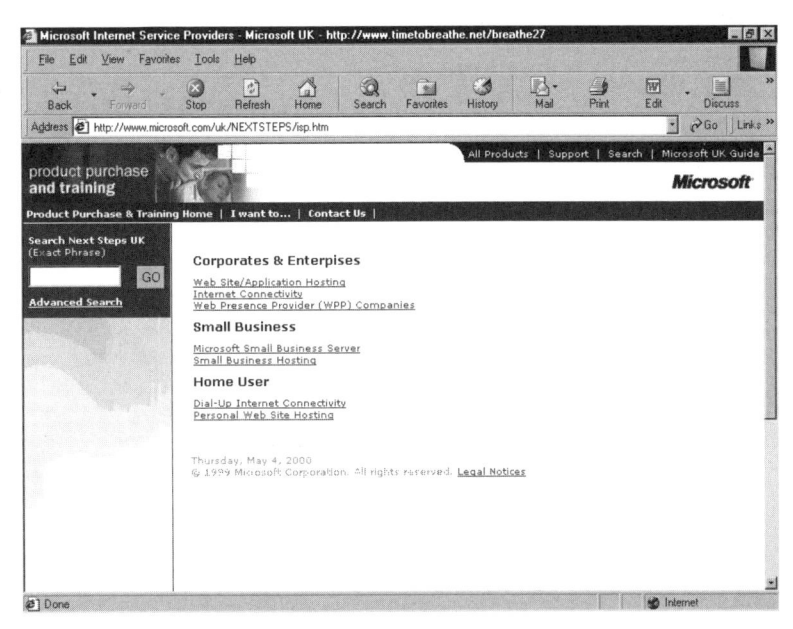

1. Introducing FrontPage 2000 | 11

Your Web site address

The form that your Web site address (URL) takes will depend on the type of ISP account that you use, and the way in which you acquire your Web space.

The Web space will be identified by a server or network domain name, a Web space folder name and a Web page name.

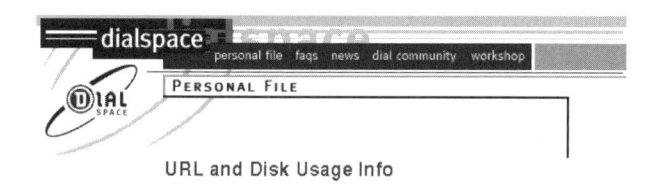

URL and Disk Usage Info

For example, if you use a Dial Pipex ISP account, your Web space would have URLs of the form:

http://dialspace.dial.pipex.com/town/plaza/acctid/

Server name   Web space folder   User ID

Web space is grouped to put the users of similar types in a "community" to make it easier to locate sites of possible interest.

The e-mail alias for the account is used to construct a short form synonym for the URL that does not rely on knowing the location of the Web space:

http://www.alias.dial.pipex.com/

Some ISPs allow you to choose an account name which becomes part of the server address. The Web site for an account called Queensmead on the Freeserve ISP would have this URL:

http://www.queeensmead.freeserve.co.uk

Larger organisations would have a dedicated server and full time access to the Internet, and register a domain name for the server, such as:

mycompany.com

However, for an annual fee of around $35 you can register your own virtual domain name for Web space hosted by a WPP. This would give you a URL such as:

http://www.queensmead.com

With this facility, size no longer matters and even the smallest company can operate over the Internet on equal terms with large corporations.

FrontPage 2000

FrontPage has the flexibility of a simple HTML editor, with the professional finish you'd expect from a bespoke design service.

FrontPage 2000 allows you to design and build Web pages and Web sites that look professional and include all the functions and features you want, without you having to deal with all the intrinsic details of the underlying HTML code. It also provides help in getting the Web pages and data files from your system to your Web space on the Internet, or onto your network server if you are designing an Intranet site.

FrontPage is not just for the Internet – it can be used to publish pages on your local area network.

FrontPage 2000 lets you share the task of creating and maintaining your Web site with other members of your group.

FrontPage 2000 is a tool for both Web site creation and Web site management. With it, you can make sure that there is a consistent style and appearance applied to every page. It does not restrict you to the features it offers. You can add and change items using native HTML codes and you can incorporate advanced Web technologies. It gives you full control over the page, and you can position the items exactly where you want them.

When you have created your Web site, FrontPage 2000 allows you to set up and maintain it as a unit. You can monitor the status of your site, and apply updates and changes. If you are a member of a workgroup, you can collaborate with other members who are also updating or extending the Web site.

Because FrontPage 2000 was designed as a part of Office 2000, you will find that the processes and procedures are familiar, and you can easily share documents and data with the other applications in Office 2000.

FrontPage packages

You can choose the FrontPage package that suits you best – Full or Upgrade, Stand-alone or in Office.

FrontPage 2000 is shipped as a component of the Office 2000 Premium Edition. It is also included in the Developer Edition, which is itself based on the Premium edition. The other editions of Office 2000 (Standard, Professional and Small Business) do not include FrontPage 2000.

The Office product and hence FrontPage can be purchased as a full package for installation on a new system, or as an upgrade package. This requires you to have a qualifying product already installed on your PC, for example Office 97.

If you do not plan to install the full Office 2000 product, you can obtain FrontPage 2000 as a product on its own CD-ROM. As with Office, there is a full version, or an upgrade for users of previous versions.

Microsoft made a trial offer for the USA and Canada. This trial was extended to Europe, via prelaunch sessions. The trial was based on pre-release code, and it expired 45 days after installation.

Whether stand-alone or part of Office, FrontPage 2000 uses the Windows Installer program. For operating systems that support the Installer shortcuts (Windows 98 and Windows 2000), the features are only copied at the first time of use. Most users spend 80% of their time with an application using just 20% of the features, and many features never get accessed, so this approach can avoid wasting disk space on unused items.

FrontPage also shares other features introduced in Office 2000, including the personalised menus and toolbars, and the self-repairing capability. This latter function means that when it starts up, FrontPage checks to see if any essential files are missing or invalid, and then reinstalls them from the server or CD. You will be asked for the CD if required, but otherwise the repair needs no intervention on your part.

Requirements

The minimum requirements are not large, but you'll find Webs place high demands on your system, especially if you like lots of animation and video effects.

To use FrontPage 2000, the following components are required (or recommended):

- PC with a 486 or higher processor (Pentium class processor preferred).

- Windows 95/98, Windows NT 4, Windows 2000 or Windows ME.

- 16 MB memory for Windows 95/98 or 32 MB memory for use with Windows NT/2000/ME (64 MB advised).

Internet Explorer 5 (or higher) isn't mandatory, but some features won't work without it on your system.

- 50-80 MB hard disk space, just for the FrontPage application (plus additional space for the Web sites and pages that you will be creating).

- CD-ROM or DVD-ROM drive.

- VGA display adapter (SVGA, 256 colour 800 x 600 or higher recommended).

Have copies of other Web browsers, if possible, so you can check out how your site looks from other users' viewpoints.

Internet access is needed to use Internet features, so you will need a modem, a cable modem or other mechanism for connecting to the Internet. You'll need a Web browser, but it doesn't have to be Internet Explorer, since FrontPage works with any browser.

There will be other components that you need, for Windows or for multimedia applications, including a mouse, printer, audio adapter, speakers, microphone, scanner or digital camera.

Features of FrontPage

There is an ongoing debate between Web designers, with the purists preferring HTML, and the pragmatists welcoming tools to relieve the tedium. FrontPage lets you choose the best of both these approaches.

FrontPage 2000 includes many features to make it easier for you to create and manage your Web site, without having to become involved at a programmer level. It allows you to control the way your pages look, using WYSIWYG (what you see is what you get).

Among the features of FrontPage 2000 are:

Pixel precise positioning and layering
This allows absolute and relative positioning to place page elements such as graphics and text exactly where needed, using layers to overlap elements.

Pre-designed themes
Themes provide ready-made settings for a consistent look across the page and the Web site. Add your own themes or customize existing themes to suit your preferences. Office applications also use FrontPage themes.

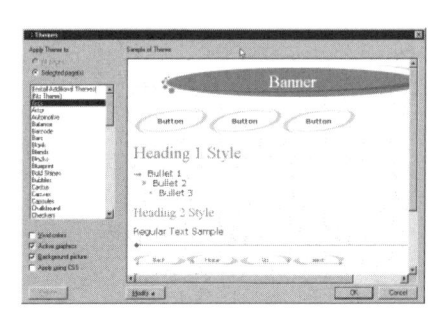

You don't need Office 2000 to use FrontPage 2000, but the two do work hand in hand, since Office applications support HTML as a native format.

Dynamic HTML
DHTML supports effects such as text and graphics animation and collapsible outlines, which work with Netscape Navigator as well as Internet Explorer.

Cascading Style Sheets
CSS apply consistent formatting, over a related set of pages, or across the whole Web site.

Office 2000 integration
FrontPage can integrate data from Office applications. For example, you can incorporate database queries directly into Web pages, and even update the database from Web pages.

...cont'd

HTML editing
Choose how you want your HTML code stored – what indents, tag colours and capitalization rules to follow – and FrontPage will apply these rules as the code is saved.

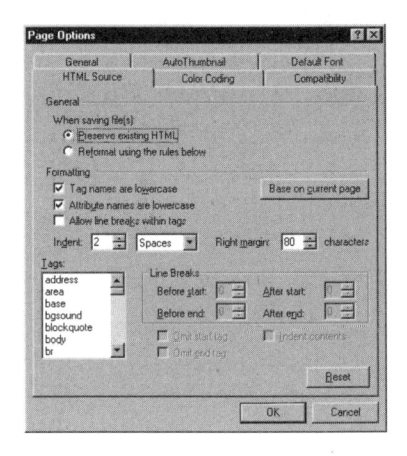

When you edit HTML and scripts from other sources, FrontPage respects the existing structure and layout.

FrontPage 2000 doesn't make gratuitous changes to existing code.

Other coding languages
As well as HTML, you can edit and debug JavaScript and Visual Basic script, and take advantage of pre-built Web components and snap-in tools and utilities.

Extend the features of FrontPage to support special applications such as online shopping and e-commerce.

Workgroup support
FrontPage 2000 is not just for individuals. You can work as a group to set up and maintain a shared Web site. As well as providing the various views, FrontPage eases the task of publishing by letting you flag pages or by sending changed pages only. Tasks such as document updates and hyperlink adjustments are automatically carried out.

Compatibility
You can pre-select which type and version of browser and which type of Web server your Web site will display with. You can also enable Server Extensions and other Web technologies. FrontPage will restrict features used in the site to those supported on the targeted systems.

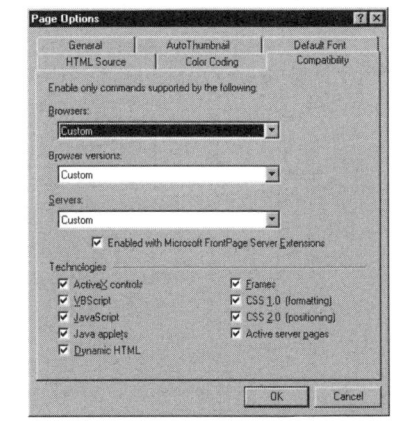

Restricting the Web features means missing out on some effects, but will increase your potential audience.

1. Introducing FrontPage 2000 | 17

FrontPage Webs

FrontPage manages Webs, which are Web sites that can be stored on your hard disk or on your Web server.

A FrontPage Web is like any Web site that consists of a home page plus the associated Web pages, graphics, documents, multimedia, and other files that it references. The FrontPage Web site also contains files that support the FrontPage-specific functions that allow the Web to be opened, copied, edited, and administered in FrontPage. The Web site is created in FrontPage and stored directly on a Web server or on the PC hard disk, for use on an Intranet or for later transfer to a Web server. The Web is stored in a folder or directory. There can be other folders nested within the main folder. The top level is known as the root or parent.

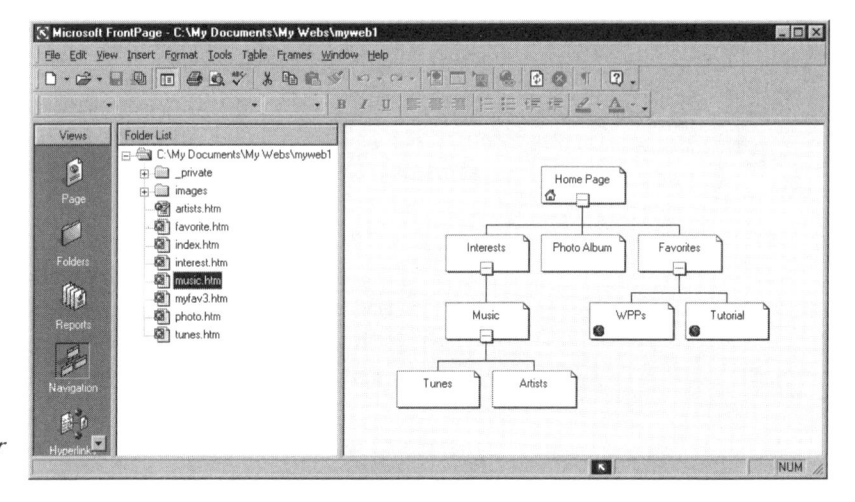

The Web server must support the FrontPage server extensions for you to use nested subwebs.

These subfolders of the root Web may themselves be complete FrontPage Webs. They are known as subwebs, and can have independent administration, authoring and browsing permissions. The subwebs can be used to organise the Web into separate sections for different departments or different groups of visitors. Searches and hyperlinks can be limited to the subweb. For example, you could create a business Web for all users, and include a private subweb for employees and another subweb for existing customers. FrontPage is installed with a root Web named RootWeb or C:\My Webs, ready for you to create Web pages and subwebs.

Building your Web site

FrontPage 2000 is designed to handle all the tasks, with assistance from your browser and FTP (file transfer program).

There are a number of stages involved in creating your Web site. The exact process will vary, depending on the level of complexity in your requirements, and you may need to iterate through some of the stages a number of times, until you achieve the effect you want. However, the basic stages are as follows:

Define the requirements:
Decide exactly what purpose you have in mind when you establish your Web site. This may be as simple as "gaining experience with the Internet", or you may have specific aims related to your hobbies or your business. Whatever the objectives, you should identify your aims and your goals before you start establishing the Web site.

Design the Web site:
The Web site will be a series of interconnecting Web pages, plus graphics, documents and other files and components. Choose one of the FrontPage templates to get started.

See also the links on page 183, for various style guides for Web sites, Web pages and HTML code.

Create the components:
Build the Web pages, collect data, prepare graphics, add links and put everything together to complete the site. Use your browser to preview the results.

Publish the Web:
Transfer the components to the Web server or LAN server that will host your Web site, and check that everything fits together the way it should, without, for example, relying on items that exist on your own hard disk. Access the site from a different PC, and try out the scenarios that your visitors will face, so that you can ensure that their visits will be effective.

You can publish updates of any size to your Web site. However, for major changes, you'd do better to repeat the whole process and build a replacement Web site.

Maintain the Web:
You must keep the information on the Web site up to date, respond appropriately to the feedback that you receive, and resolve and eliminate any problems or issues that arise.

FrontPage views

> **HOT TIP**
> *Previous versions of FrontPage had an Editor to create and edit Web pages, and an Explorer to build, test, publish and maintain Web sites.*

In FrontPage 2000, all the design and build tasks are carried out in the one application, with different views for the different stages and activities.

The vertical bar at the left of the FrontPage application window is the View Bar and contains the buttons that switch to different ways of looking at the information in your Web site.

Page view is the view you use for creating, editing, and previewing Web pages. It displays Web pages as they will appear in a Web browser.

Folders view shows how the content of the Web is organized, in the same style as Windows Explorer. You can create, delete, copy, and move folders in this view.

Reports view allows you to analyse the contents of your Web and calculate the total size of the files, show which files are not linked to any other files, identify slow or out of date pages, and group files by task or assignee.

Navigation view is used to create, display, print, and change the navigation structure of a Web. It includes a folder-like view, from which you can drag and drop pages into your site structure.

> **HOT TIP**
> *FrontPage wizards automatically generate some tasks, but you can add your own tasks and use the task view to manage them.*

Hyperlink view shows the status of the hyperlinks in your Web, and includes both internal and external hyperlinks. It indicates graphically those hyperlinks that have been verified and those that are broken.

Tasks view maintains a list of the tasks associated with the Web site that are required to complete or maintain the site.

Installing FrontPage 2000

You can add FrontPage 2000 to any PC with Windows 95, Windows 98, Windows NT, Windows 2000 or Windows ME. The usual way of installing FrontPage 2000 is as part of the Office 2000 installation. You won't have to select it specifically, since it is a part of the default setup.

To install Office 2000:

> **HOT TIP**
> *If you have disabled AutoRun, open the CD-ROM and double-click Setup.exe.*

1. Insert the Office 2000 program CD and the Windows Installer program starts up automatically.

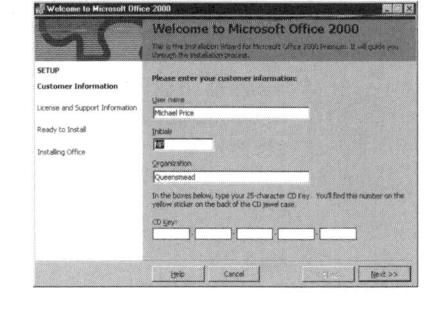

> **HOT TIP**
> *Note that FrontPage includes a set of files used to help build Web pages during the tutorial. See page 25.*

2. Add your personal details and enter the CD-key for validation.

3. Click to accept the terms and conditions.

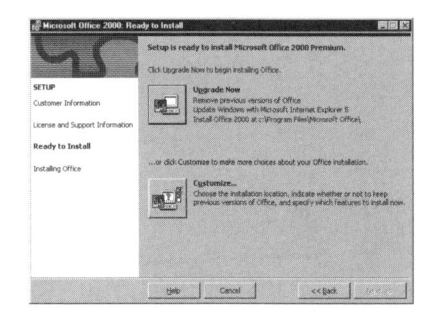

> **HOT TIP**
> *You follow similar steps to install the stand-alone FrontPage 2000 product from its own CD. It still uses the Windows Installer but has just the one application.*

4. Press Upgrade Now for the default Office 2000 setup, which includes FrontPage.

5. Press Customise to see details of the selections, and make any changes needed.

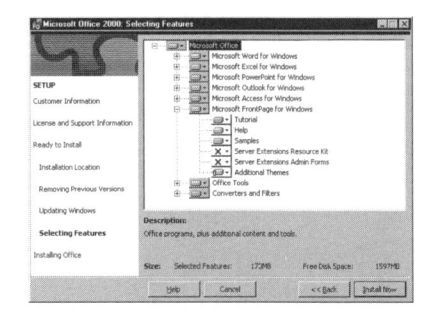

...cont'd

Autoplay does not run Setup if it finds that Office is already installed.

If you had left FrontPage out of your initial Office installation, or if you need to reinstall it for any reason, you can start up Windows Installer in maintenance mode.

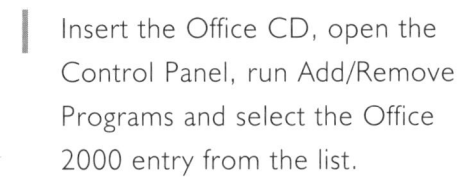

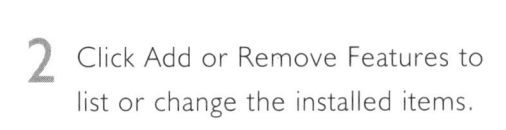

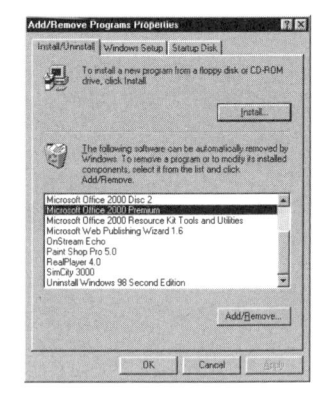

1. Insert the Office CD, open the Control Panel, run Add/Remove Programs and select the Office 2000 entry from the list.

Maintenance mode provides options to remove Office completely, modify the selection of features, or repair the installation by replacing any invalid files.

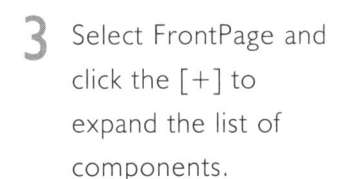

2. Click Add or Remove Features to list or change the installed items.

3. Select FrontPage and click the [+] to expand the list of components.

4. Click Update Now and the FrontPage components will be installed on the Start menu and the initial files copied.

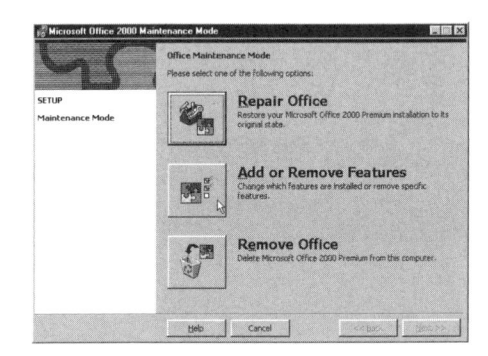

As with all the Office 2000 programs, you will need your setup CDs close to hand (or a copy available on a server) until you have exercised all the features that you want.

When the Installer completes, the application is ready for use, with some features completely installed and others set up ready for transfer on first use.

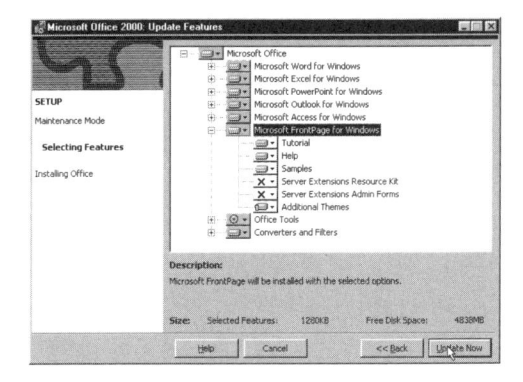

22 | FrontPage 2000 in easy steps

Using FrontPage 2000

This provides an introduction to FrontPage by stepping through the creation of a simple Web site. It uses image and text files supplied with FrontPage, so you can repeat the steps on your own PC.

Covers

Starting out | 24

The FrontPage tutorial | 25

Creating your first Web site | 26

Make a FrontPage Web | 27

Navigation view | 28

Page titles and names | 29

Building the home page | 30

Adding a link | 32

Adding an animated picture | 33

Arranging the items | 34

Viewing the page | 35

Previewing the page | 36

Closing down | 37

Starting out

As with all Office applications, a FrontPage shortcut is added to the Start menu. To start FrontPage 2000:

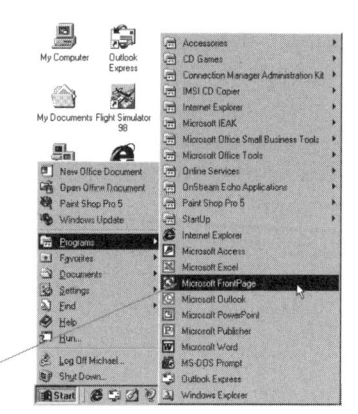

> *Whenever you run FrontPage, it validates the files and will refresh any that have errors.*

1 Press Start, and click Programs.

2 Select the entry Microsoft FrontPage 2000.

This displays the main FrontPage window, showing the toolbar and view bar, but with a blank contents screen since by default no Web site will be opened.

> *You can instruct FrontPage to open the latest Web site you've worked on, the next time it starts up. See page 38.*

Parts of FrontPage 2000:

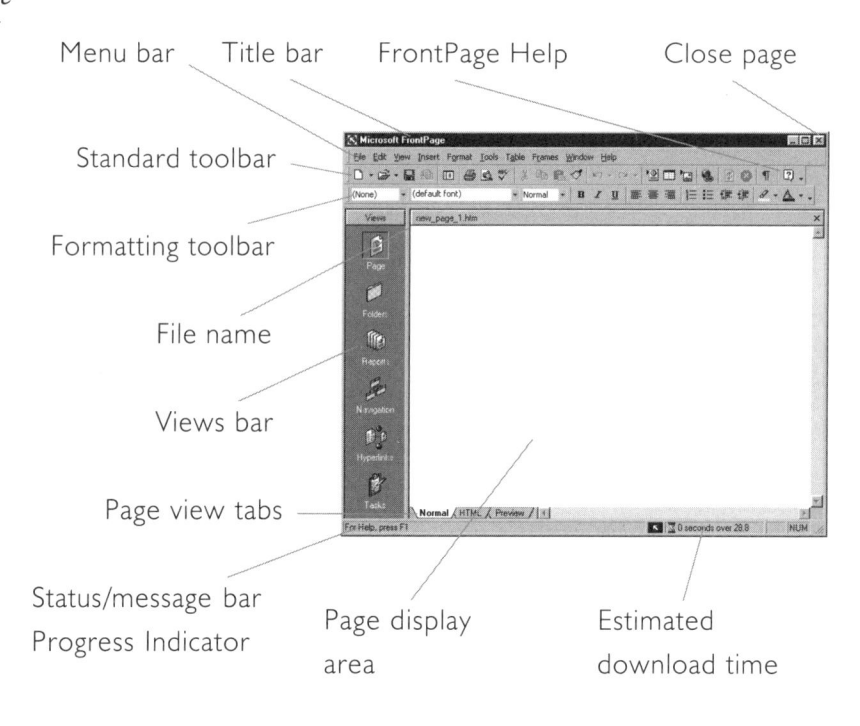

- Menu bar
- Title bar
- FrontPage Help
- Close page
- Standard toolbar
- Formatting toolbar
- File name
- Views bar
- Page view tabs
- Status/message bar Progress Indicator
- Page display area
- Estimated download time

24 | FrontPage 2000 in easy steps

The FrontPage tutorial

If you are new to FrontPage you'll find an introduction on the Internet in the form of a tutorial. Chapters two and three cover similar material, but let you work off-line.

FrontPage includes a set of files used for an introductory tutorial. This isn't mentioned in the Help information, but currently (Microsoft may change this reference in future – this is unavoidable) you'll find the tutorial at the URL:

http://msdn.microsoft.com/c-frame.htm#/workshop/languages/fp/2000/tutorial2000/003fp.asp

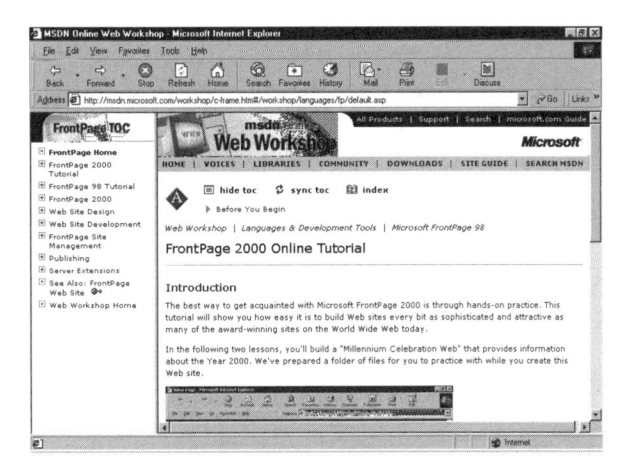

Using these files saves you having to type in lots of text or create suitable pictures, so you can concentrate on the functions.

You can take this tutorial by signing on to the Internet and accessing the URL specified. The first lesson is to create and edit Web pages and design the Web site. The second lesson is to add navigation, apply a theme and publish the Web site.

The files used in the tutorial are already installed on your hard disk, in the Tutorial folder. With these as the starting point, you can try out the techniques and build a sample Web site. You won't have to sign on to the Internet until the Web site is finished.

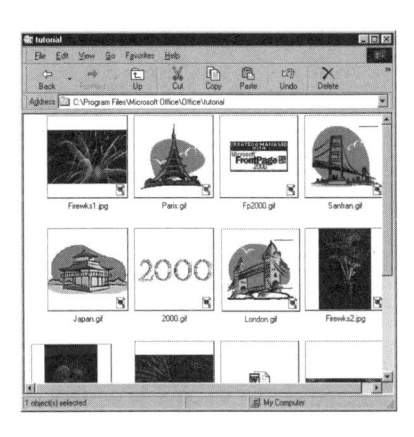

Creating your first Web site

The steps involved, discussed on page 19, are to define the purpose, design the Web, create the pages, publish and maintain the Web site.

The easiest way to find out about FrontPage is to go right ahead and create a Web site. This will introduce you to the style of working that it offers, and show you some of the components and procedures that it supports. You can then examine these in more detail.

The following sections describe how to create and publish a Web site with information about the millennium. The online tutorial also builds a millennium Web site, though the sequence of activities and the resulting Web pages are different. It may be worth visiting the Tutorial site to compare the effects.

The purpose of the Web site is to tell your visitors about the new millennium and associated celebrations. The end product will be a Web site with five pages that are linked something like this:

Draw a sketch showing the main pages and files or documents to give a pictorial image of the Web site you have in mind.

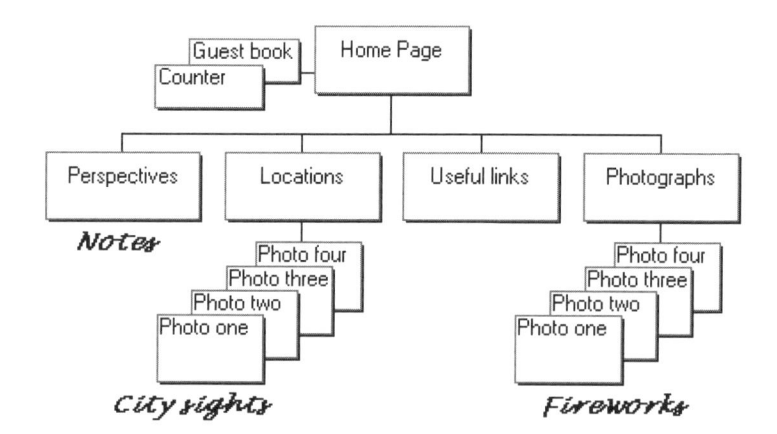

The Web site will keep a count of the number of visitors, and will capture any comments that they care to leave.

You will begin by building pages on your hard disk, so you won't need to connect to the Internet until you are ready to publish the site. When that is done, anyone on the Internet can view your pages. However, you can still make changes to the information, adding or removing elements, or inserting new pages whenever you wish, and visitors will see the latest version.

Make a FrontPage Web

> **HOT TIP:** *You could start by creating the pages, but it is usually better to set up the outline structure first.*

FrontPage will create a Web as a unit, with all the information needed to manage the site for you. This allows it to spell check and validate hyperlinks across the site, and it can maintain dynamic navigation links. You can change or add pages and links, to modify or extend the structure.

To create a FrontPage Web site:

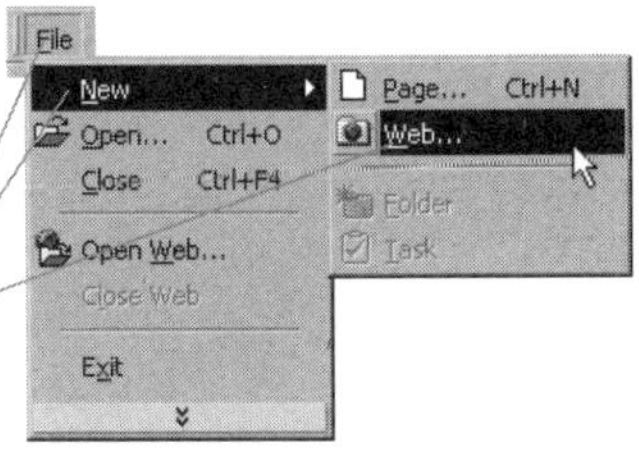

1. Select File from the Menu bar then New, and choose Web.

2. Select the One Page Web template and then Tab to the Name field.

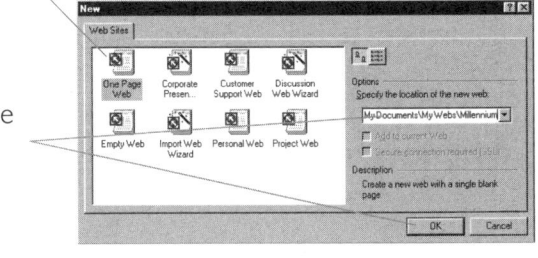

3. Specify the Web location and name (for example: C:\My Documents\My Webs\Millennium) then click OK

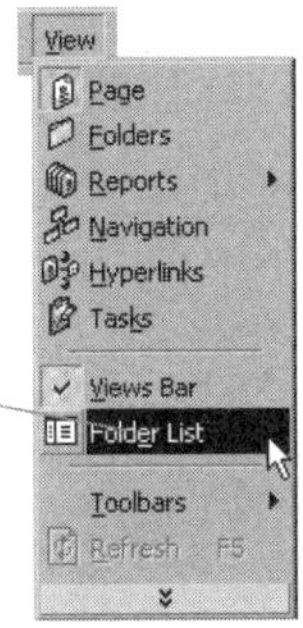

4. Click View, Folder List to see the files that have been created.

> **HOT TIP:** *The home page is given the default name Index.htm, so that it will be automatically displayed when visitors enter the URL for your site.*

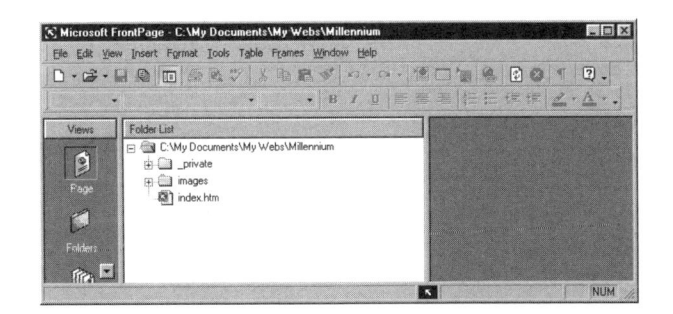

2. Using FrontPage 2000 | 27

Navigation view

> **HOT TIP**
> *Creating the Web site in Navigation mode makes it possible to have navigation bars and references updated automatically when you add or remove pages.*

1. Press the Navigation button on the Views bar.

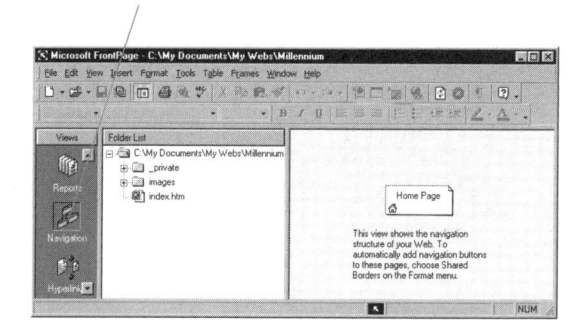

Navigation view shows the structure of your Web site. To modify the Web site structure:

2. Press the New Page button on the toolbar.

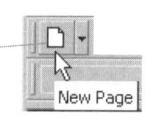

> **HOT TIP**
> *Even though you start with a single page Web, you can change the structure and add more pages.*

3. FrontPage creates "New Page 2" below the home page.

4. Press Ctrl+N to create a second page.

5. Press Ctrl+N two more times to bring the total number of pages to five.

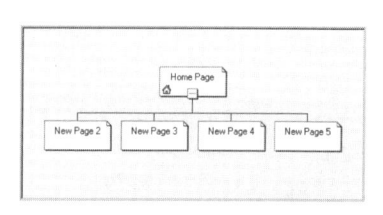

> **DON'T FORGET**
> *The new page is a placeholder until you edit it or import an existing page.*

You can also right-click an existing page and press the New Page entry on the context menu, to add an extra page.

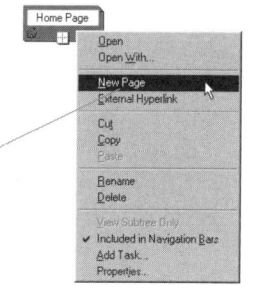

28 | FrontPage 2000 in easy steps

Page titles and names

The new pages are added to the page currently selected. This is coloured blue, while the rest are coloured yellow.

The new pages added below the home page are not immediately given file names, so you can re-title the pages and set the file name.

1 With the home page selected, press Tab to switch to the next page in the structure, with the page title ready to edit.

2 Type Perspectives and press Tab again.

You can change the title of a page by right-clicking it and selecting Rename.

3 Type Locations and press Tab again.

4 Type Useful links and press Tab again.

Internet standards require URLs and file names with plain ASCII characters, so that all visitors can follow URLs, without relying on a particular type of PC, operating system or browser.

5 Type Photographs and press Enter.

6 Right-click a clear area and select Apply Changes. The files for the new pages are created, using titles as file names.

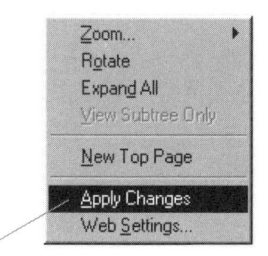

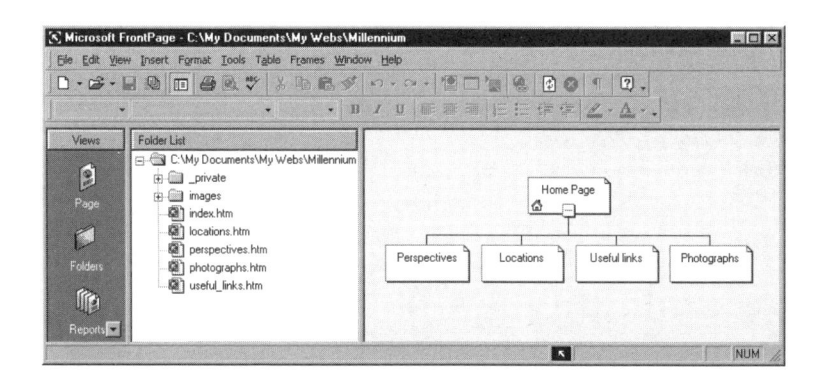

2. Using FrontPage 2000 | 29

Building the home page

Provide enough on your home page to motivate visitors to stay to view more pages. Think also what encourages repeat visits and recommendations.

Start with the Home page, which is the most important page on the Web site. It is the default page, the first page that your visitors will see, and it contains the links to the other pages in your Web site.

To edit the home page:

1. Double-click the page in Navigation view to open Index.htm as a blank sheet in Page view.

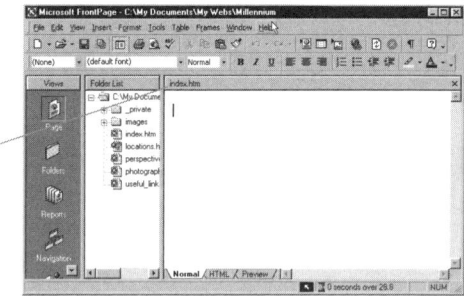

2. Select View and click Views Bar and Folder List to give more space.

3. Type the title for your Web site and press Enter.

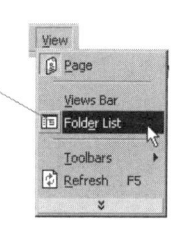

The initial versions of FrontPage 2000 failed to switch dictionaries and spell-checked in US English. You can obtain a fix from the Office Update site (see page 175).

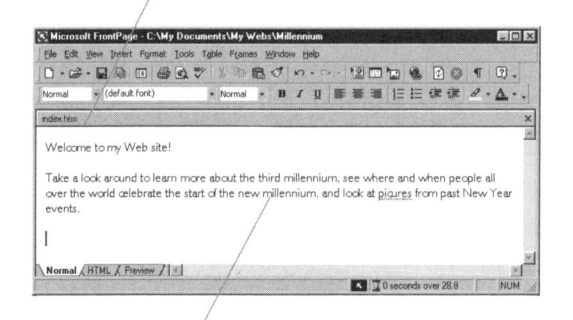

4. Type the introductory message then press Enter.

5. Right-click any underlined words to correct typing or spelling errors.

30 | FrontPage 2000 in easy steps

...cont'd

> **Hot Tip:** *You can insert the text and images onto the page and then format and arrange them later.*

Now you can add a picture to the page. A picture may be a scanned photograph or drawing, or a graphics file created on the PC as a drawing or bitmap. For the example, the picture to insert is a graphical image of the FrontPage 2000 Web site logo, and it will be used as a button to select that site.

To insert a picture:

1. Select Insert from the menu bar, choose Picture, and From File.

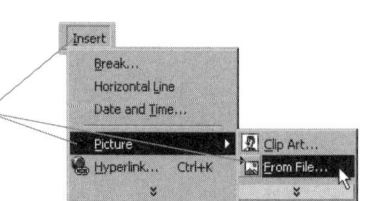

2. Click the button to select a file on your computer.

3. Locate the Tutorial folder and the Fp2000 file.

4. Click OK to insert the file onto the page.

5. Press Enter to create a new line.

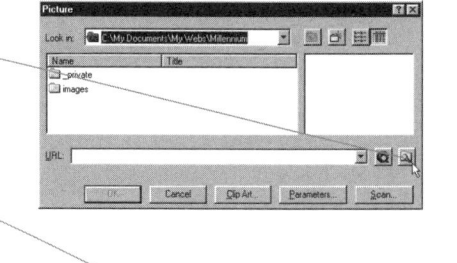

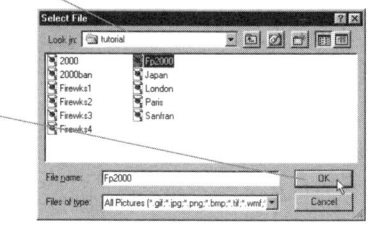

> **Hot Tip:** *The file is just a .GIF image so you must associate a suitable hyperlink with it to make it functional.*

This file is a picture button to indicate that your site is based on FrontPage 2000.

The button will be converted into an active link to the Microsoft FrontPage information Web site.

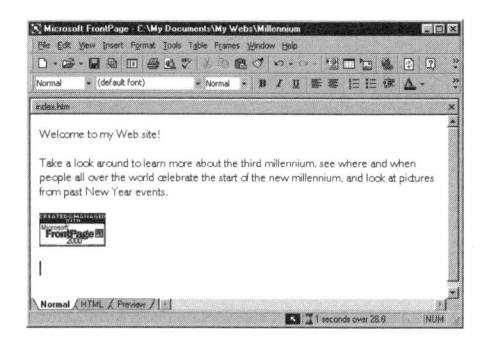

2. Using FrontPage 2000 | 31

Adding a link

The main mechanism for moving around the Internet is the hyperlink, a pointer that contains the address of the target page, file or location.

You can make a picture, word or phrase clickable, so that it switches to another Web page or a different position on the same page. This needs a hyperlink associated with the item.

To associate a hyperlink with the picture button:

1. Click to select the picture on the page – file handles and the Pictures toolbar are displayed.

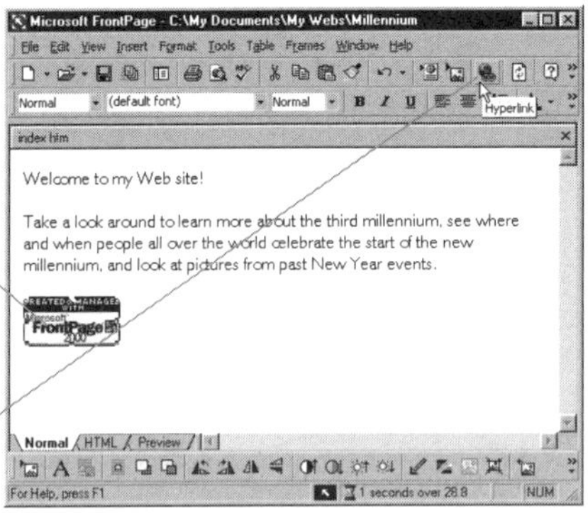

2. Press the Hyperlink button on the Standard toolbar – FrontPage displays the Create Hyperlink box.

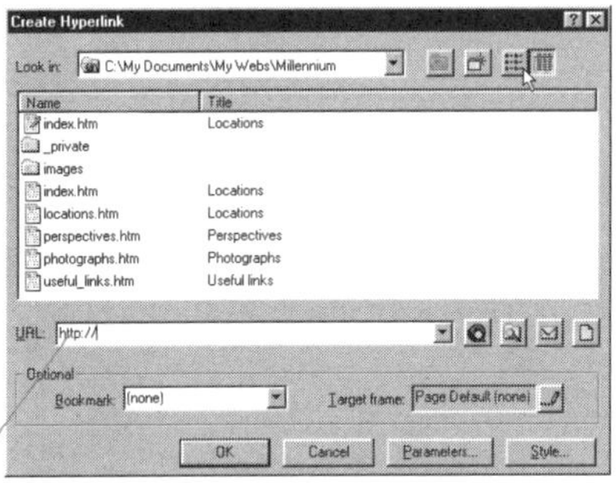

You can enter the target address of a page or file in your Web site, on your hard disk, on a Web server, or on another Web site.

3. Enter the URL 'www.microsoft.com/frontpage' (omit the quotes) immediately after the http:// prefix provided for you.

4. Click OK to finish creating the hyperlink:

The appearance of the button doesn't change, unlike the text hyperlinks. When you select a section of text and create a hyperlink, the text is coloured and underlined.

32 | FrontPage 2000 in easy steps

Adding an animated picture

You can create an animated picture using Animation Shop, a program that comes with Paint Shop Pro.

Pictures on the Web page can contain multiple images, and the browser will display each image in quick succession. Usually, each image varies slightly so as the images are presented, you get the effect of an animated picture. The Tutorial file contains the file 2000.gif, which has 43 frames, including:

To insert an animated picture on the home page:

1. Press Ctrl+Home to jump to the beginning of the current page.

FrontPage remembers Tutorial since it was the last folder used.

2. Select Insert, Picture, and then From File.

3. Double-click the file named 2000 (or 2000.gif) to insert it – FrontPage inserts the animated picture of the number 2000 into the open page:

You can Preview the page to see the animated effects in action (page 36).

4. Press Enter to move the title text down a line.

While you are in Page view edit, FrontPage displays a static view, using the first frame of the animation.

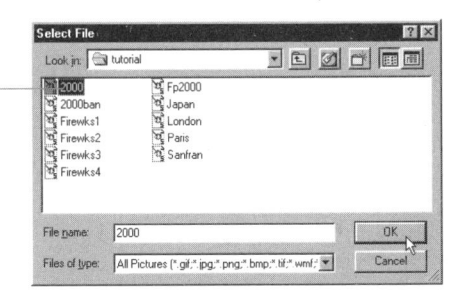

2. Using FrontPage 2000 | 33

Arranging the items

You can change the alignment, adjust the spacing, and apply indentation for text and graphics.

You can select one or more text and graphics items from the page, and apply changes to layout and orientation.

To centre items on the page:

1 Select Edit from the Menu bar and choose Select All.

2 Press the Centre button on the Formatting toolbar. This centres both text and image items.

3 Click anywhere on the page to deselect all page elements.

To save the current page:

1 Press the Save button on the Standard toolbar.

2 Press Change Folder and select the Images folder for this Web site.

3 Click OK to save a copy of the embedded files.

4 Select, View, Folder List (or select the Folders view) to see all the files that are included in your Web.

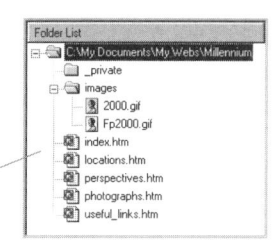

Viewing the page

You create and edit your Web pages in Page view which shows text and images as they will appear, but without animation effects.

HTML tags define the page setup and contents, but these codes are normally hidden.

To display all the HTML tags on the current page:

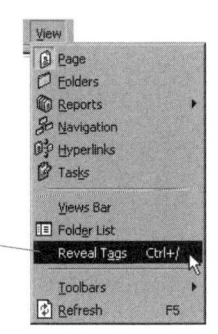

1. Select View from the menu bar and click Reveal Tags.

2. Move the mouse pointer over any of the tags to see the details of the tag, in the ScreenTip shown.

You can view the HTML tags in a graphical form, so you can see where the tags are placed on the page.

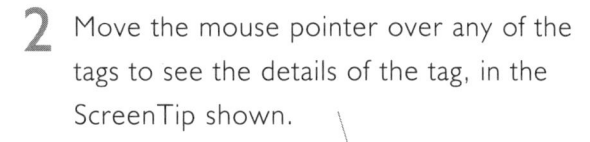

3. Select View, Reveal Tags again to turn off the display.

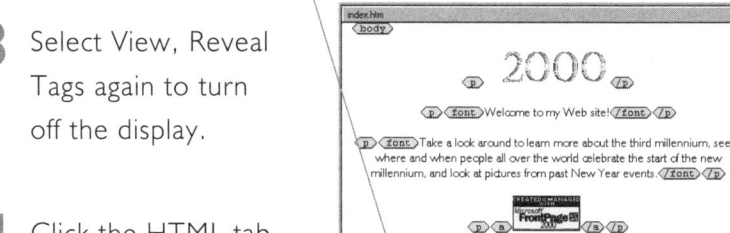

4. Click the HTML tab at the bottom of the page to show the actual coding statements.

Do not change the entries in the source code unless you are sure of the effect that will be created.

Note that this view is meant for use by experienced Web site designers and Web programmers, to supplement or adapt the HTML codes that are entered into the page by FrontPage.

2. Using FrontPage 2000 | 35

Previewing the page

If you use Microsoft Internet Explorer on your PC, you can preview the page as it will appear when it has been published to the Web site.

To see the page in its final form:

> *You can view the page the way the browser will show it. You are still running FrontPage, but it utilises code from Internet Explorer.*

1 In page view, click the Preview tab at the foot of the display area.

2 Animation effects for text and graphics will be enabled.

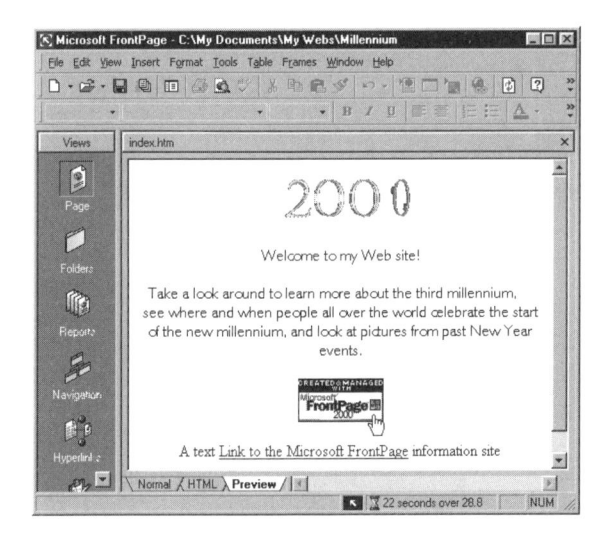

3 Hyperlinks will become live, and will navigate appropriately (though you must be online to access Web sites).

> *You need access to the target Internet or Intranet Web server, in order to follow hyperlinks.*

4 Press the Normal tab to end this preview.

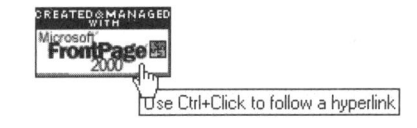

Note that you can still navigate hyperlinks in Normal view, by holding down the Ctrl key as you click the link.

Closing down

You should save your Web pages regularly while you are working on them, and again when you finish the working session.

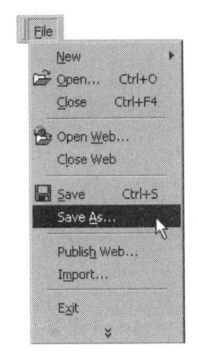

To save the current page:

1. Click the Save button on the Standard toolbar, or select File, Save.

To save the page with a new title or file name:

1. Select File, Save As.

2. Press the Change button.

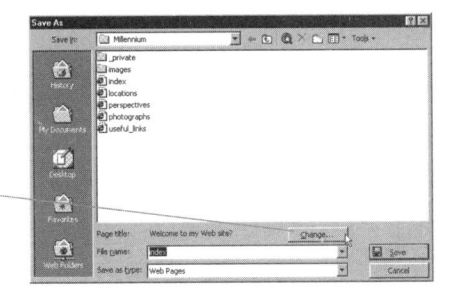

You can also change the title by right-clicking the page and selecting Page Properties.

FrontPage displays the Set Page Title box. The title is used by the browser to identify the Web page and appears on the browser title bar. The default title is based on the first line of text on the page. You can make it more meaningful, for example by putting Millennium III, rather than the vague Welcome message.

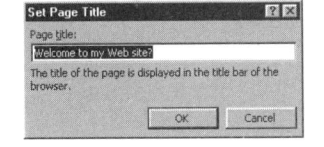

3. Press OK to record the title, change the file name if desired, and press Save to save the page.

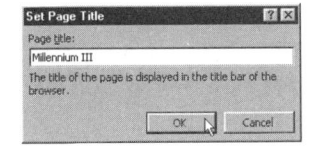

When you select Save As, you'll see a message to remind you that the page already exists, even if you don't change the file name.

2. Using FrontPage 2000 | 37

...cont'd

If you have several pages open, you can close the whole Web:

| Select File from the menu bar and click Close Web.

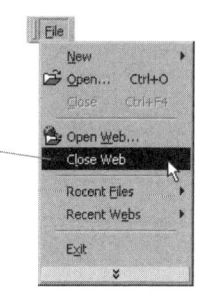

All open pages will be closed. You are prompted to save any changes or new embedded files. You do not have to save the Web as such. It is actually a folder, with the set of Web pages, files and subfolders which contain all the data for the Web.

You can return to the Web site files later by reopening the Web.

To open an existing Web site:

Choose the Recent Webs item from the File menu, if you want to choose a different Web.

| Select File, Open Web.

FrontPage remembers the last Web, and offers it as the default selection.

If you plan to expect to work on the same Web site over a number of sessions, you can tell FrontPage to open the last Web automatically when it starts up:

The next time you start up FrontPage, it will load the Web site that you were working with most recently.

1 Select Tools from the Menu bar and click Options.

2 Click the General tab and click to turn on the option to Open last Web automatically when FrontPage starts.

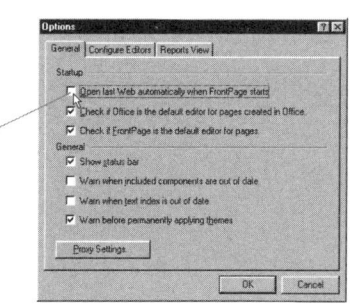

38 | FrontPage 2000 in easy steps

Adding to your Web

Continue to build the sample Web, completing the remaining pages and showing how to insert text and pictures, check that the pages will download effectively, and create and validate hyperlinks.

Covers

Inserting plain text | 40

Adding formatted text | 42

Adding files to your Web | 44

Wrapping up images | 46

A page of photographs | 48

Display timings | 49

Thumbnail images | 50

Useful links | 51

Creating text hyperlinks | 52

Verified hyperlinks | 54

Inserting plain text

This adds text to the Web page in order to set up the Perspectives page.

You can choose to open by default in the last Web that you worked on. See page 38.

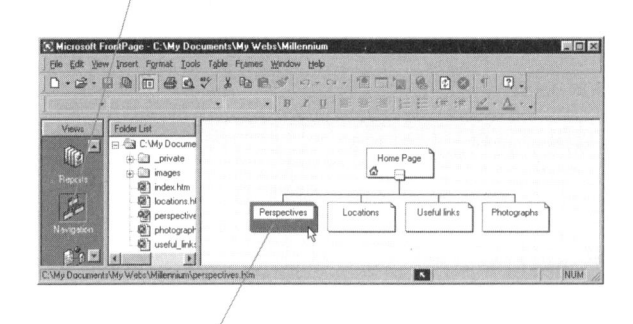

The text that puts the millennium into perspective has already been created, so you can carry on building your Web without having to type the information.

To add the text file to the Perspectives page:

1. Start FrontPage and open the Millennium Web and press the Navigation button on the Views bar to display the Web site structure.

2. Double-click the Perspectives page to open it as a blank sheet in Page view.

3. Select Insert from the Menu bar and click File. You'll need to expand the menu list, the first time you insert a file.

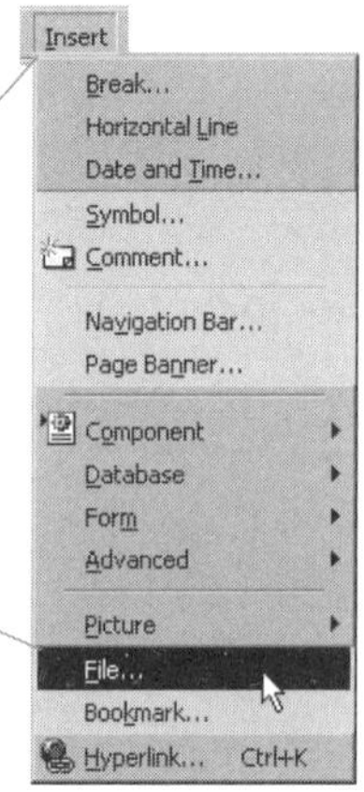

4. Switch to the Tutorial folder in C:\Program Files\Microsoft Office\Office.

5. Select files of type Text (*.txt), click on the file Year2000 and press the Open button.

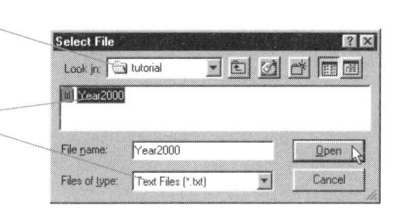

40 | FrontPage 2000 in easy steps

...cont'd

Hot Tip: Since the file is plain text, not a Word Doc or HTML format, you must say how the text should be handled.

6 Choose Normal paragraphs (or Normal paragraphs with line breaks if you want to preserve line ends) and click OK.

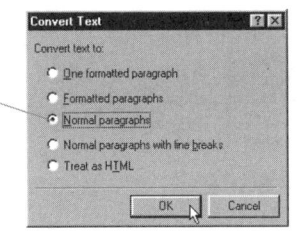

7 The text is inserted into the page.

Hot Tip: It looks very plain, but don't format the text at this stage. You should apply the themes and any across-the-site formatting before adjusting the layout of individual pages.

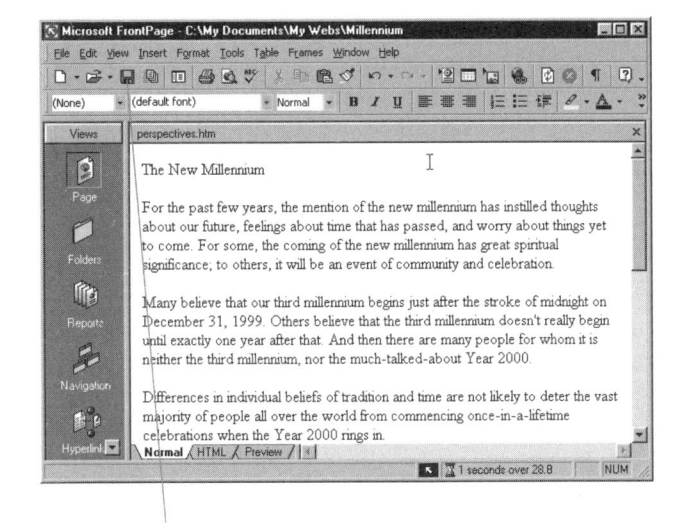

8 Press the Save button on the toolbar to capture the text.

You can insert text from files of various formats, including HTML, Word, Works, Lotus, Excel, WordPerfect and Write.

The first time you use a particular file type, you may need the Office or FrontPage CD to complete the installation, since the conversion routines are not installed until they are actually needed.

3. Adding to your Web | 41

Adding formatted text

There's more text describing events and locations, ready to use, in the Tutorial folder.

The Locations page describes events and locations associated with the Millennium celebrations, and adds some pictures to lighten the effect.

To edit this page:

1. Press the Folder List button on the toolbar to display the Folder List in Page view.

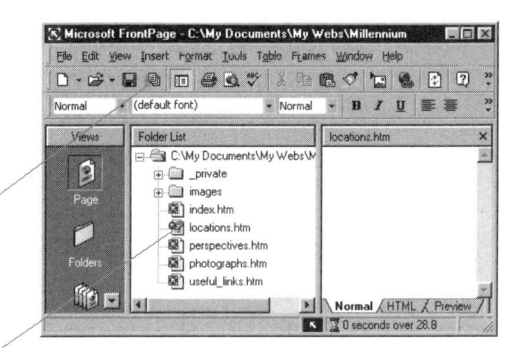

2. Double-click the Locations.htm file to open the page.

3. Select Insert from the menu bar, and File.

4. Change file type to Rich Text Format (*.rtf) and double-click Events.rtf to open it.

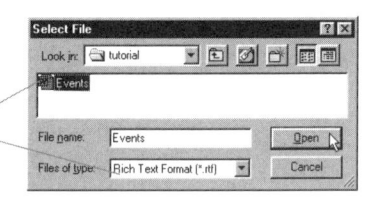

Although rtf files have some formatting they may not have the style you want, so you can make changes once the text is inserted.

Since the text in this file is already formatted, FrontPage will convert it into HTML form, without requiring instructions.

5. Select File, and Save to record the changes made so far.

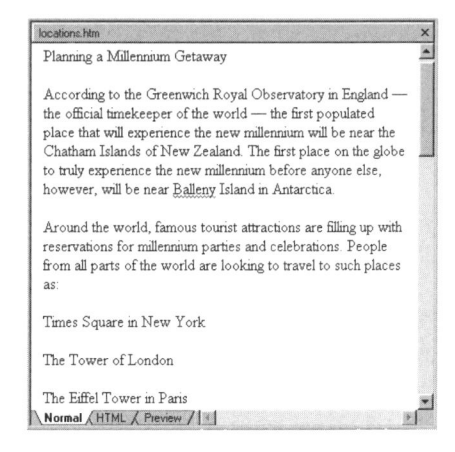

42 | FrontPage 2000 in easy steps

...cont'd

To convert a simple list into a bulleted list:

The actual style of bullet will be defined when you select the Theme for your Web site. See page 64.

6 Find the list of locations on the page. It starts with 'Times Square, New York' and the last is 'The Acropolis in Greece'.

7 Highlight the list, and press the Bullets button.

8 The selected text is displayed with bullets.

FrontPage supports the usual word processing formats. To see a list of the functions available:

1 Click the down arrow at the end of the Formatting toolbar.

2 This displays the option to add or remove buttons.

3 Pause the mouse pointer over this command, to display the list of the formatting buttons with their names and keyboard shortcuts.

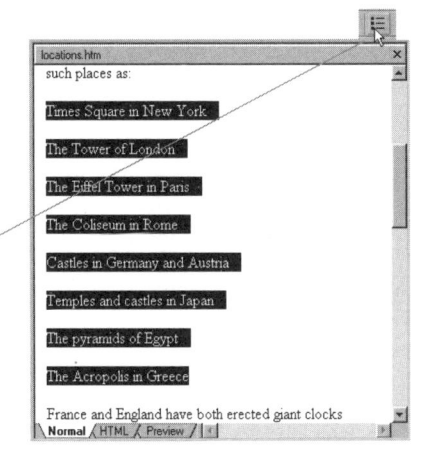

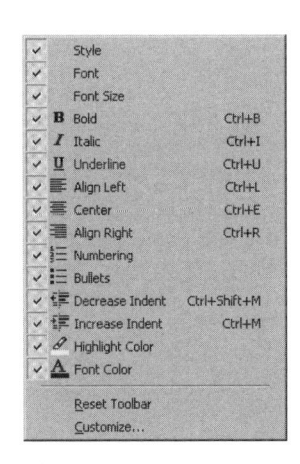

3. Adding to your Web | 43

Adding files to your Web

When you insert pictures and text files in a Web site, FrontPage assumes that the files are already part of the site, so add the files en bloc ahead of time.

To add files to the current Web site:

When you import a file, a copy is added to your Web, and the original stays in the source folder.

1 Press the Folders button on the Views bar to switch to Folders view, and open the target folder Images.

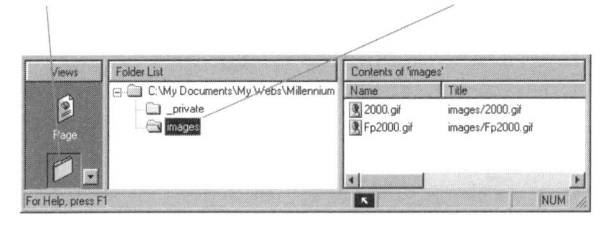

You can import files from your hard disk, from a LAN file server, or from the Internet, from a Web server.

2 Select File from the menu bar, then Import and then click Add File.

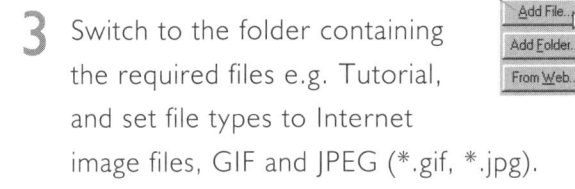

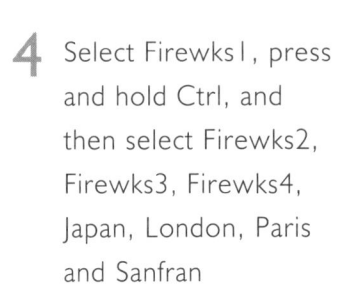

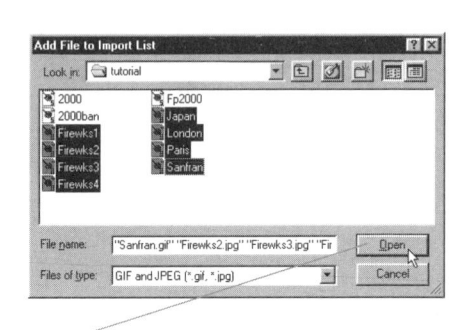

3 Switch to the folder containing the required files e.g. Tutorial, and set file types to Internet image files, GIF and JPEG (*.gif, *.jpg).

4 Select Firewks1, press and hold Ctrl, and then select Firewks2, Firewks3, Firewks4, Japan, London, Paris and Sanfran

5 Release the Ctrl key and click Open to have the selected files added to the Import list.

...cont'd

6 Press Add File, Add Folder or From Web to collect any other items required.

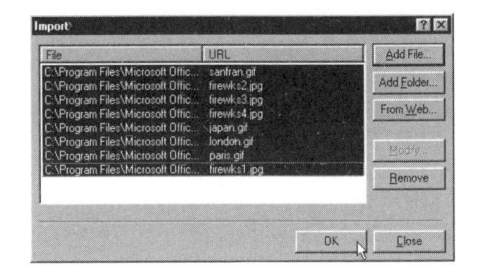

To change the file name or the target folder of any file before importing it:

To quickly import a file or a selection of files to the current Web, drag them into the Folder List from Windows Explorer.

7 Select the file and click Modify. In the File location type a URL relative to the root of the current Web, then click OK.

8 To save the import list, and import the files and folders at a later time, click Close.

9 Click OK to import the selected files to the target folder in your Web.

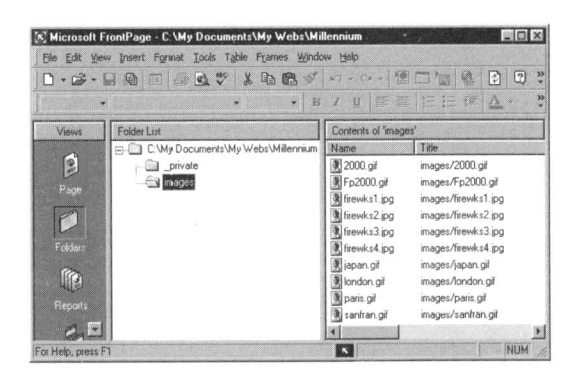

This procedure will help ensure that all the items required for your Web are stored in its folders and available to be published to the Internet.

3. Adding to your Web | 45

Wrapping up images

As well as pictures, you can insert clip art from the gallery in FrontPage.

Having copied the image files to the Web site folders, the pictures can now be placed in the Web page.

1. Select Folders view and double-click Locations.htm to open it in Page view.

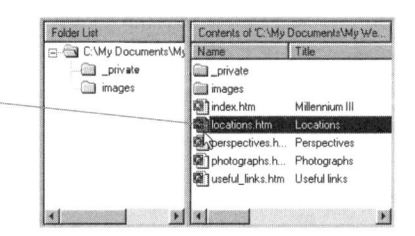

2. Select Edit, Find and locate the word France.

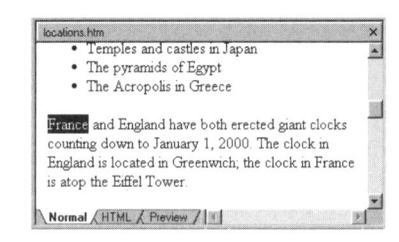

3. Press Home, and click to Insert Picture From File.

When you select a picture file FrontPage displays a preview so you can check that it is the right image.

4. Open the Images folder if necessary, select the Paris.gif picture, and click OK.

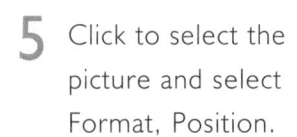

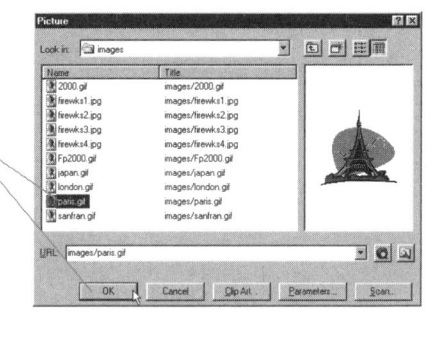

5. Click to select the picture and select Format, Position.

Press the Save button from time to time, to record your changes.

6. Choose Wrapping style, Right and press OK.

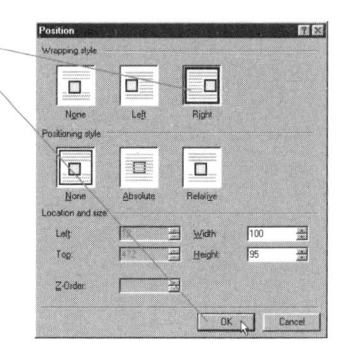

This will align the picture with the right margin of the page and the text will flow around it on the left side of the image.

46 | FrontPage 2000 in easy steps

...cont'd

Position the other three pictures in a similar way:

Don't Insert a picture while the text is highlighted, or the text item will be deleted and replaced by the picture.

1. Find the word Reconstruct, click on it to clear the highlight, and Insert the picture London.gif.

2. Select the picture and press Align Left on the toolbar.

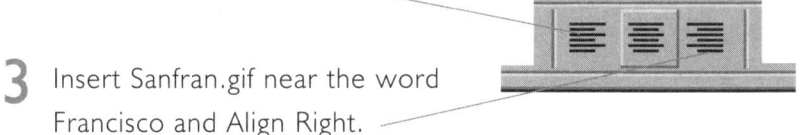

3. Insert Sanfran.gif near the word Francisco and Align Right.

4. Insert Japan.gif near the word Agency and Align Left.

Positioning pictures in the margin protects your page layout when the page is viewed at different screen sizes and resolutions in the visitor's Web browser.

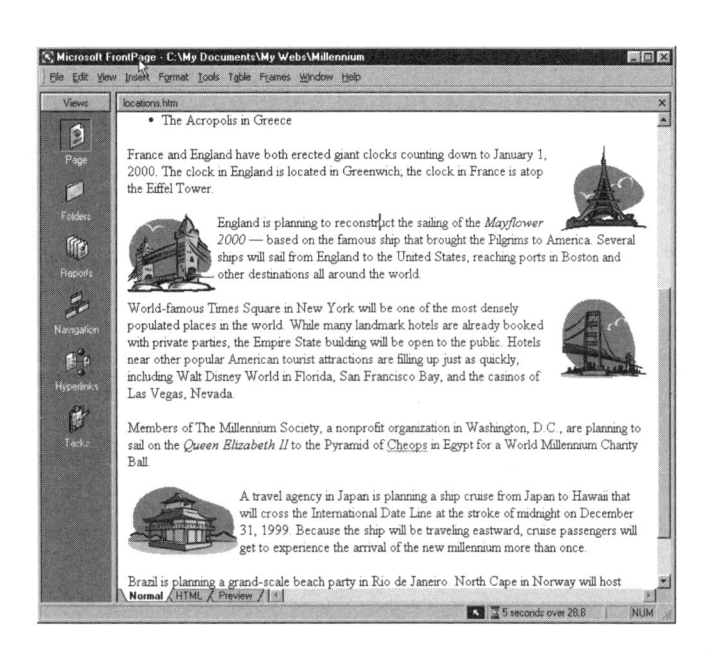

3. Adding to your Web | 47

A page of photographs

DON'T FORGET: *It is easy to obtain digital images, with a scanner or digital camera. You can also have your photographs developed and transferred to a CD-ROM.*

One type of Web page that is very popular with Web builders is the page of photographs.

1. Select Folders view and open the Photographs page.

2. Type 'New Year's Fireworks' as the first line and title, then press Enter.

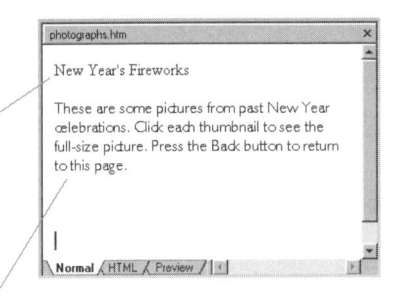

3. Type 'These are some pictures from past New Year celebrations. Click each thumbnail to see the full-size picture. Press the Back button to return to this page.' Then press Enter a couple of times.

HOT TIP: *The page will use thumbnail images that point to the full size pictures.*

The four fireworks photographs from the Tutorial folder have already been copied to the Image folder in the Web.

4. Press Centre on the toolbar, press Insert Picture From File, select Firewks1.jpg, click OK and press Enter.

5. Repeat this for the files Firewks2.jpg, Firewks3.jpg, and Firewks4.jpg.

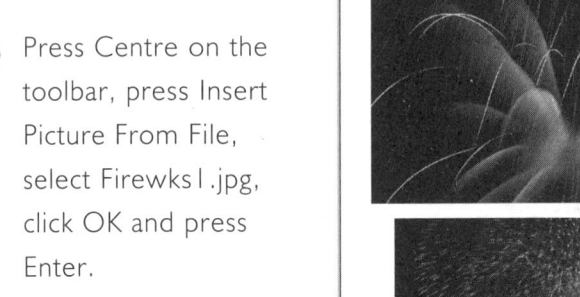

DON'T FORGET: *You will now need to adjust the size and position of the images seen on the page.*

Display timings

Unless your visitor has a very high speed connection, the download times with full pictures will be far too long.

The page as created, with the four photographs inserted, will not be welcomed by most visitors. This is simply because they will have to wait a long time for the page to download, before they can decide if they are interested in the contents.

The status bar displays an estimated time for the page to download over the Internet, assuming a speed is 28.8K.

To check the timing for other speeds:

1 Click the hourglass symbol and choose another speed or connection type.

These are best case estimates assuming that there are no delays anywhere over the links between your PC and the Web site server.

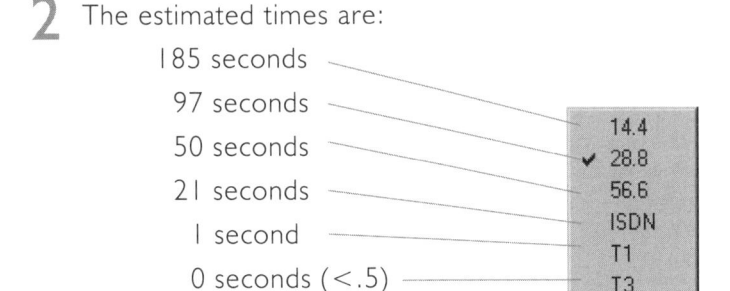

2 The estimated times are:

185 seconds — 14.4
97 seconds — 28.8 ✓
50 seconds — 56.6
21 seconds — ISDN
1 second — T1
0 seconds (<.5) — T3

With these times, many visitors may lose interest, press Stop on their browsers and abandon your site before seeing what is there. If you want your visitors to be pleased with your site, make sure that delays are minimised and that visitors know when they will be transferring larger amounts of data.

See page 50 to convert pictures into thumbnails.

Replace the pictures with smaller thumbnail versions. The page will appear quickly, with enough of a preview to urge a closer look. By selecting an individual thumbnail, the visitor explicitly requests the full picture, and only one picture at a time need be downloaded.

3. Adding to your Web | 49

Thumbnail images

To view and adjust the default options for thumbnails:

> **HOT TIP**
> FrontPage creates a thumbnail of the selected picture with a blue border to show a hyperlink to the original picture. Visitors can click a thumbnail to download the full-size picture.

1 Select Tools, Page Options and then AutoThumbnail.

2 Select a border (indicates a hyperlink) and a bevelled edge (to simulate a button) and change the default setting from Width to Height.

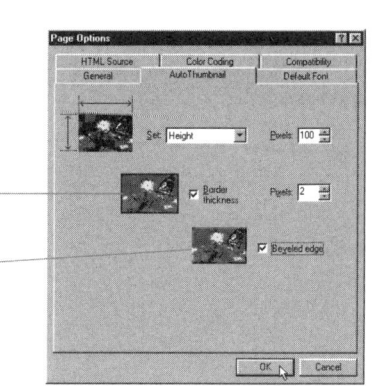

3 Press Ctrl+Home to jump to the beginning of the current page and click on the first fireworks picture.

> **HOT TIP**
> FrontPage doesn't alter the original picture files. It makes a copy of each picture, resizes and resamples it to reduce the display resolution, and associates a hyperlink to the original picture file.

4 On the Pictures toolbar, press the Auto Thumbnail button.

5 Press AutoThumbnail for each of the other three pictures.

6 Arrange the thumbnails neatly, e.g. by placing tabs between the pictures.

7 Press Save, OK to record the changes to the page and save the embedded thumbnail pictures.

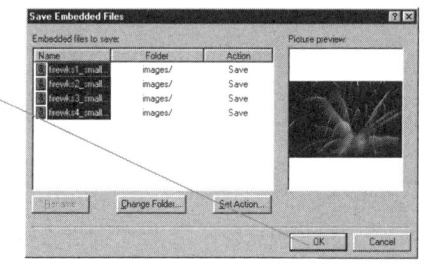

Useful links

The sign of a good Web site is that it will direct you on to other places of interest, so you don't have to retrace your footsteps, and you get the benefit of searches others have already performed.

When you create your own Web sites, provide suitable links to other Web sites dealing with the same subject or related topics. This allows visitors to browse on without having to perform further searches.

To set up a Useful links page:

1. Select Folders view and open Useful links.htm.

2. Type 'Links to My Favourite Sites' as the first line/title and press Enter.

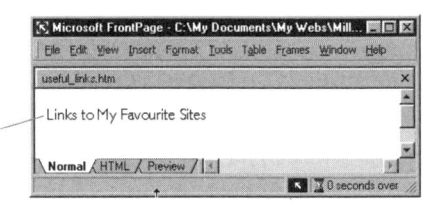

Dynamic HTML is an extension of the HTML language for presentation effects for text and objects, without the need for programming.

To make this heading more distinctive, add an effect:

3. Click anywhere in the text and select Format, Dynamic HTML Effects.

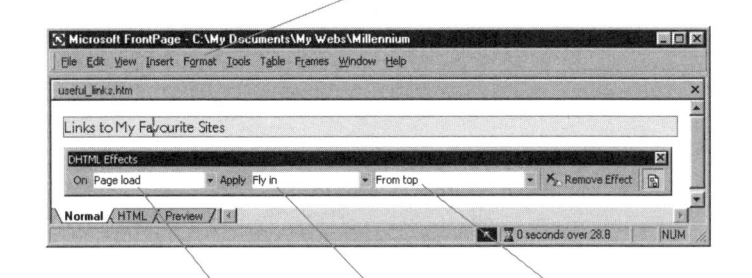

To change the effect, click the text in Normal Page view, select Format, Dynamic HTML Effects and choose Elastic, Drop in by word, or Hop etc.

4. Choose On Page Load, Apply Fly In and From Top, then click the Close button.

5. Press the Preview tab, or select Preview in Browser from the Standard toolbar.

Creating text hyperlinks

HOT TIP: You can turn a selected item of text into an active link.

To create hyperlinks from text:

1 Press the Down-arrow, type 'MSN - The Microsoft Network' and press Enter.

2 Highlight the text and select Insert, Hyperlink.

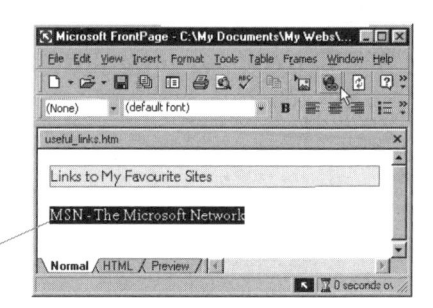

DON'T FORGET: You can associate a URL with a graphics to create a picture button (see page 32 for an example).

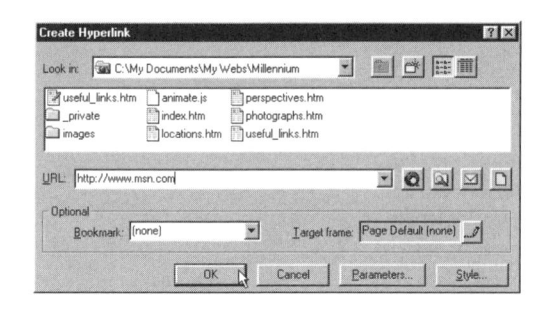

In the Create Hyperlink box, specify the target of the hyperlink. This could be a page or a file in your Web site, on your local file system, on a Web server, or on another site on the Internet.

3 In the URL box, type 'www.msn.com' (without the quotes) immediately after the http:// prefix, and then click OK.

4 Press the Down-arrow to deselect the text.

The words change from black to blue and are underlined to denote a hyperlink. When this page is displayed in a browser, clicking this text will display the MSN home page.

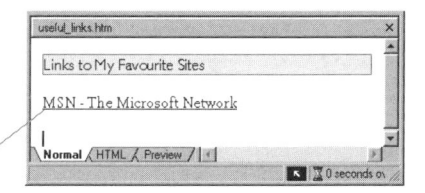

...cont'd

> **HOT TIP**
> MSN is a trademark, so you can insert the appropriate symbol into the hyperlink text.

To insert a symbol:

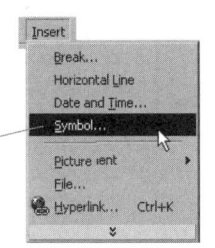

5 Click in the text just after MSN and select Insert, Symbol.

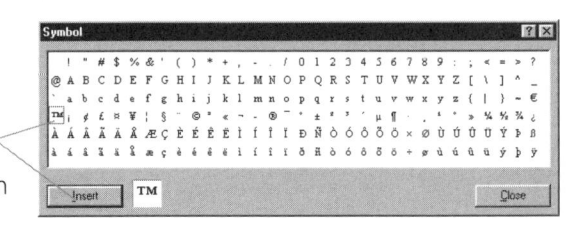

6 Select the trademark TM symbol, click Insert, and then click Close.

Create an automatic hyperlink:

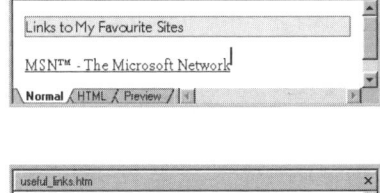

> **HOT TIP**
> You can create an automatic hyperlink, bypassing the Create Hyperlink box.

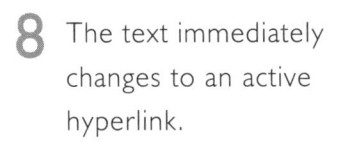

7 On a new line, type 'http://www.yahoo.com', and press Enter.

8 The text immediately changes to an active hyperlink.

9 Highlight the link and type a descriptive title such as 'Yahoo! Home Page'. The active text changes, but the hyperlink URL associated with it remains unchanged.

You can also copy URL shortcuts from your Favourites list, or from an existing hyperlink on a Web page, by right-clicking and selecting Copy Shortcut, then Pasting into the URL box or straight onto the Web page.

3. Adding to your Web | 53

Verified hyperlinks

> **HOT TIP:** The best approach is to use your Web browser to validate the URLs, though you must be connected to the Internet to check Web site addresses.

To create a verified hyperlink:

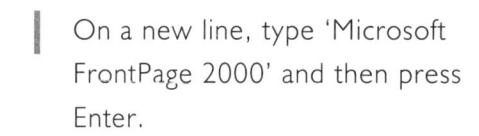

1. On a new line, type 'Microsoft FrontPage 2000' and then press Enter.

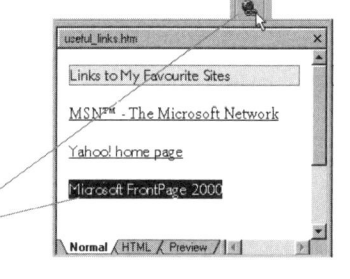

2. Highlight the text, click the Hyperlink button.

3. In the Create Hyperlink box, click the Web Browser button.

4. Connect if needed then enter the URL in the Web browser address box, press Enter, and follow links if necessary to display the required Web page.

> **HOT TIP:** Add the links that you find helpful and want to tell your visitors about. When you have finished entering links, press the Save button on the toolbar to record the changes.

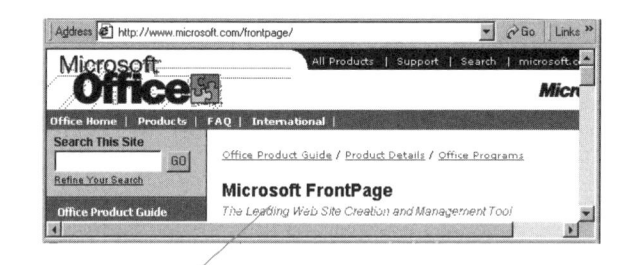

The Web browser displays the Microsoft FrontPage home page and the URL is copied to the URL box in the Create Hyperlink screen.

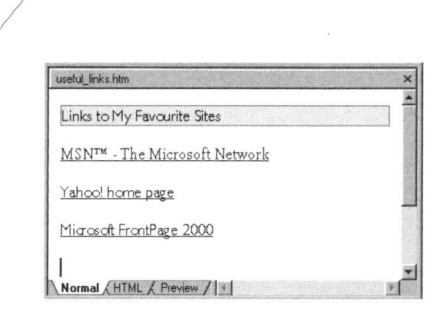

5. Switch back to FrontPage and press OK.

Enhancing the Web

Continue working with the Millennium Web, adding formatting and navigation bars and graphical themes. Preview and test the Web site and prepare it for publication on the World Wide Web.

Covers

Formatting headings | 56

Connecting pages | 58

Bookmarks | 60

Shared borders | 61

Navigation bars | 62

Graphical themes | 64

Customising the theme | 66

Arranging files and folders | 68

Adding a new page | 70

Chapter Four

Formatting headings

Choose fonts and formats that make your Web site look interesting, but try to be consistent.

When you have created the pages for your Web site, you can apply font and text style changes to the contents. It is helpful to tackle the pages as a group, so you can easily compare the pages and provide similar effects.

To open all the pages in the Web and apply styles to the paragraph headings:

1. Select Page view, open all five pages by double-clicking each file name in turn.

FrontPage always opens a Web with a new, empty page ready for use. You can ignore this since it goes away when you open one of your existing pages.

2. Select Window from the menu bar, and choose Index.htm.

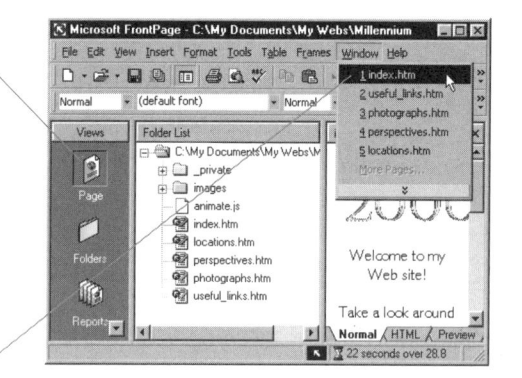

3. Click in the heading text, click the down-arrow to display the Style list and choose Heading 3.

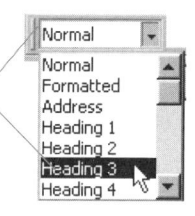

Heading styles are universal HTML standards, and range from level 1 to level 6.

4. Select Window and the Locations page. Click in the heading and apply Heading 4.

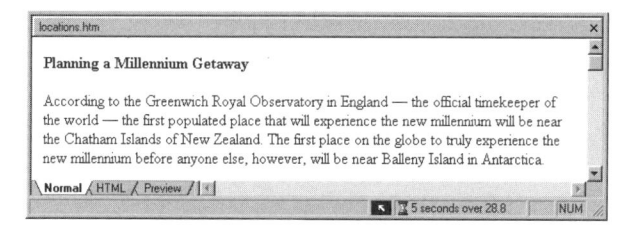

56 | FrontPage 2000 in easy steps

...cont'd

> *FrontPage, like other Office applications, has a Format Painter to replicate settings.*

To make it less tedious to repeat the same formats, and to minimise mistakes, you can use the Format Painter to copy an existing format:

1 Click the Locations heading and click the Format Painter button on the toolbar.

2 Select Window, Photographs and click the heading to apply the format.

You'll have to reset the Format Painter each time you want to apply the format to another heading.

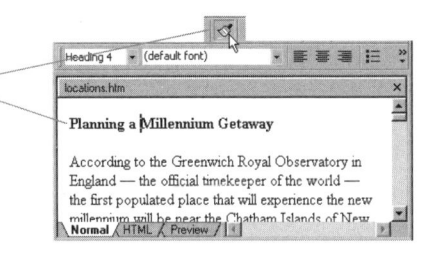

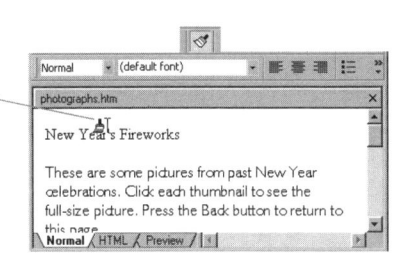

However, it is possible to apply the new format to several sets of text in succession:

3 Click in the Photographs heading and double-click the Format Painter.

> *The heading changes format, but the Format Painter button remains depressed.*

4 Click the Perspectives page, and click in the first heading.

5 Click in the second heading to change its format.

6 Click the Format Painter button to release it.

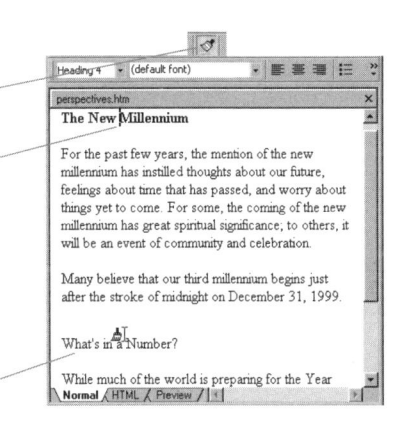

4. Enhancing the Web | 57

Connecting pages

You must link your Web pages together to make them into a Web site.

| Start FontPage and open the Millennium Web site.

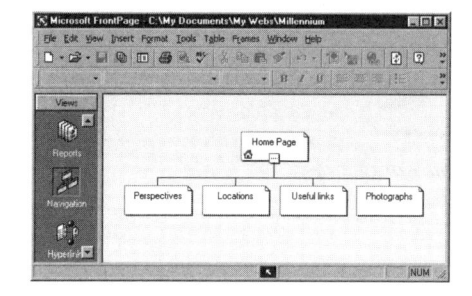

The steps so far have created a Web site of five pages, with hyperlinks to picture files and links to other Web sites. However, there are as yet no links between the pages within the site.

There are several ways you could add links between the pages:

Manual hyperlinks
You can manually create hyperlinks on the Home page to the other four pages, and also put links on those pages, i.e. back to the Home page. These links will allow your visitors to navigate around your Web site. This method gives you the most control over the connections between the pages.

You must define Shared borders for your Web pages, to store the Navigation bars (see page 61).

Navigation bars
FrontPage will create, manage, and automatically update hyperlinks that connect the pages in your Web. You can make changes and additions to the Web without having to explicitly update the hyperlinks.

Frames
Frames divide the browser window into different areas, each of which can display a different page. These are known as Frames pages. One of the frames can be used to contain a list of hyperlinks to the pages in the Web.

See page 138 for more details about frames and frames pages.

This requires more manual intervention when pages change, but the same Contents frame can be used on all the pages, so the amount of updating is minimised.

The FrontPage template for Banner and Contents provides a layout that includes a Contents frames page.

...cont'd

> **HOT TIP:** Use the techniques described on page 52 to add hyperlinks, or simply drag a page file name from the Folders list.

2 Open Index.htm, press Ctrl+End, Centre and drag & drop the file name Perspectives.htm onto the foot of the page.

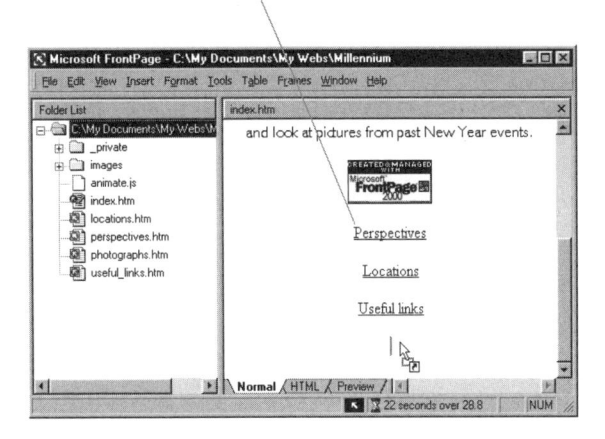

> **BEWARE:** This makes it easy to create hyperlinks, but you'll have to revise the links when you add, remove or rename any pages.

3 Press Ctrl+End, Centre and drag & drop, for each of the three file names, to add them onto the Index page.

4 Open each page in turn and drag & drop the Index.htm file name onto the foot of the page.

5 Select View, Hyperlinks (or press Hyperlinks on the Views bar) to see the links.

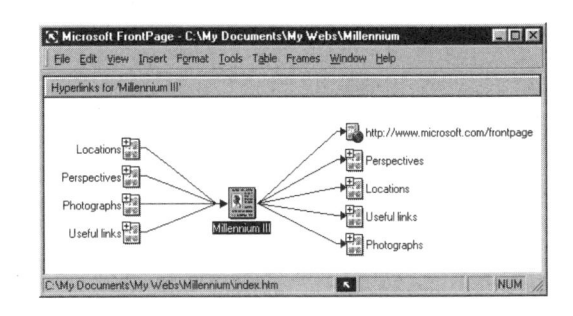

> **HOT TIP:** You can try out changes and then reverse them or end the edit without saving.

6 You can click the Undo button to reverse the latest action. Click the down-arrow to list the most recent actions and select how far back you want to go.

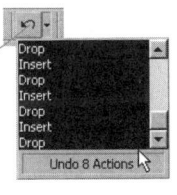

4. Enhancing the Web | 59

Bookmarks

HOT TIP *You can define a location or a set of characters on the page as a bookmark and use it as the target for a hyperlink.*

Use a bookmark as the target of a hyperlink, to create a contents list for a page, or to direct the visitor to a specific paragraph on another page.

To bookmark a heading in the Perspectives page:

1. Open Perspectives, highlight the second heading, and press Insert, Bookmark.

2. Click OK to accept the name. The text is underlined with dashes.

3. If you bookmark just a location on the page, supply the name, and a flag will be added.

4. In the Home page, create a text hyperlink to the bookmark.

When you click on this hyperlink, the browser will switch to show the Perspectives page at the second heading.

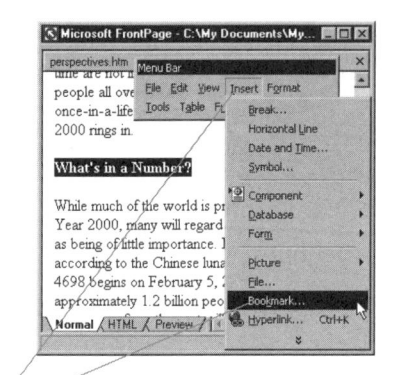

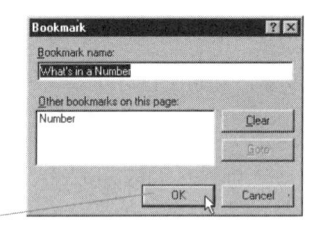

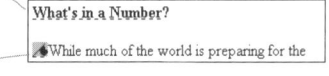

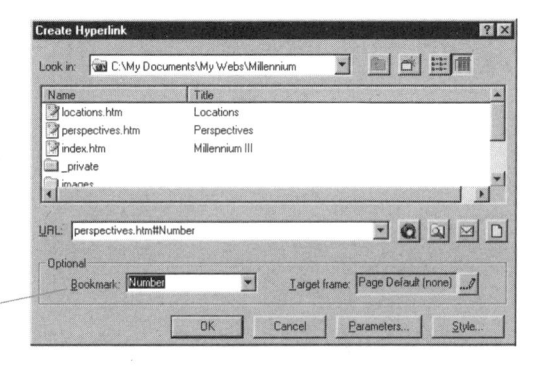

60 | FrontPage 2000 in easy steps

Shared borders

Shared borders give your pages a consistent look.

A shared border is a region that is common to some or all of the pages in your Web. It may be along any edge of the page (top, bottom or either side). You use shared borders to position the same content (for example logo, copyright notice or contact details) on multiple pages, to save changing each page individually. It also means that you only have to modify content in one place to update all pages.

You can set shared borders defaults for the Web as a whole, and apply individual changes to the settings for particular pages, for example turning off a shared border on certain pages.

You add shared borders, page banners and navigation bars to Webs created through Navigation view only.

Shared borders can be used to hold page banners. These display the page title or other text. You also use shared borders to hold the FrontPage navigation bars.

To create shared borders across a Web site:

1 Open the Web in Navigation view and select Format, Shared Borders.

2 Select the All pages option.

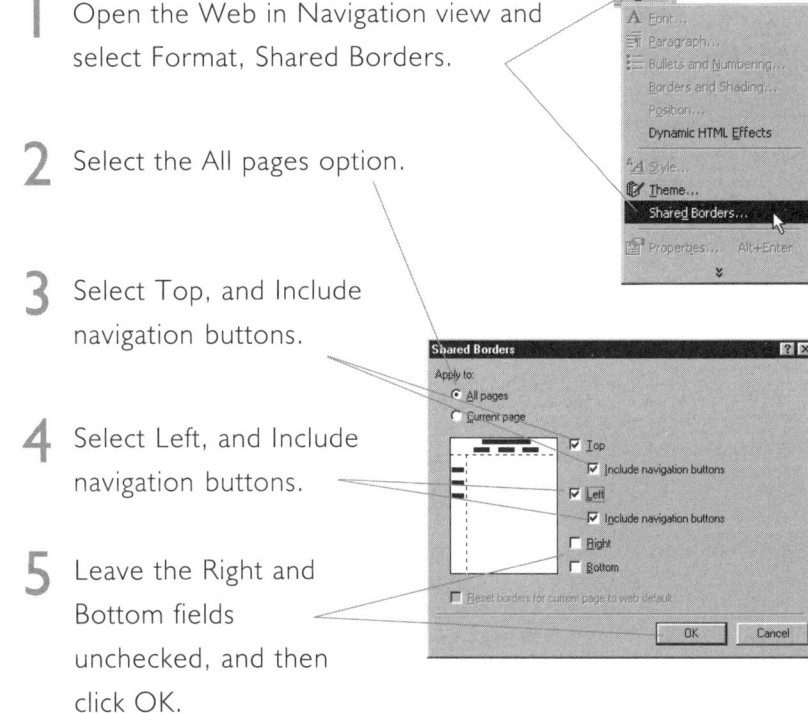

FrontPage creates shared borders and default navigation bars for all the pages in the Web site.

3 Select Top, and Include navigation buttons.

4 Select Left, and Include navigation buttons.

5 Leave the Right and Bottom fields unchecked, and then click OK.

4. Enhancing the Web | 61

Navigation bars

Hot Tip: *Instead of creating links, let FrontPage create and maintain them through the navigation bars in the shared borders.*

1 From Navigation view, double-click the Home Page.

With shared borders enabled, the Home page has a page banner and an empty links bar at the top. On the left is a bar with hyperlinks to the lower level pages.

2 Hold down Ctrl and click Perspectives.

The Perspectives page (like the other second level pages) has the navigation bar on the top border, but no links in the left border.

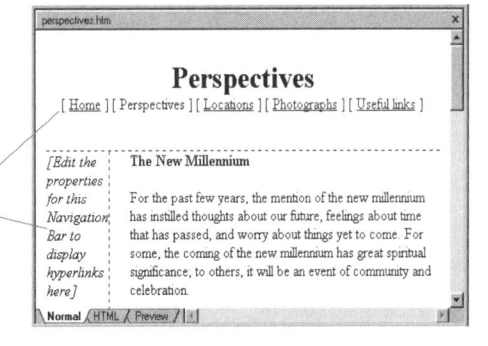

Hot Tip: *By default, the top border shows pages at the same level and the left border shows pages below the current pages. No bar appears when there are no qualifying pages.*

To view the settings for this navigation bar:

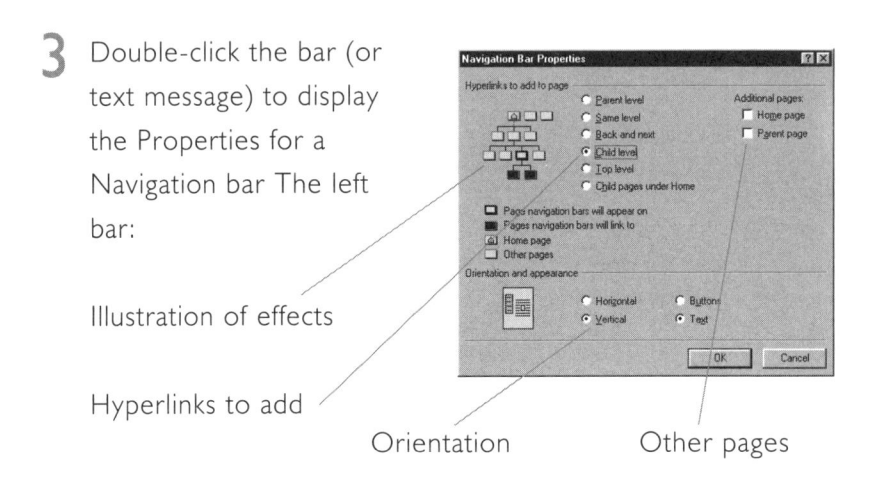

3 Double-click the bar (or text message) to display the Properties for a Navigation bar The left bar:

Illustration of effects

Hyperlinks to add

Orientation

Other pages

62 | FrontPage 2000 in easy steps

...cont'd

4 Open the Properties for the Left bar and set Child pages under Home, and add the Home page.

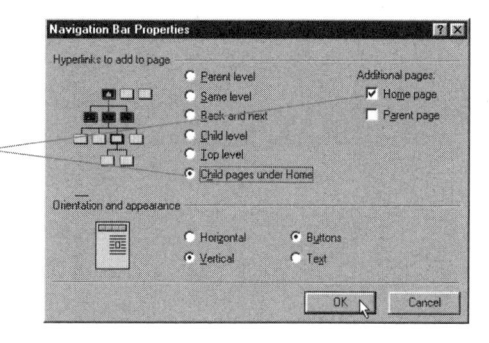

Since there are no top level pages, this switches off the top bar, leaving the banner page.

5 Open Properties for the Top bar and set Top level only.

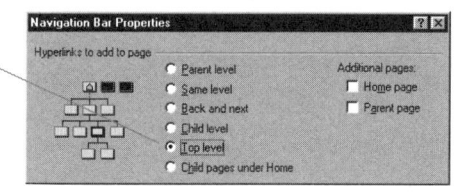

The Top border shows the page banner only.

The left navigation bar shows all five site pages and will include any new pages at one level below Home.

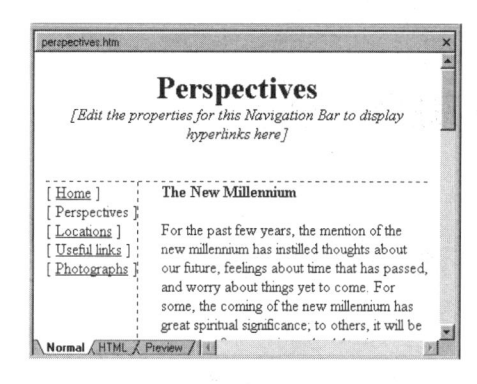

Use the Preview in browser rather than the Preview tab, to see the bars in their final form.

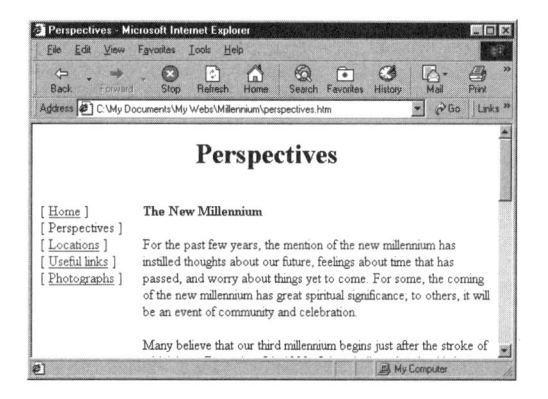

6 Select File, Preview in browser to see how the pages will display.

4. Enhancing the Web | 63

Graphical themes

Despite all the effort so far, the Web pages are still quite plain. It takes colour and graphics to liven them up and make them into a real Web site. FrontPage provides this with Themes. These offer designs for bullets, fonts, pictures and buttons, and are applied to pages, page banners and navigation bars, to produce an attractive and consistent appearance.

> **HOT TIP** *You are saved the detailed design job, since FrontPage has more than 50 professionally designed themes to apply to your Web site.*

To apply a theme to your Web:

1. Select Format, Theme, and click on any name to explore the options.

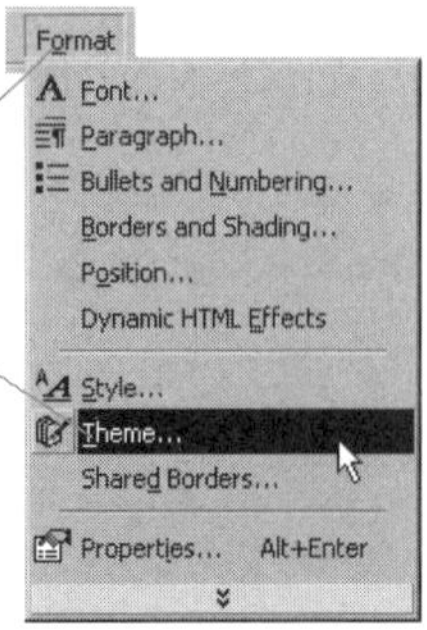

2. Choose to apply the theme to all of the pages in the Web site.

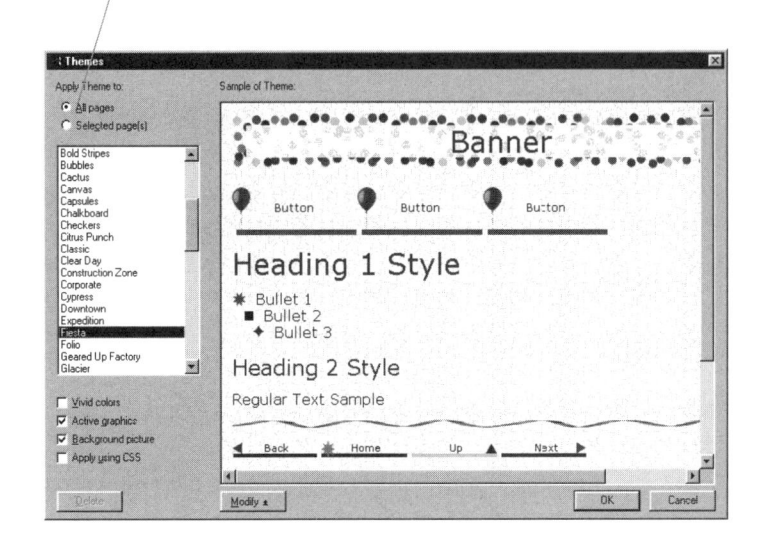

> **HOT TIP** *Try the options to see how they affect particular themes. You may need to apply the theme and preview in the browser to get the complete impact.*

...cont'd

3 Select the theme Fiesta, choose the active graphics and background picture options. Click OK to apply the theme.

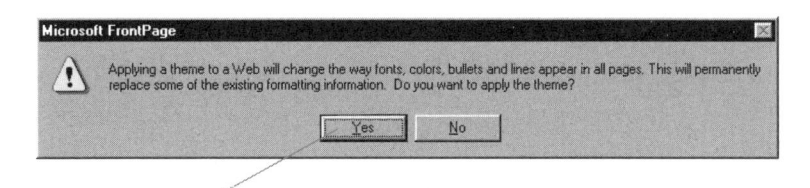

4 Reply Yes if asked to override manual format changes.

The theme will be applied to all the pages and borders in your Web.

5 Press the Save button to capture the change.

6 Select File, Preview in browser to see how the pages will display on the Internet.

4. Enhancing the Web | 65

Customising the theme

> **HOT TIP**
> *You can edit the colours used in any portion of the theme, replace any of the graphics, and modify the styles for text items.*

You can change any element of the themes provided, to make your own custom theme. For example, you could change the page banner for the Web site to something that relates to the Fireworks motif. The Tutorial folder contains a suitable file: 2000ban.gif.

To modify the theme:

1. Open the Web site and the Home page, and select Format, Theme. Fiesta is the default theme for this Web.

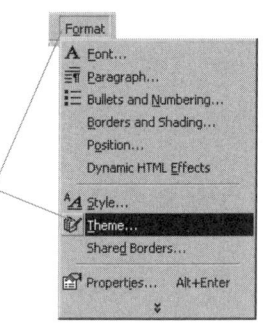

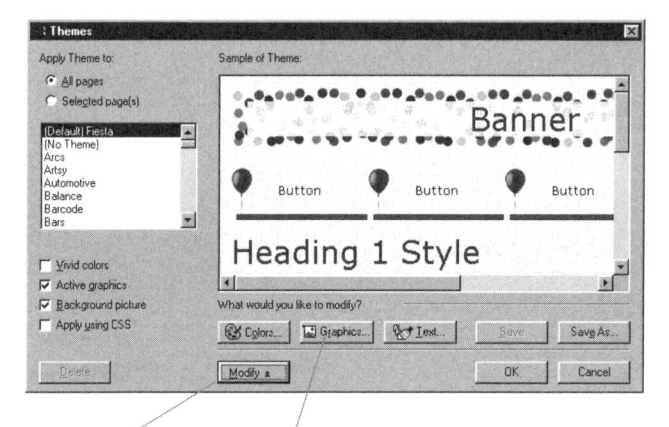

2. Click Modify, and then Graphics from the set of option buttons added to the panel.

3. Select Banner from the Item list. Click the Browse button and locate 2000ban.gif in the Tutorial folder. Press OK to insert the new graphic into the theme.

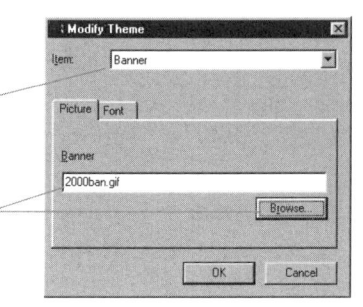

66 | FrontPage 2000 in easy steps

...cont'd

HOT TIP: *The new banner file replaces the banner from the original theme.*

4 The theme is updated and the new banner is added to the display in the sample panel.

5 Press Save As to save the theme, as Copy of Fiesta or another name.

DON'T FORGET: *A theme is marked as read-only, so you must save an existing theme under a new name.*

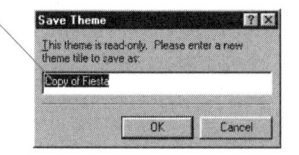

6 Click OK to apply the new theme to the Web site.

DON'T FORGET: *The new theme is applied to all the pages in the Web. To see the effect, press the Preview in Browser button.*

4. Enhancing the Web | 67

Arranging files and folders

You can arrange the files and folders in your Web site using the Folders view. With it you can change the locations of files without worrying about invalidating hyperlinks or losing access to banners, buttons or navigation bars.

To view the contents of the Web:

1. Open the Web and press the Folders button on the Views bar (or select View, Folders).

Don't use Windows Explorer or other file managers to rearrange the contents of your Web – it would break the hyperlinks.

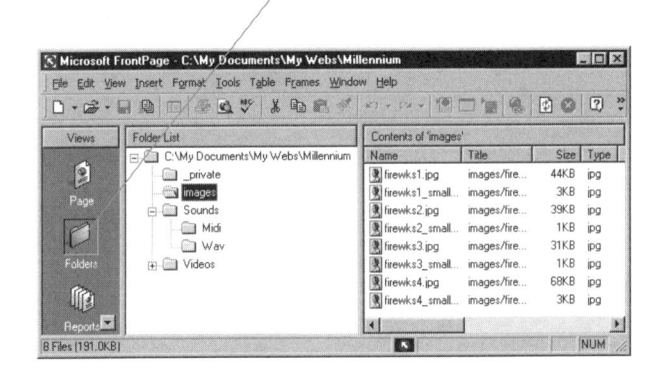

2. Select a folder name to see the contents. Click the [+] to expand a folder list.

If you save embedded files into the default folder when you create pages, you could have a mixture of file types in your main folder. It is much easier to maintain the Web if you group files together. For example, you should put all picture files into the Images folder.

To move picture files to the Images folder:

Click once to sort in ascending order, and click again to sort in descending order.

3. Click the top-level folder for the Web site, and click the Type column to sort by file type.

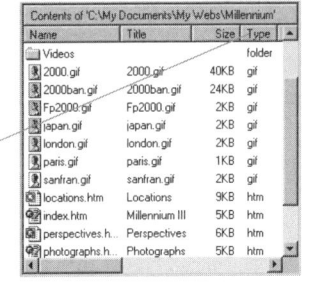

68 | FrontPage 2000 in easy steps

...cont'd

HOT TIP: *Use the Ctrl key to select a group of nonconsecutive files.*

4 Select the first picture file, hold down the Shift key and select the last picture file.

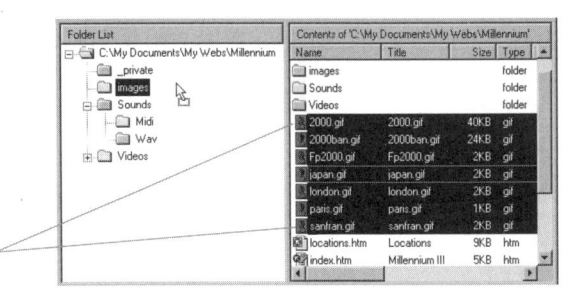

HOT TIP: *FrontPage displays Rename while it moves files since it is updating all the hyperlinks to those files.*

5 Click and hold the left mouse button to drag the selection onto the Image folder. Release the button to drop the files into the folder.

You can create new folders in Folders view as desired, to store related types of files together, such as sound files, movie clips or application data.

To create a new folder for Applets:

6 Right-click the folder within which you want to create the new subfolder.

7 Select New Folder from the context menu displayed.

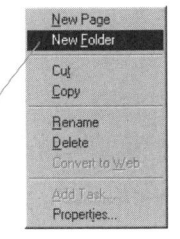

BEWARE: *You can create a new page in Folders view, but it won't use shared borders or navigation bars (see page 70).*

8 Overtype the New Folder name with the name you want, for example 'Applet'.

9 Drag and drop the animation file into the new folder. FrontPage makes any adjustments needed to the Web site.

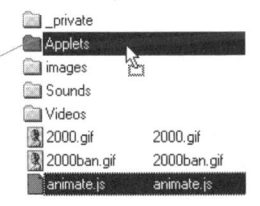

4. Enhancing the Web | 69

Adding a new page

When you use themes and shared borders for all pages in the Web, new pages that you create will inherit the attributes that you have specified.

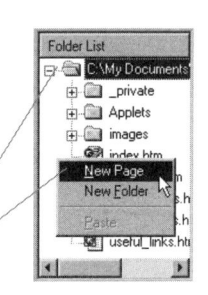

To create a new page:

As well as creating a new page, you have to show FrontPage where the page fits in the overall Web structure.

1 In the folder list, right-click the target folder and select New Page.

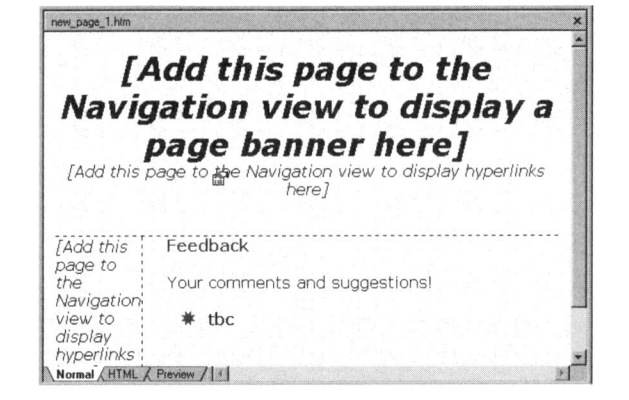

Depending on its level in the structure, the new page may be added to the navigation bars in the shared borders and appear on the other pages.

2 Add the text (Feedback, Your comments and suggestions!) then select Save. The default name is the first line of text.

3 Switch to Navigation view, and drag the new file from the folder list to the appropriate position on the Web structure.

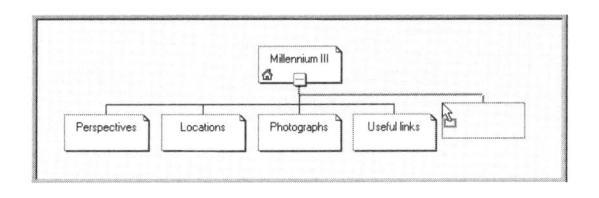

This page will be completed in the next chapter (see page 72).

The page will now display the page banner themes etc.

70 | FrontPage 2000 in easy steps

Finalise the Web

Add the final items, such as a feedback page. Display reports to check that the Web is complete, and confirm that the Web is ready for publication on the Internet or the Intranet.

Covers

Requesting feedback | 72

View page | 74

Which browser? | 75

View the Web | 76

Modify text | 78

Check spelling | 80

Completing tasks | 82

Web reports | 84

Backup | 86

Chapter Five

Requesting feedback

With a feedback option on your Web site, you can gain information as well as distribute it.

The last page added to the Web was Feedback. The purpose of this page is to provide a means for visitors to the Web site to contribute their comments and information.

To create a form for this information:

1. Open the Web and the Feedback page.

2. Replace the initial text with an invitation to send comments on the topic.

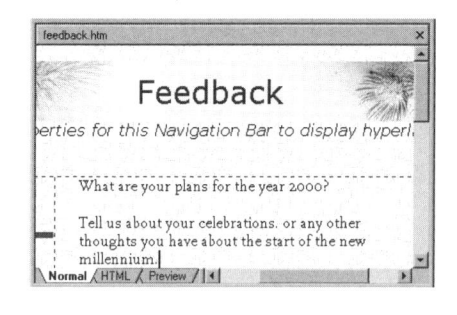

The form makes it easier to collate and interpret feedback, especially if you want the analysis to be automated.

3. Press Enter to create a new line, select Insert from the menu bar, then click Form. Select Form from the next menu.

FrontPage inserts a new form on the current page. The dashed lines indicate the form's boundary. By default, a new form contains Submit and Reset push buttons.

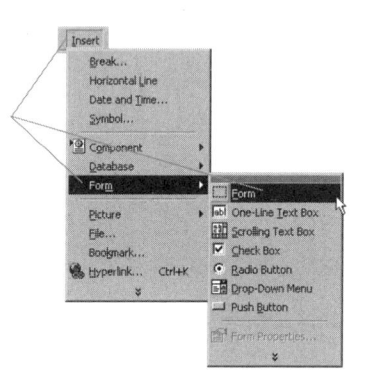

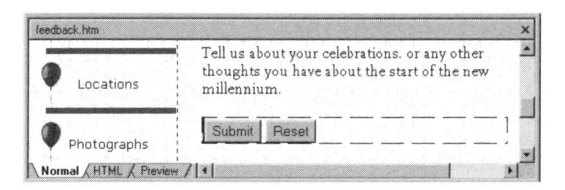

4. With the cursor left of the Submit button, click the Centre button on the toolbar and then press Enter to add space. Press the up-arrow to go to the top of the form.

72 | FrontPage 2000 in easy steps

...cont'd

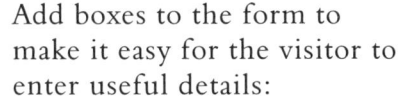

Add boxes to the form to make it easy for the visitor to enter useful details:

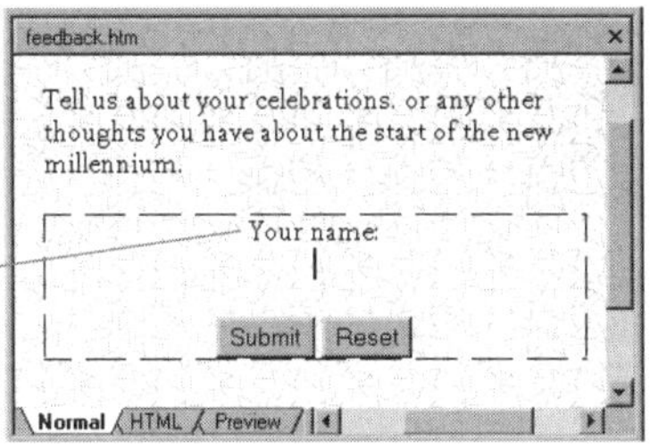

1. Type Your name: and then press Shift+Enter to create a line break.

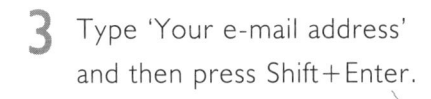

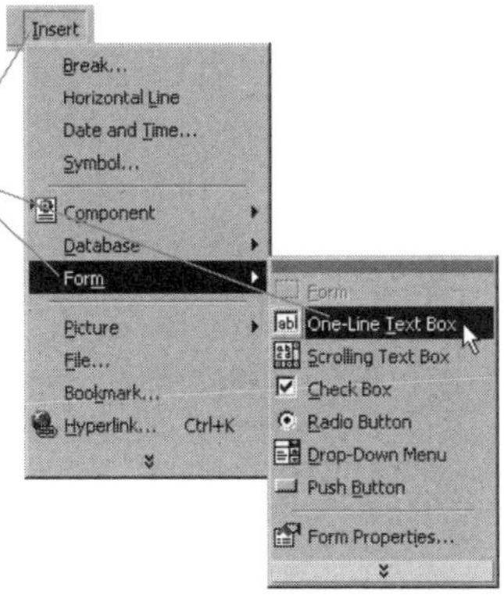

> **HOT TIP**
> You can add text boxes, check boxes, menus, radio buttons, pictures and push buttons, to your forms.

2. Select Insert, Form, click One-Line Text Box, and then press Enter.

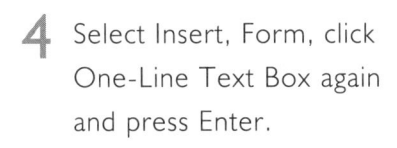

3. Type 'Your e-mail address' and then press Shift+Enter.

4. Select Insert, Form, click One-Line Text Box again and press Enter.

> **HOT TIP**
> The default scrolling text box is very small but can easily be enlarged (see page 74).

5. Type 'Your millennium thoughts:' and then press Shift+Enter.

6. Select Insert, Form, click Scrolling Text Box, and then press Enter.

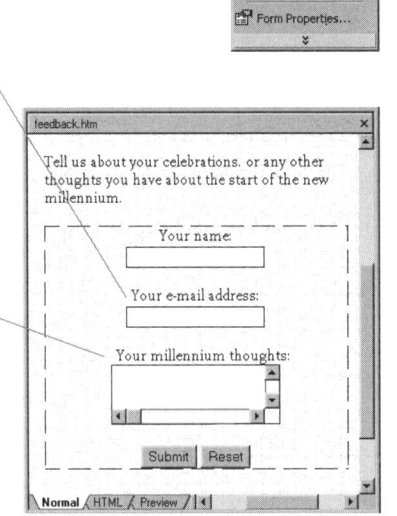

This provides a scrollable text box with a default width of 20 characters, and allowance for two lines of text in the viewable area.

View page

When you display the properties for text boxes or scroll boxes, you can change the default names.

1. Double-click the scrolling text box to display the Properties for the Scrolling Text Box.

2. Change the width to 35 characters and the number of lines to 7, and press OK.

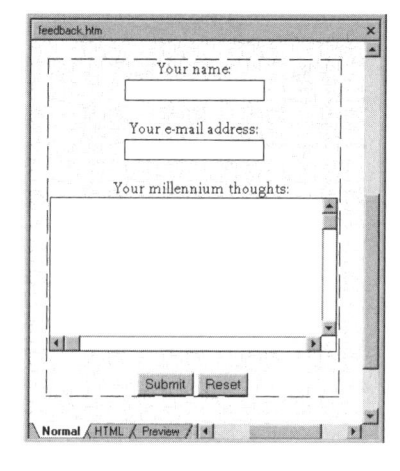

Make sure that your text boxes are large enough for their intended contents, to encourage responses.

3. The scrolling text box is enlarged. Press Save to capture the revisions.

4. Press the Preview in Browser button to view the page in its final form.

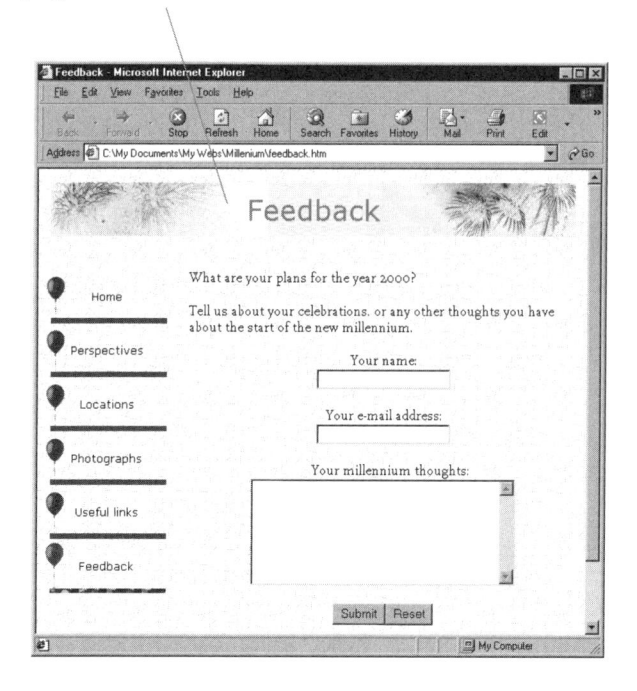

Which browser?

A browser is not essential for making a Web, but one is required to view the pages in their final form.

When you view your Web pages with your browser, you will see what your visitors will see, as long as they have the same browser as you, or one with support for all the functions that you use.

This may be more difficult to achieve than you might think. There are many browsers available on the Internet. This is the list for machines running Windows operating systems:

Cello	Thomas Bruce
Communicator	Netscape
HotJava	Sun Microsystems
I-Comm	Talent Communications
I-View	Talent Communications
InterGo	InterGO Communications, Inc.
Internet Explorer	Microsoft
Internet Workhorse	MarketNet
Lynx	Lynx Team
Multilingual Mosaic	Accent Software
NeoPlanet	NeoPlanet
NetCruiser	NetCom
Navigator	Netscape
Opera	Opera Software
Mosaic	Quarterdeck
SlipKnot	Peter Brooks
Softerm	Plus Softronics, Inc.
Tango	Alis Technologies Inc.
Tiber	Video On Line

Of course, visitors to your site are not restricted to Windows, so there may be other browsers not available on a Windows platform.

To add a new browser:

The new browser must be already installed on your system, since FrontPage checks the command line.

1 Open a page in your Web, select File, Preview in Browser, and click Add.

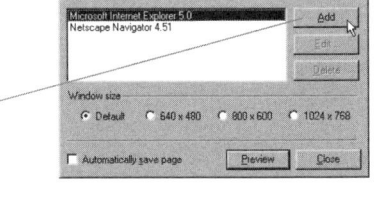

2 Enter the name and the command line for your browser, and press OK.

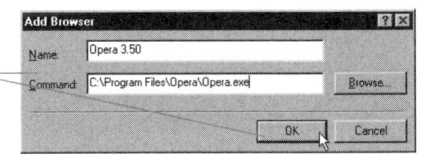

5. Finalise the Web | 75

View the Web

You can't dictate the resources that your visitors will have available, but you can avoid conflicts or at least warn visitors of potential mismatches.

At the minimum, you should examine your Web using Internet Explorer and Netscape Communicator, which are the main browsers in use. Even if your Web design requires a particular type or version of browser, you should see what other visitors will find, and understand how they may react.

To view your Web site:

1. Click this button on the toolbar to view the current page in your default browser:

2. Press File, Preview in Browser to change the default browser or to adjust settings.

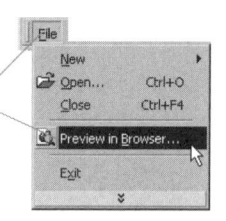

Your choices become the new defaults (as used by the Preview in Browser button) until you set different values.

3. You can choose a browser, select the window size, and elect to save the current page automatically. Press the Preview button to display the current page.

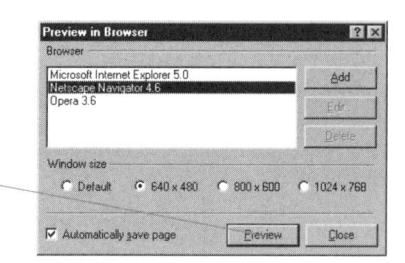

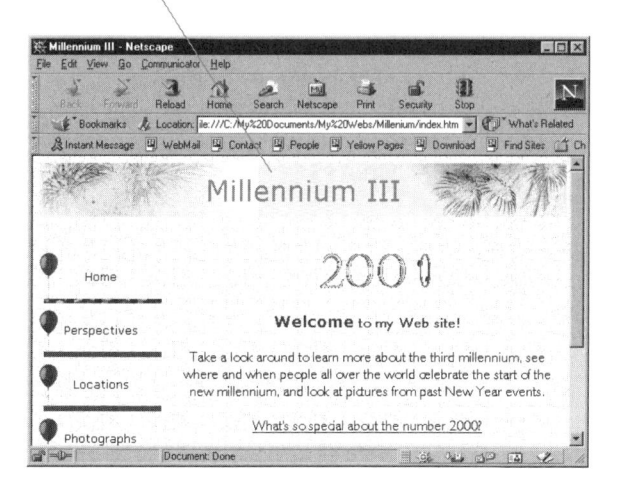

76 | FrontPage 2000 in easy steps

...cont'd

View all the pages in your Web site. Note any items that fail to operate as expected. Repeat the checks with other browsers. If there are browser-based limitations, you can modify the items, or add a suitable caution to the page.

1. Select the window that you will use as your preferred size, for example 600 x 800.

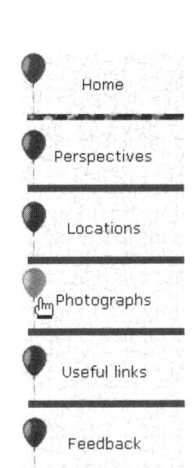

2. Click on the Navigation bar to change pages. For example, select the Photographs page.

3. Observe the layout and note problems. For example, the photo thumbnails could be moved up slightly. Delete the blank line (in FrontPage, Page view).

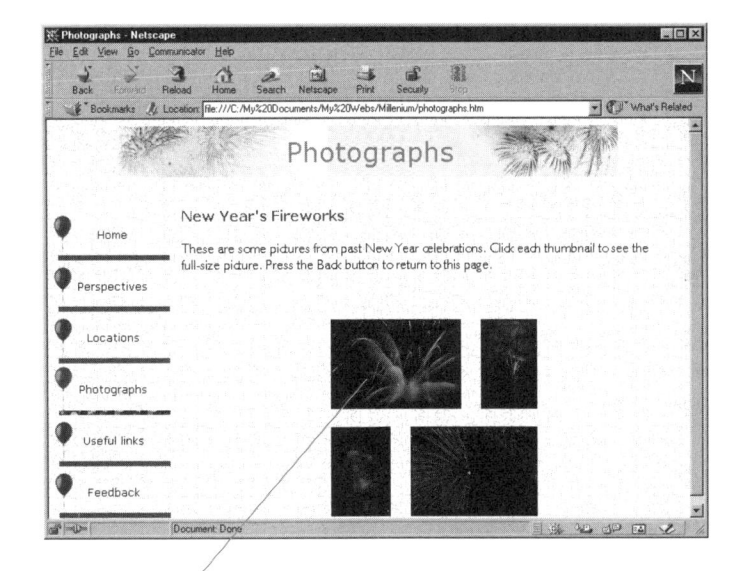

4. Click on a Thumbnail to display a photograph.

5. Click the Back button to return to the main Web page.

When you make any changes in FrontPage, Save the page, and press Reload or Refresh in your browser.

5. Finalise the Web | 77

Modify text

You can make global changes to the Web site if there are terms that you use on several Web pages, and you decide that they need adjusting.

> **HOT TIP:** You can make a change to selected pages or all pages in the Web site, but you can only replace text in parts of the page that can be edited directly. Text in page titles must be modified individually.

To modify a section of text:

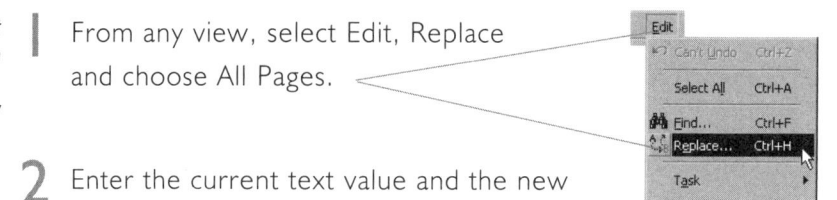

1. From any view, select Edit, Replace and choose All Pages.

2. Enter the current text value and the new text value.

3. Set Match case or Whole word if needed and press Find in Web.

> **HOT TIP:** You can select individual pages instead of working through them all, if you see that changes to some pages are not appropriate.

4. Double-click the first entry to open the page.

5. Click Find Next to skip a change, or Replace to change and find next.

6. Press Replace All to change all the occurrences immediately.

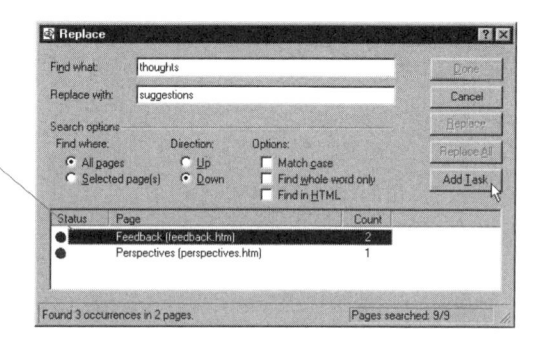

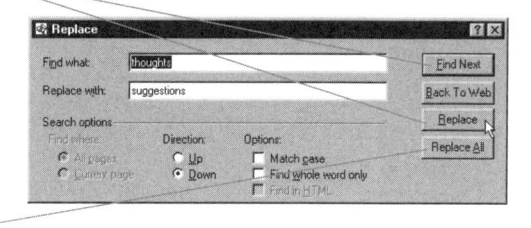

...cont'd

FrontPage guides you through the changes, reminds you to save the changed files and makes sure that you do not leave out a page by mistake.

7 When each page is finished, you are prompted to save and close the current document and move on to apply the changes to the next page.

8 When the final page is completed, you are prompted to save and close the last document.

9 Press Replace All to change all the occurrences immediately. The report shows which pages have been edited. Press Cancel to end the operation.

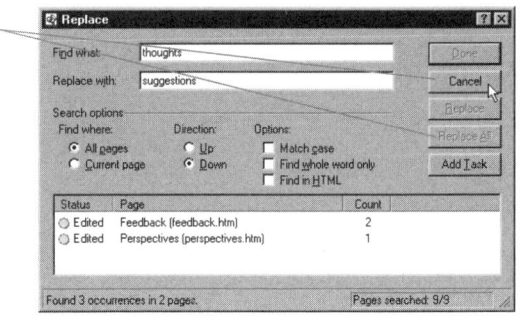

If there are several persons making changes to the pages in your Web site, or if you want to keep a log of the changes, click Add Task instead of double-clicking the results. This will add the Replace operations to the Task list. The replacement will not be applied until you complete the task in Tasks view, as shown in the Spelling example on page 80.

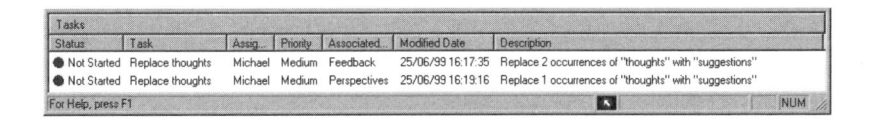

5. Finalise the Web | 79

Check spelling

You also need to check the content of the pages. The FrontPage spell checker helps with this.

The background spell-checking will identify possible spelling errors with underlines. You can retype the words or use the spell checker to correct them, as you build the individual pages. However, you should also make it a practice to carry out a full spell check of all the Web pages, just before you are ready to publish the Web site.

To check the spelling for the entire site:

1. From any view except Page press F7, or click Tools, Spelling.

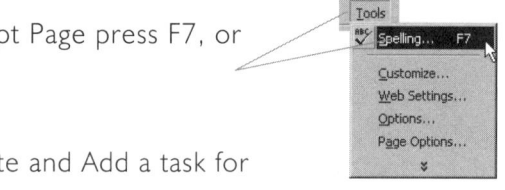

In Page view, you can check only the current open page. Global checking is not offered.

2. Select Entire Web site and Add a task for each page with misspellings.

3. Click Start and FrontPage displays progress and results for the spell check.

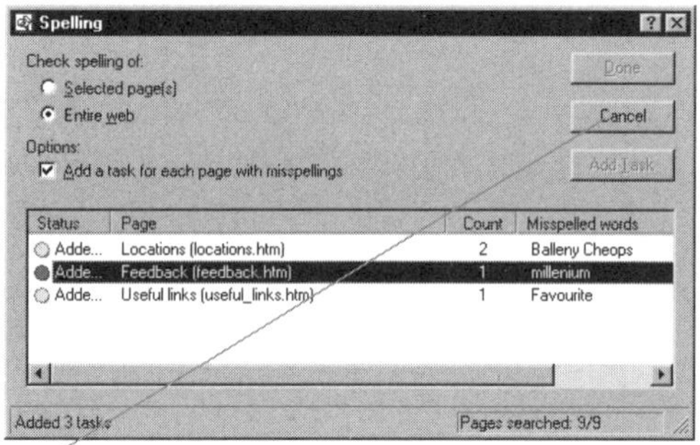

Text on items such as page titles in page banners will not be included in the check and must be checked in the Page edit view.

FrontPage displays the misspelled words and the number of tasks added to the Tasks list – one for each page that has any spelling errors.

4. Click Cancel to finish with Spelling.

The spell check is complete, but corrections are not yet applied.

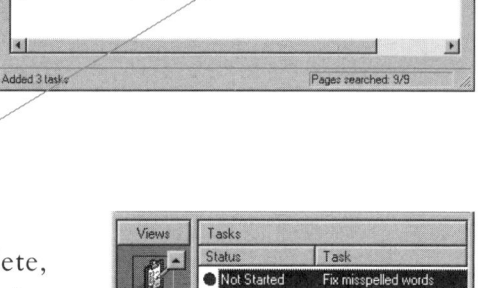

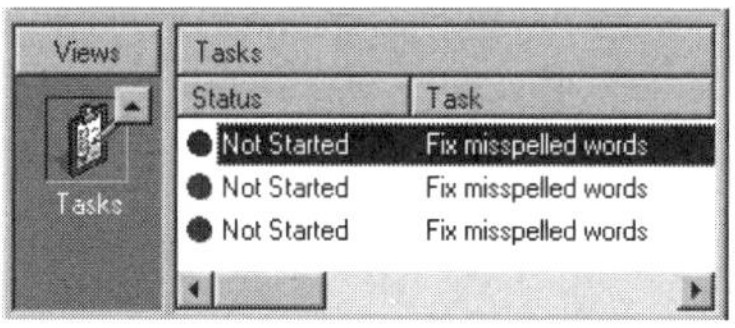

...cont'd

> *The Tasks mechanism makes it possible for several people to schedule changes, and then have all the tasks completed at one time. This reduces the possibility of multiple concurrent changes that could cause some changes to be lost or overridden.*

The spell checking and the Replace operation can both add tasks to the task list. To display the list:

1. Select the Tasks icon on the Views bar, and the Tasks list is displayed.

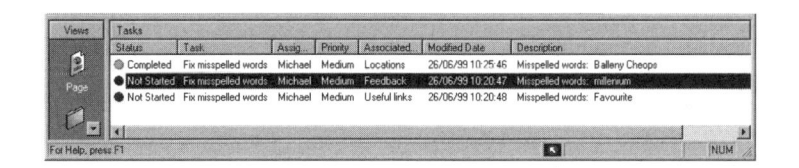

2. Double-click a task on the list, or right-click the task and select Edit Task in the menu.

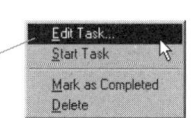

   The details of the selected task are shown. Change the task name, set the priority, assign it to someone else in your group. Click OK to save changes, or click Cancel. To perform the task:

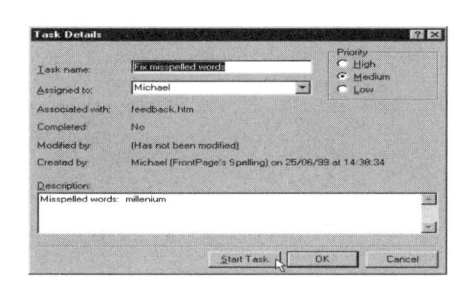

> *Additions are made to the custom dictionary used by the other Office applications, so you won't have to add special terms for every application separately.*

3. Click Start Task, or right-click a task and select Start Task, to open the page.

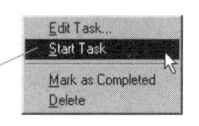

   Ignore special terms that are rarely used. Change to one of the dictionary suggestions. Add terms and names that are frequently used in your documents.

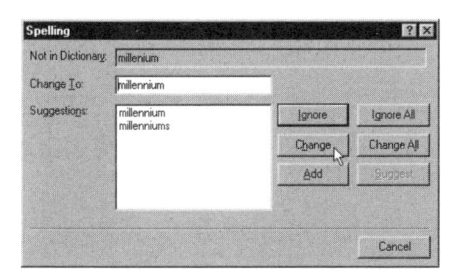

5. Finalise the Web | 81

Completing tasks

1 Click OK when the spelling corrections for a page are completed.

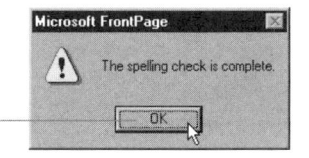

> **HOT TIP** *It is best to mark tasks as completed, since they are then removed from the list of outstanding tasks.*

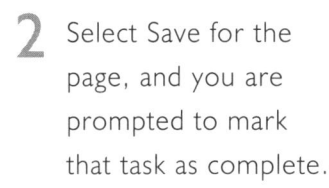

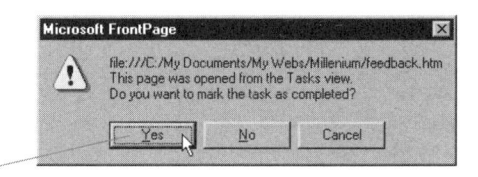

2 Select Save for the page, and you are prompted to mark that task as complete.

3 Alternatively, right-click the task and select Mark as Completed.

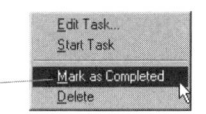

4 Start the next task, and continue until all the tasks can be marked as completed.

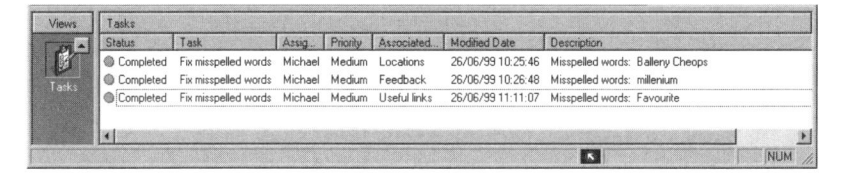

> **HOT TIP** *For example, you could assign a research task to an individual in your group, and log the task in the list. When the research report has been produced, mark the task as completed.*

You can use the Tasks list to record the need for any type of activity. You can assign tasks, prioritise them, and link them to a page or any other files in your Web. When the tasks are finished, you can mark them as completed, in the Tasks list.

To create a task:

5 Open the Web, and select File from the menu bar, then New and then Task.

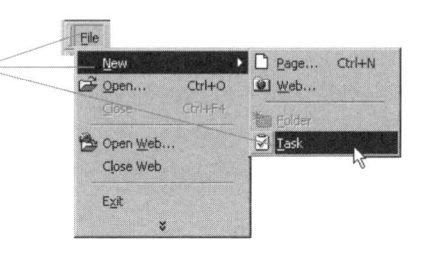

82 | FrontPage 2000 in easy steps

...cont'd

If you create a task in Page view while editing a page, the task is automatically associated with that page. To associate a task with a page or file in another view, select the file, and then create the task. If no pages are open, the task will carry no file association.

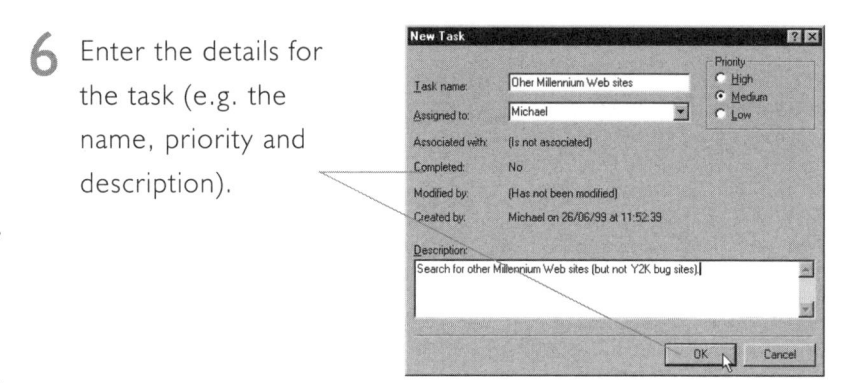

6 Enter the details for the task (e.g. the name, priority and description).

The tasks are added to the Tasks list, just like the tasks automatically generated by FrontPage.

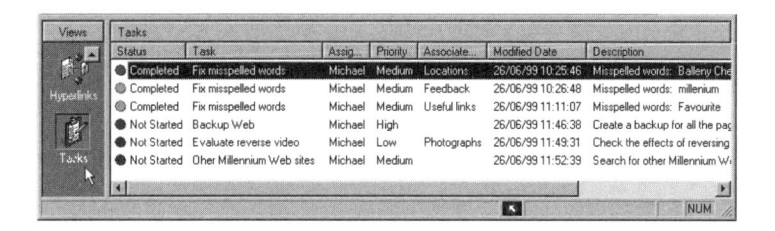

When you refresh Tasks view or switch to another view, Microsoft FrontPage by default hides completed tasks.

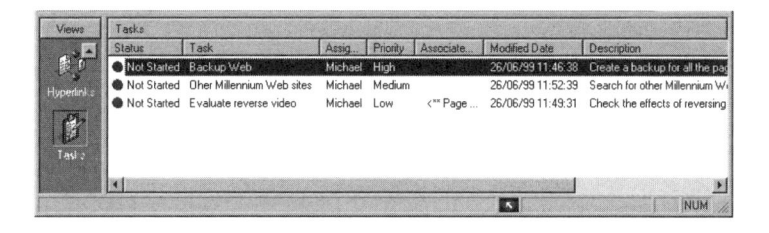

To show completed tasks:

7 Right-click the background in Tasks view and click Show Task History. Select again to hide the tasks.

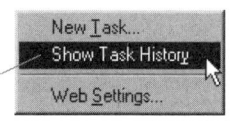

5. Finalise the Web | 83

Web reports

> **HOT TIP:** *FrontPage provides reports to help you identify any problems with your Web, before you send the files or the updates to the Web server.*

The Reports view gives you information about the status and condition of your Web, so that you can find and resolve any shortcomings before you publish it. There are over a dozen report categories, but the place to start is the site summary.

To display the default report:

1. Open the Web and press Reports on the Views bar to display the default report (the site summary).

2. To reset the default, you'd select Views, Reports and click the Site Summary from the list offered, to make it the default.

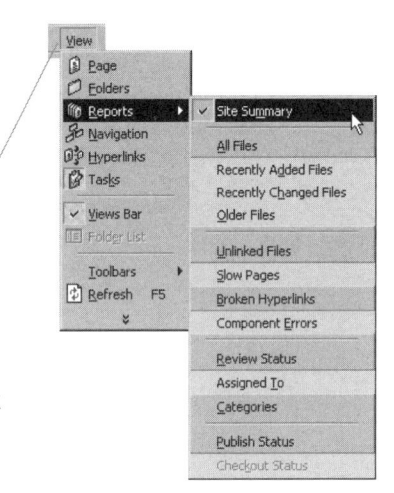

> **HOT TIP:** *All files tells you the disk space you will require at the Web server. Slow pages warns of any pages that may be a problem during download.*

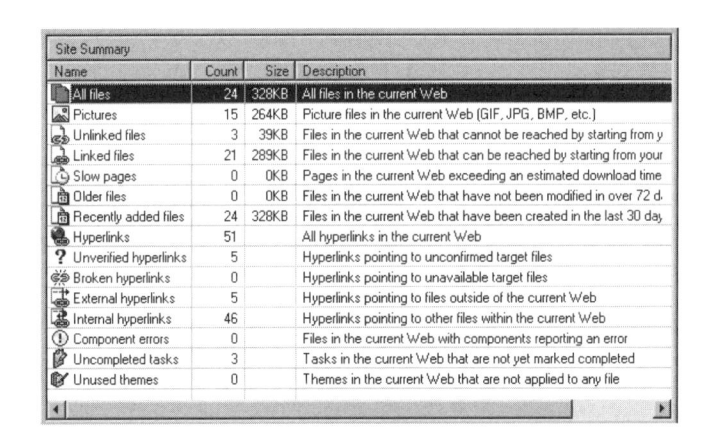

Name	Count	Size	Description
All files	24	328KB	All files in the current Web
Pictures	15	264KB	Picture files in the current Web (GIF, JPG, BMP, etc.)
Unlinked files	3	39KB	Files in the current Web that cannot be reached by starting from y
Linked files	21	289KB	Files in the current Web that can be reached by starting from your
Slow pages	0	0KB	Pages in the current Web exceeding an estimated download time
Older files	0	0KB	Files in the current Web that have not been modified in over 72 d.
Recently added files	24	328KB	Files in the current Web that have been created in the last 30 day
Hyperlinks	51		All hyperlinks in the current Web
Unverified hyperlinks	5		Hyperlinks pointing to unconfirmed target files
Broken hyperlinks	0		Hyperlinks pointing to unavailable target files
External hyperlinks	5		Hyperlinks pointing to files outside of the current Web
Internal hyperlinks	46		Hyperlinks pointing to other files within the current Web
Component errors	0		Files in the current Web with components reporting an error
Uncompleted tasks	3		Tasks in the current Web that are not yet marked completed
Unused themes	0		Themes in the current Web that are not applied to any file

FrontPage switches to Reports view and generates the default report which is the Site Summary. This report provides statistics on the Web pages and files, giving the sizes and providing information about the links used in the Web site.

...cont'd

If you rename or relocate files using the Folders view, the integrity of URLs will be maintained. Using normal Windows commands will invalidate the URL references.

The Broken Hyperlinks report will alert you to any errors in hyperlinks. These could be due to mistyping of URLs, or to changes in file names or locations made after the URL was set up.

For the detailed list of the broken hyperlinks in the Web:

1. Click the down-arrow on the Reports toolbar, and select the Broken Hyperlinks report.

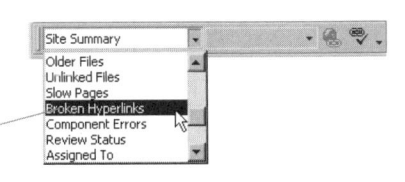

2. Any invalid hyperlinks are displayed. FrontPage will also list unverified external hyperlinks.

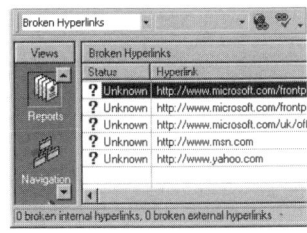

If there are many external hyperlinks in the Web, it may take some time to carry out this command, since FrontPage must connect to each external Web site to verify the hyperlink.

3. Click the Verify Hyperlink button on the Reports toolbar. You can verify all hyperlinks, resume an interrupted check, or verify a selected hyperlink.

4. FrontPage connects to the Internet to check the links.

5. Right-click a hyperlink and select Add Task to create a reminder, or click Edit Hyperlink or Edit Page to correct the URL.

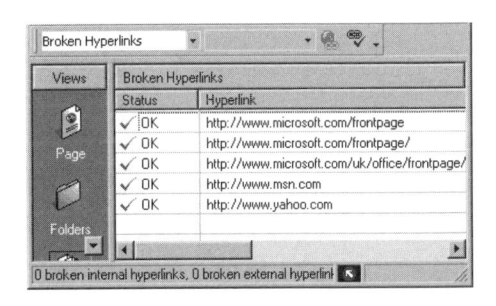

5. Finalise the Web | 85

Backup

When you have checked your Web site and corrected any errors, you should make a backup copy before publishing.

You can make a backup copy of all the files and folders in the Web. However, the preferred way is to publish the Web to a folder on your hard disk. This ensures that all necessary files are saved, in the correct structure.

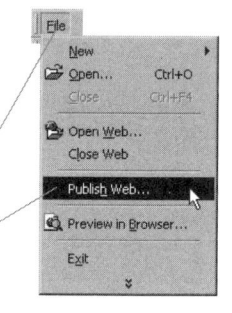

1. Open the Web, and select File, Publish Web. Click Options to expand the options panel.

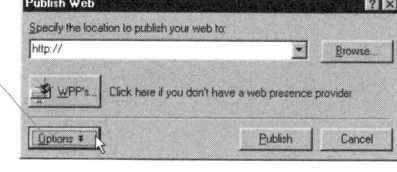

For future backups, you can choose to publish changed pages only.

2. Click Browse and locate the backup folder.

3. Specify Publish all pages and Include Subwebs.

4. Click Publish and FrontPage transfers the files and folders of your Web to the specified destination.

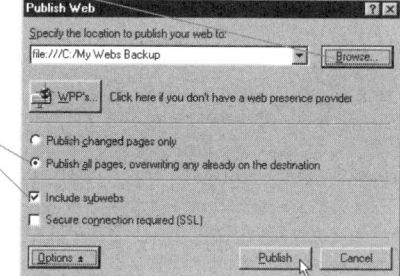

If you cancel publishing in the middle of the operation, files that have already been published remain at the destination.

When transfer has completed, you can choose to view the new copy of the Web through the default Web browser, or just press Done to end.

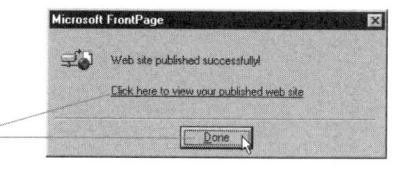

86 | FrontPage 2000 in easy steps

Publishing the Web

When you have all the components, and you have checked all the links, you can finally transfer the Web to the Internet. The process depends on the type of ISP or WPP you are planning to use.

Covers

Ways to publish | 88

ISP and FTP | 89

Try the form | 91

Select a WPP | 92

ISP with WPP and HTTP | 93

Using Hypermart | 94

Form results | 96

Using banners | 97

Full function WPP | 99

Selective publishing | 100

Chapter Six

Ways to publish

When you are ready to display your Web on the Internet or on your company intranet, you must publish your Web, which means copying all the files and folders in your Web to a Web server, where visitors can browse. You should already have checked for broken hyperlinks, and verified that the pages look the way you expect.

To publish to the Internet, you need an ISP, preferably offering a Web server with the FrontPage Server Extensions installed. You also need the Web server location, and your user name and password.

FrontPage Server Extensions

The server extensions are not essential, but they give your Web the full FrontPage functionality, such as form handlers, search forms, hit counters, and component features. FrontPage will maintain your files and hyperlinks. Each time you publish the Web, FrontPage compares the files on your local computer to the files on the Web server. If you move a file in your Web on the hard disk, FrontPage will update and correct any hyperlinks to it, and then make the same corrections to the Web server files, the next time you publish the Web.

You can also edit the Web directly on the Web server, though in that case the hard disk version will not stay in sync.

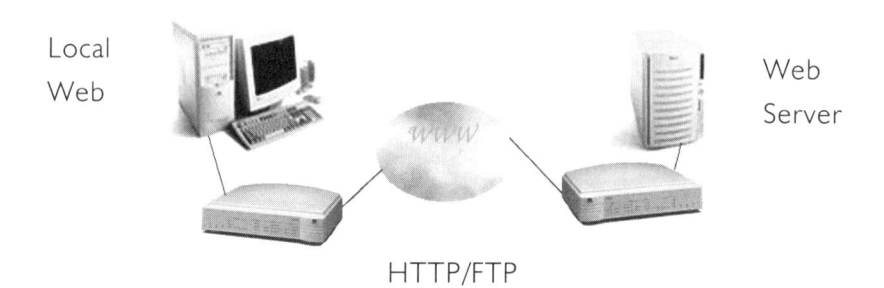

Local Web — HTTP/FTP — Web Server

HTTP or FTP

The server extensions also influence the way you publish the Web. If your Web server has the extensions, then FrontPage can publish using HTTP (Hypertext Transfer Protocol). Otherwise, your Web will be published using FTP (File Transfer Protocol).

ISP and FTP

Even if the ISP does not have support for the FrontPage Server Extensions, you can use FTP and FrontPage will still manage the Web files for you.

This is the method to use if your ISP does not have explicit support for FrontPage 2000:

To publish using FTP:

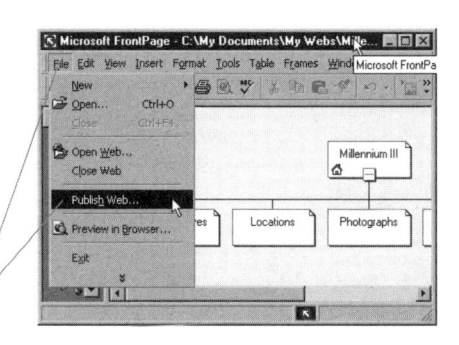

1. Open the Web. Select File, Publish Web.

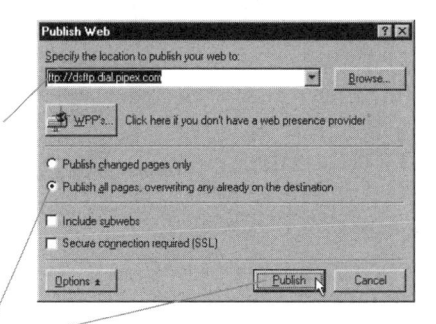

2. Enter the FTP address for the Web server providing your space.

There may already be a page called Index.htm at the Web site, since it is the usual default.

3. Specify All Pages the first time to replace existing files, and click Publish.

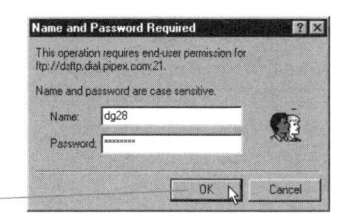

4. Enter the account ID and password for your ISP account, and click OK.

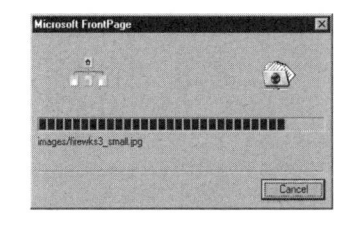

5. FrontPage connects to the Internet, and then opens the folders in the Web and transfers the files to the Web server.

Try asking your ISP (or your network administrator for an Intranet) to install the features. At least they'll then know that there is a demand.

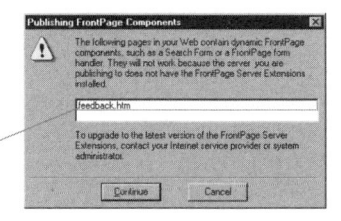

6. FrontPage detects that the server does not support the extensions, and warns you of pages that use their functions.

6. Publishing the Web | 89

...cont'd

Don't try the link suggested with the message, since it is an FTP link. Use the URL provided by your ISP to view the Web site.

7 When all of the files have been transferred, the Web site published successfully message is displayed.

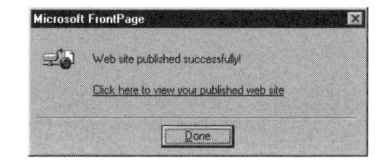

8 Open the browser and enter the URL for the Web site.

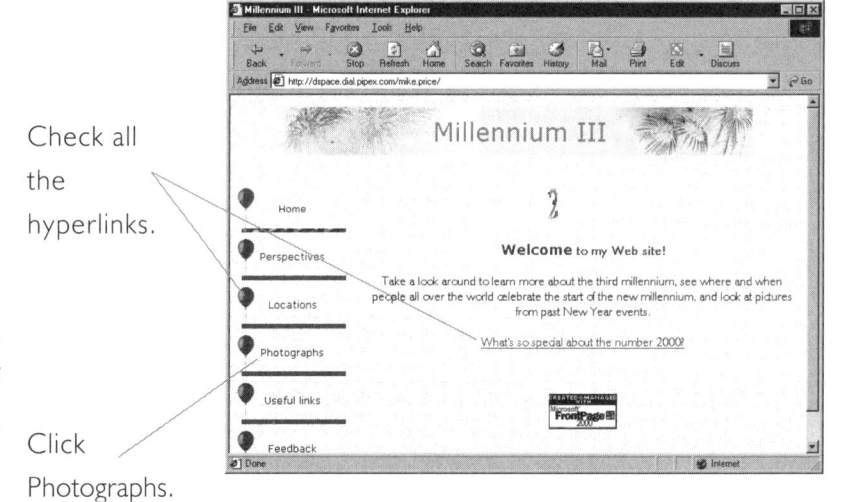

Check all the hyperlinks.

Click Photographs.

You'll find that most functions work as they should, though with a much slower response, compared to the local Web, since everything must be downloaded from the Web server.

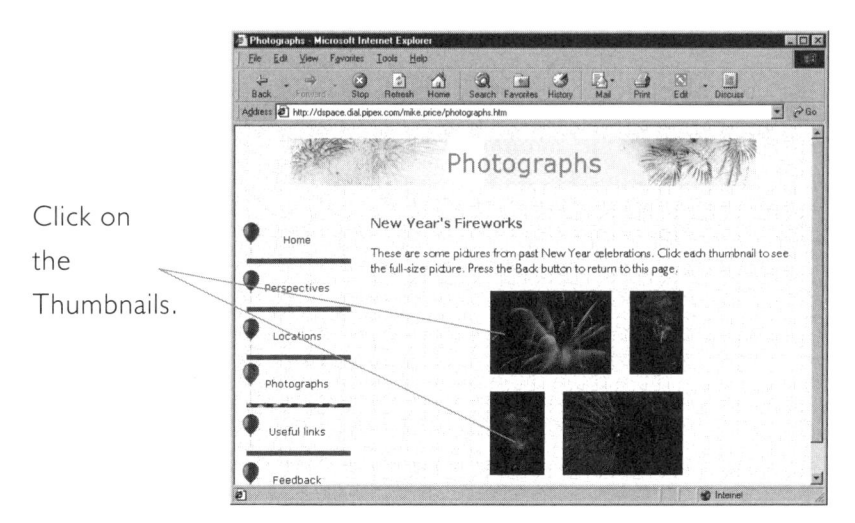

Click on the Thumbnails.

90 | FrontPage 2000 in easy steps

Try the form

Dynamic features such as FrontPage forms may appear to work but won't complete properly without the server extensions.

1 Select the Feedback button to display the page.

2 The form displays correctly, and your browser will allow you to fill in any of the fields on the form.

3 When you press the Submit button however, there is no server extension to process the data in the form.

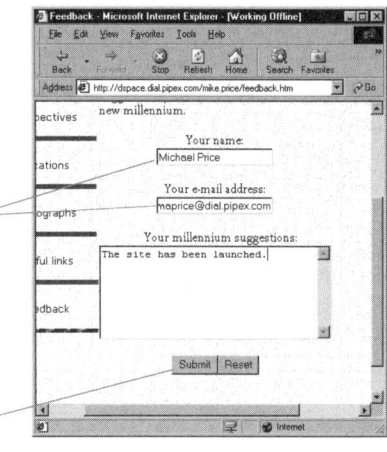

Various Internet sites offer Guest Book facilities that manage responses for you without requiring special functions on your Web server.

You need to change the page to use a different method that does not depend on the extensions. For example, insert a MailTo address:

4 Click the 'Hyperlinks' and 'Make a hyperlink that sends E-mail' icons.

5 Enter an e-mail address for responses. Click OK to add the link to the Web page.

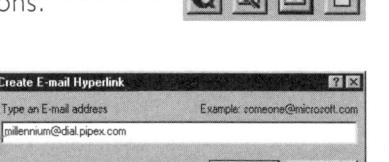

mailto:millennium@dial.pipex.com

6. Publishing the Web | 91

Select a WPP

If you want to find an ISP that offers support for FrontPage enabled Web sites, you'll find help at Microsoft's Web site.

To view lists of Web Presence Providers:

> **HOT TIP**
> *The URLs and the ISP names are changed from time to time, but the WPP button should direct you to the latest lists.*

1 Click the Publish button on the toolbar, and press the WPP's button.

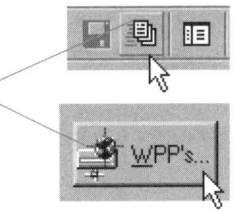

> **DON'T FORGET**
> *You can use a USA provider just as easily as a UK provider, although it may be more difficult to call technical support due to time zone differences.*

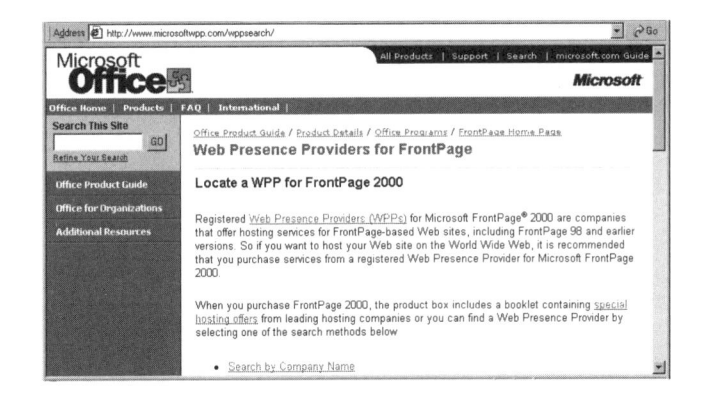

2 The USA Web page for WPPs supporting FrontPage 2000 is displayed.

3 Follow links for International and UK, to find a list of ISPs for home Web sites. There are also lists for ISPs hosting small business and corporate Web sites.

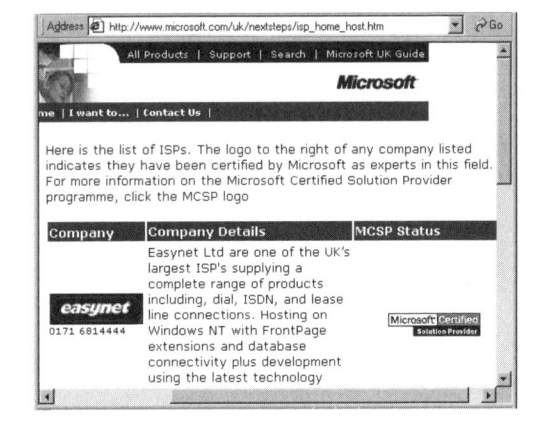

ISP with WPP and HTTP

Stay with your ISP and get FrontPage Server Extensions from a Web space provider.

You can continue to use an ISP such as Dial Pipex that does not support FrontPage extensions, but store your Web site with a Web space provider. You'll have to pay for an ad-free service, or you can have free Web hosting if you are happy to accept advertising banners.

As an example, Hypermart offers 10 MB of free Web space when you register for an account at the Hypermart site:

The free Web space accounts rarely include support for database linkage, so they'll need the premium service.

The sign on, enable and install processes at the Hypermart Web server are automated, so they complete very quickly.

1 Sign up, and wait for e-mail with the startup information.

2 Enable your account and choose to install the FrontPage Server Extensions on your Web site.

3 A few minutes after the confirmation arrives, you are able to publish FrontPage aware Webs to Hypermart's Web server.

6. Publishing the Web | 93

Using Hypermart

Publishing to a Web space provider such as Hypermart will give you the FrontPage Server Extension support that your ISP may be missing.

To publish using HTTP:

You must connect to the Internet using your ISP, when you publish to the Web server.

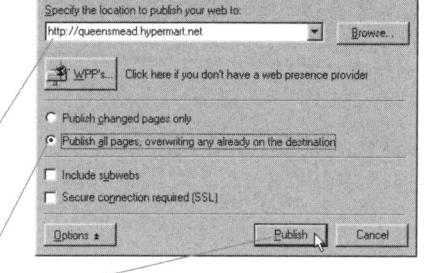

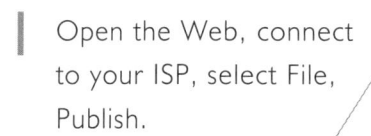

1. Open the Web, connect to your ISP, select File, Publish.

2. Enter the URL address for the Web server, select Publish all pages and click Publish.

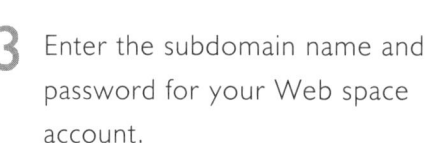

3. Enter the subdomain name and password for your Web space account.

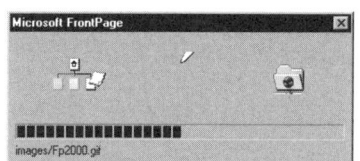

You will not see warnings about the dynamic FrontPage components, when there is support installed at the Web server.

4. FrontPage copies the files and folders from your Web to the Web server.

5. When the transfer completes, you should be able to use the link provided, to go to the new Web site.

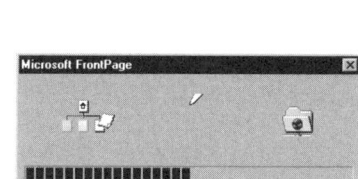

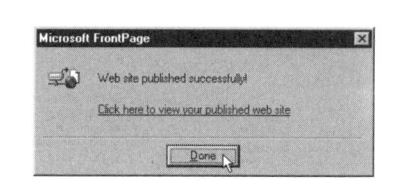

When you open the site, all the pages and features of your Web site should operate just as they did with the ISP setup. However, this time you should be able to use the form on the Feedback page to collect observations left by visitors to the site.

...cont'd

6 Click the URL link on the message, or open your browser and enter the URL for the Web site.

The Home page for your Web is displayed, but over it is a second, smaller window containing a banner advert.

There's no point in closing this – it reopens every couple of minutes – so get used to hitting Minimise when it reappears.

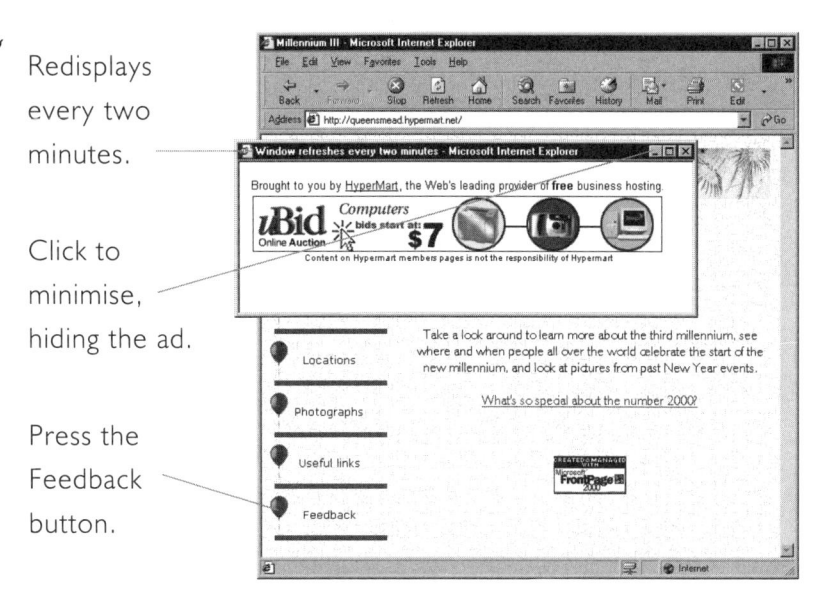

Redisplays every two minutes.

Click to minimise, hiding the ad.

Press the Feedback button.

The feedback form displays, ready to be completed.

7 Enter your name, e-mail address and comments in the text boxes.

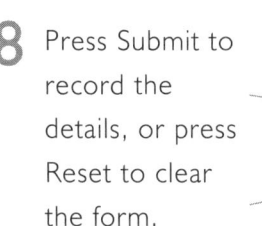

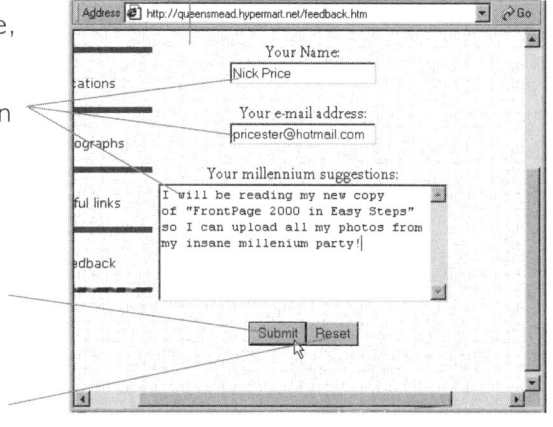

The form contents are written to a file in the Web site (see page 96).

8 Press Submit to record the details, or press Reset to clear the form.

6. Publishing the Web | 95

Form results

> **HOT TIP**
> *By default, FrontPage forms use simple field names such as T1, T2. You can choose meaningful names when you create the form, using form field properties (see page 74).*

When you submit a form, the details are written to file, and the confirmation messages show the fields recorded.

To view the contents of the results file:

1. Click to return to the form (or press the Back button).

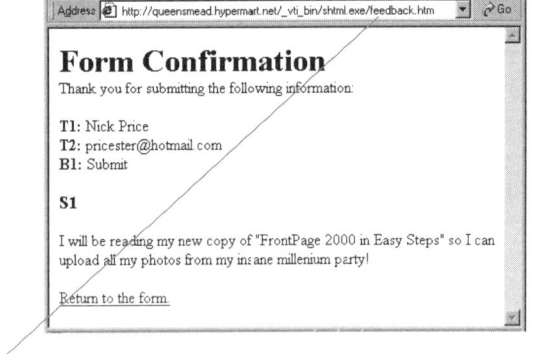

2. On the address bar, replace the 'feedback.htm' by the file name _private/form_results.htm.

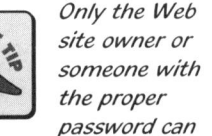

3. Provide the account name and the password as authorisation to view.

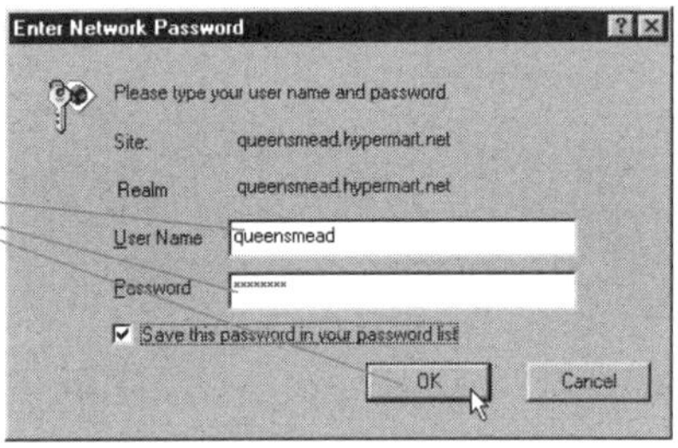

> **HOT TIP**
> *Only the Web site owner or someone with the proper password can access the results file.*

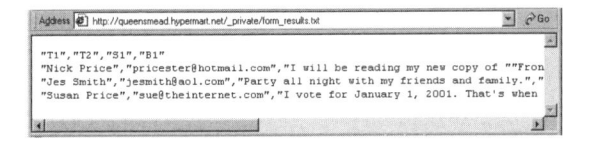

4. The contents are displayed in a comma delimited form, with the field names as headings.

This file is at the Web site, and won't automatically be downloaded. You can select File, Save As, and save the contents to a file on your hard disk. The file can then be imported into a Word document as a table, or into an Excel spreadsheet for analysis of the responses.

Using banners

If you feel that the separate windows are too intrusive, you could try an ad banner instead.

Hypermart offers different ways for you to insert the advertising that qualifies you for free Web space. For example, you can add code to every page to display a banner. This should be placed where it can be viewed without scrolling the default 640 by 480 browser.

Add the banner to the top border on any page, then it will appear on all pages.

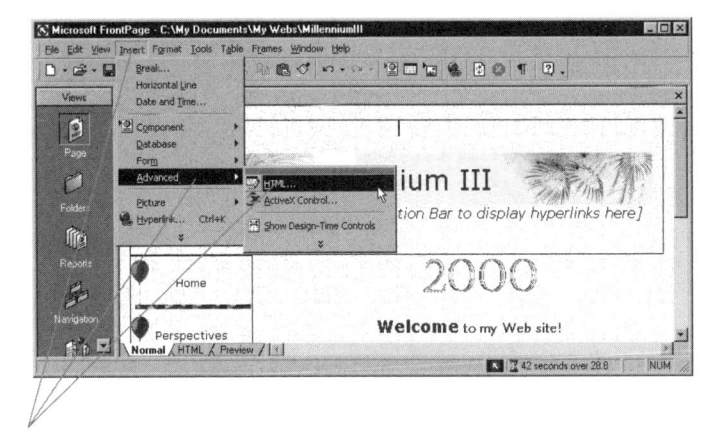

1 Open the Index.htm page, add a blank line at the top, and select Insert, Advanced, HTML.

You can't type HTML code directly into the page, since FrontPage would display rather than process the code.

2 Insert the code provided by the WPP to define the banner, in this case `<!--#echo banner=""-->`

3 Save the changes, connect to the Internet and Publish the Web (changed pages only). The modified margin files are transferred to the Web server.

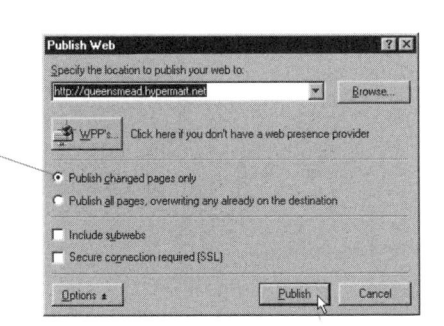

...cont'd

> **HOT TIP**
> *No second window is displayed, and the banner disappears when you scroll down to view the rest of the page.*

4 Open your browser and enter the URL for the Web site.

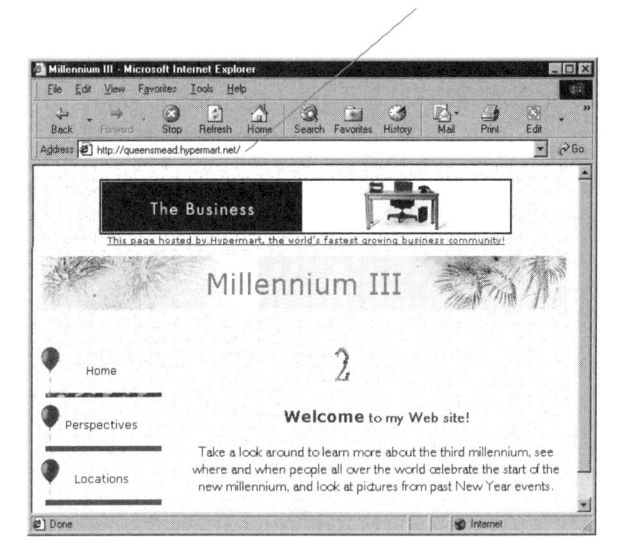

> **DON'T FORGET**
> *If you want to avoid banners altogether, sign up for the premium service, and receive more space and support for additional functions such as database links.*

The Home page for your Web is displayed, with the Hypermart banner inserted above the page banner. This banner is refreshed a couple of times and then remains static. It is hidden when you scroll the page.

You can obtain similar facilities at many Web sites.

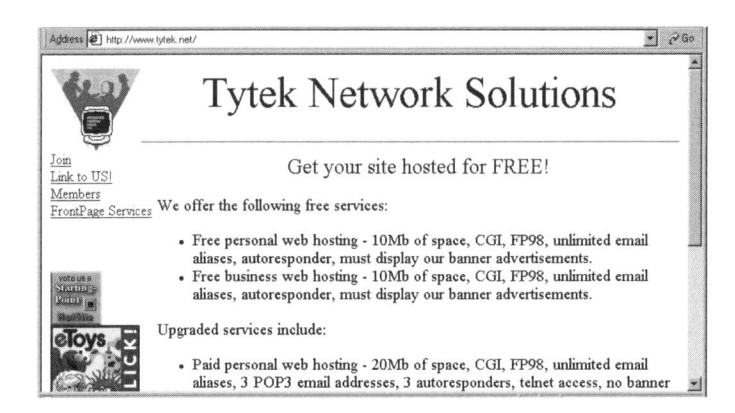

For example, you can publish personal or business Web sites at Tytek – http://www.tytek.net.

Full function WPP

For the most complete support, you need an ISP that provides support for Server Extensions, giving you a single point of contact for design assistance and technical queries.

There are a number of UK ISPs with full WPP capabilities, but these are intended for business use and won't offer subscription free accounts. You'll find lists on the Microsoft Web site (see page 92). Some, such as EasyNet, do provide a one month trial so you can see what your Web site will look like before making a commitment.

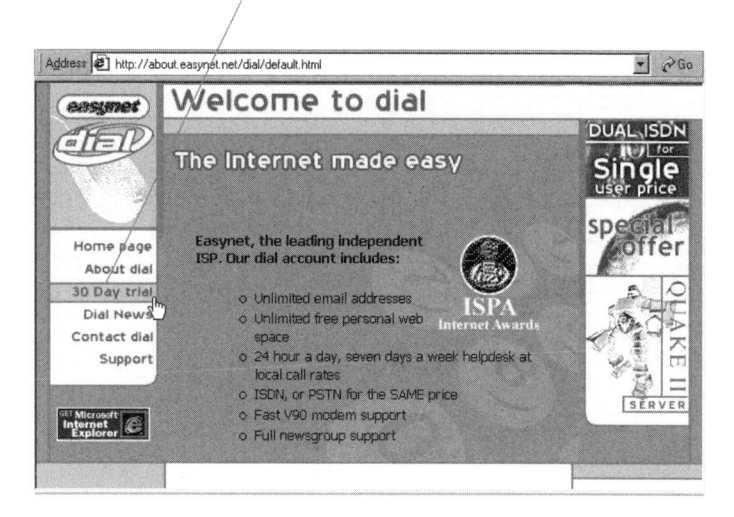

Because these are fee-based services, you will not be required to carry ad banners. Since the connection and Web space facilities are provided by the one organisation, there will be less confusion in the event that problems do arise.

You will also find full ISP and WPP facilities with FrontPage support at the CIX Web service:

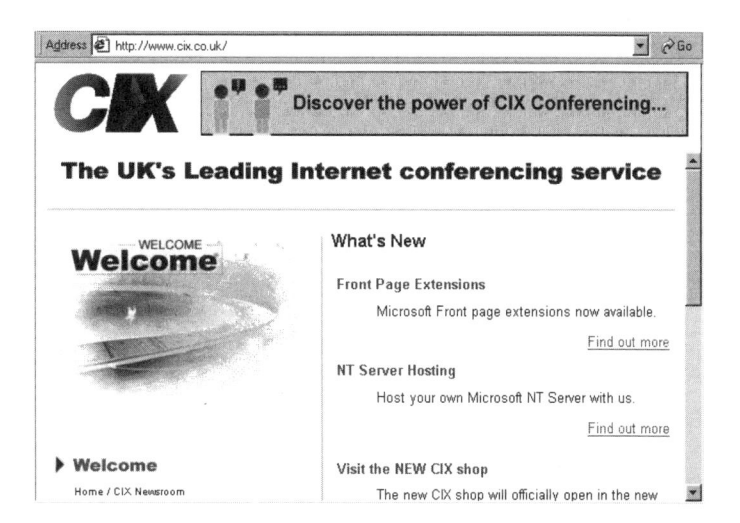

6. Publishing the Web | 99

Selective publishing

> **HOT TIP:** *You may need to restrict publication of some parts, for example while they are still under development.*

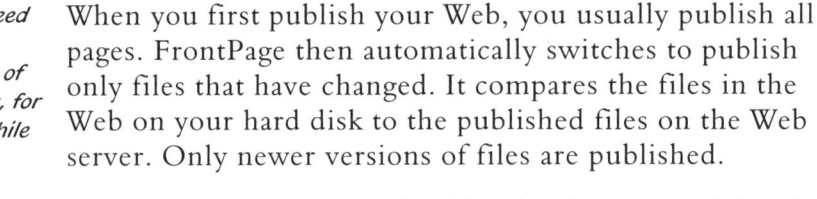

When you first publish your Web, you usually publish all pages. FrontPage then automatically switches to publish only files that have changed. It compares the files in the Web on your hard disk to the published files on the Web server. Only newer versions of files are published.

FrontPage also looks out for files that have been deleted or relocated on your hard disk copy, and synchronises the files on your local Web with the published files on the Web server.

> **HOT TIP:** *Some files are published only once, e.g. guestbook or hit counter, to avoid overwriting collected data.*

When there are incomplete pages that are still under development, or files that are not currently part of the Web, you may want to prevent publication.

To prevent a page from being published:

1. Select View, Reports and click Publish Status.

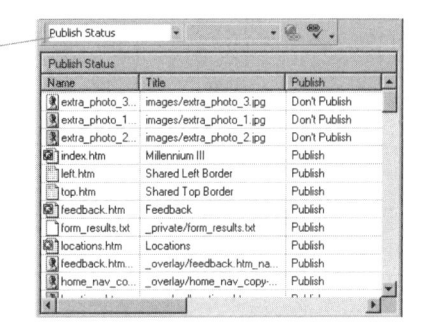

2. Select one or more files, right-click and choose Properties and then click the Workgroup tab.

> **HOT TIP:** *You can right-click the page icon from the Folder List in any view, click Properties on the shortcut menu, and then click the Workgroup tab.*

3. To prevent a file from being published, select Exclude this file when publishing the rest of the Web.

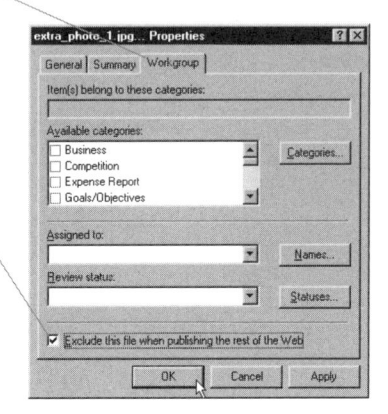

4. To mark a file for publishing, clear the Exclude box.

Promoting the Web

The best design won't help if no-one knows about your Web, so you need to add the information that will get your URL added to the search sites, to encourage visitors and references for your Web site.

Covers

Will you be seen? | 102

Your ISP or WPP | 103

Announcement | 104

Be listed by search sites | 105

Register your site | 106

Meta-variables tags | 108

Registration services | 110

Search sites | 112

Rating your Web site | 113

Apply the rating | 114

Will you be seen?

Sending your Web files to a Web server does not guarantee visitors. You have to make certain that you will be noticed.

Designing an exciting Web site and publishing it to a Web server is really only half of the job. You have to make sure that other Internet users know about your site. Then you will get visitors to enjoy the work you have put in, and perhaps some suggestions for improving the site.

There are many ways in which people might find particular Web sites, for example:

- Follow links on their ISP.

- Follow links from other Web sites.

- Find a Web site using a search engine or directory (Yahoo!, Infoseek etc.).

- Click on a banner heading.

- Find out a URL address by word of mouth.

- See a URL address in a review, advertisement or brochure.

- Receive an e-mail with a Web site URL address.

Some of these methods apply to the larger business, but many are equally applicable to the small business or the personal Web site

To get started on the process of promoting your Web site:

- Make use of the facilities offered by your ISP or WPP for raising awareness of your site.

- Tell your family, friends and business associates, with an e-mail announcement.

- Make sure that you are listed by the search sites, with a good description and in the right category.

- Run a small ad or issue a press release to a local newspaper or to a magazine dealing with your particular topic.

Your ISP or WPP

ISPs and WPPs are usually keen to provide links to their account holders' Web sites. You'd complete a form to give the title, description and category for the Web site.

Freeserve collects similar details but registers your Web site at 12 different Internet search engines, as long as you use their ZyWeb design aid. Using FrontPage, it's up to you to register the site.

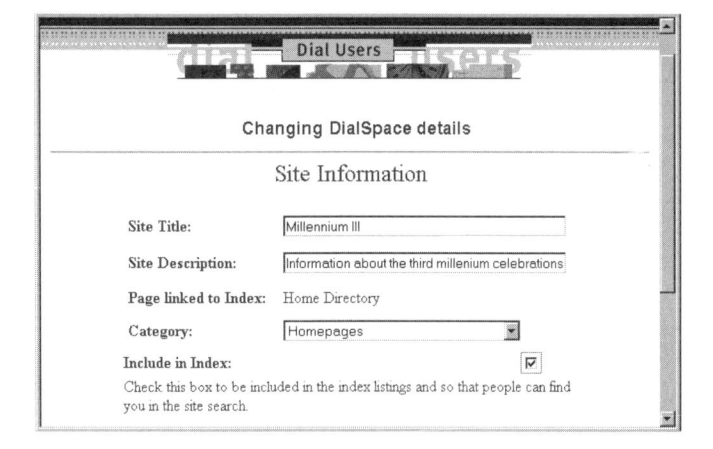

All visitors to the Dial Pipex site (account holders and guests auditing the ISP facilities) are encouraged to visit Dialspace. Their searches will be applied against the details provided through the forms.

Visitors can search all sites in Dialspace, or just a specific category. They can find your Dialspace site even if it is not registered with any Internet search engines.

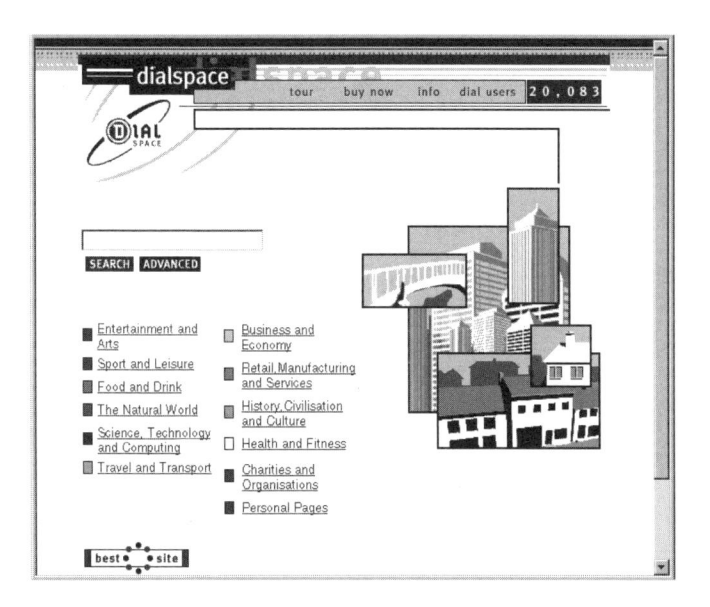

7. Promoting the Web | 103

Announcement

This may be all you need to promote your personal Web site to the people who are most likely to be interested.

1 Send a plain text announcement message with a description of the Web site content and purpose.

2 Provide the URL Internet address for your Web site.

Make the announcement text sufficiently detailed to interest and intrigue, but don't include so much of the content that curiosity is satisfied without a visit. If it is appropriate, include an e-mail address or telephone number for queries. Remember that the e-mail address you use for sending the announcement will be attached to that message. Your e-mail program should have a "send using" option, so you can select a suitable e-mail address.

Think of it as a public message, like an announcement in the newspaper, which could be seen by anyone.

Put the Send to addresses in the Bcc box, to avoid distributing all your contact addresses with the announcement. Don't make the announcement message too personal to the recipients. It should be general purpose enough that your contacts feel able to forward it to their contacts. You can always send separate, personalised notes to introduce the announcement.

3 Add your Web site URL to your e-mail signature, to act as a reminder to your contacts whenever you send e-mail.

4 Add the message to newsgroups that deal with topics related to the content of your Web site.

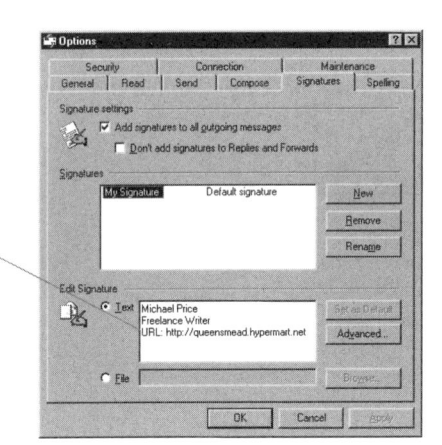

Be listed by search sites

Extend beyond the limits of your immediate circle and appeal to the Internet as a whole.

To find a Web site, page or other element, you choose a search engine such as AltaVista and enter the details of your query in the form provided:

1 Select the type of item you want to find,

Advanced search options let you state your query more precisely, to minimise the number of inappropriate matches.

2 Type keywords or phrases defining the item, or enter a question in natural language (that is, as if asking a person).

3 Press Search and await the results. There may be a long list but better matches are closer to the start of the list.

You want to be sure that searches for topics related to your Web site will include your URL in their results, near the top. This can only happen if the search engines know about your site.

There are three types of search site: search engines that use robots, directories that use people, and hybrids that are a mixture.

Search sites may rely on being told about URLs, and their staff visit and review the Web pages, to decide whether to add the URL, and what categories to use. Others send out Web robots that roam around the Internet looking for new or updated Web pages. The URL, page title, and selected text from the pages is sent to the search site. Some search sites use both methods.

To increase your chances, you can register your URL with specific search sites, or include meta-variables in your Web pages, to feed data to the search robots.

Register your site

Search sites will include a link to let you submit your URL. It may say Add URL, Register URL, Suggest a Site or similar text. See page 112 for a list of search sites, and pointers to the URL registration forms.

Registering your site with a search engine or directory is free of charge. The procedure for each search site may vary, but the examples of Excite and Snap illustrate the main techniques. To register with Excite:

1. Open the search site at http://www.Excite.com and look for the Add URL link towards the bottom of the page.

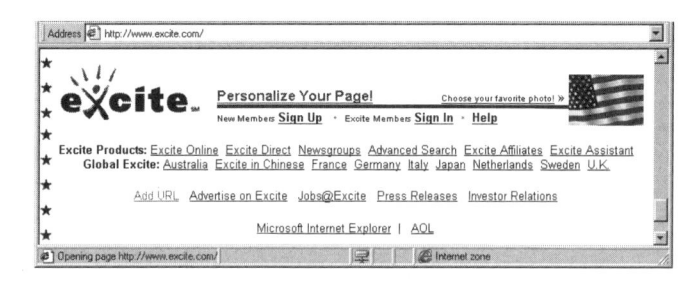

2. Locate the Add URL link and click to display the registration form.

Usually you enter the site address without the home page Index.htm, though some search sites allow you to register individual pages.

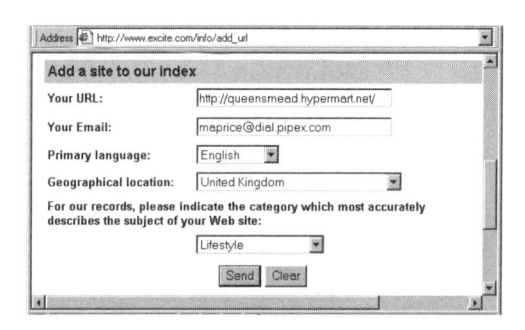

3. Enter the URL for your site, a contact e-mail address, the language and location. Select a category from the list.

When you are finished filling out the form, click the Send button to submit your request. The site should appear in the Excite index after about two weeks.

...cont'd

HOT TIP: With directory sites such as Snap and Yahoo!, you should select one of the predefined categories and subcategories, then click the Add URL link. You can usually add your URL in two different categories.

To determine the category and add the URL to Snap:

1 Open Snap.com and search with a phrase relevant to your site.

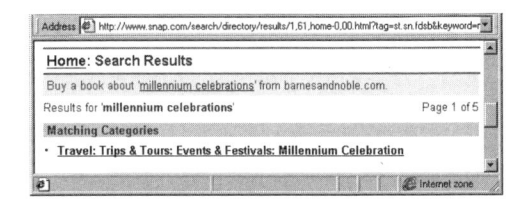

2 Select a suitable category and subcategory based on the search, and navigate through the categories to that entry.

Complete the form:

- Site title
- Site URL
- 15 word description
- New or updated

DON'T FORGET: The topic and path will be filled in for you, if you preselect your category.

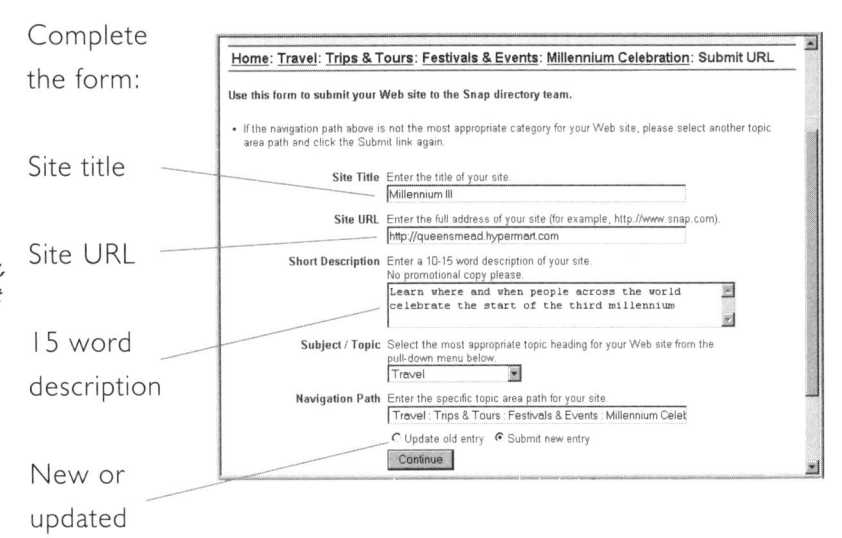

- Location details
- Contact details
- Click to Submit

HOT TIP: When you submit the request, it is sent to the directory staff for evaluation.

7. Promoting the Web | 107

Meta-variables tags

FrontPage allows you to insert data in meta-variables, to hold data for the search sites.

Many search sites will make use of Meta-variables (often called Meta-tags) if available, to collate indexing information. There are two types of Meta-variables:

System variables
<META HTTP-EQUIV="name" CONTENT="content">

These control the action of browsers, and are used to refine the information provided by HTML headers. You normally do not need system variables to index your site.

User variables
<META NAME="name" CONTENT="content">

These specify metadata, information about a document, in name/content pairs providing details. This is particularly valuable when your home page has little or no text, for example when your page is entirely graphic, or with a frames-based site where the index.htm consists of FRAME tags.

The variable types most applicable to search sites:

Description: A concise definition of the page contents. Aim to provide about twenty or so words.

Include common misspellings or include different word forms, to increase the chances of your page being selected in a search.

Keywords: Terms and synonyms related to the topic of your Web page. Choose the words you think that visitors are likely to enter into a search. Separate each word with a comma.

Author: The author or company name, if you want, this could be the target of a search.

Resource-type: Put Document for an HTML page. This is the only tag that you need to put in for indexing purposes.

Tags can also be used to exclude a Web page from being listed in an Index.

Distribution: This can be Global, Local or Iu (stands for Internal use). Normally you'd put Global.

Robots: Put Noindex, Nofollow, Noimageindex or Noimageclick to instruct the search site to avoid indexing page or image files, or to avoid following links.

...cont'd

You do not need Meta-tags in all the pages in your Web site. It is usually enough to define the Home page, and leave the rest to the search site robots.

To add Meta-tags to your Web page:

1 Open the Index.htm page in Page view, and select File, Properties to display the page properties.

> *Click Add for each variable in turn, for keywords, author, resource-type etc.*

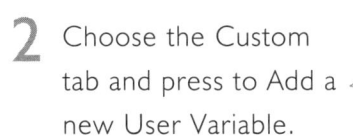

2 Choose the Custom tab and press to Add a new User Variable.

3 Enter the Name and the Value for the variable, and click OK.

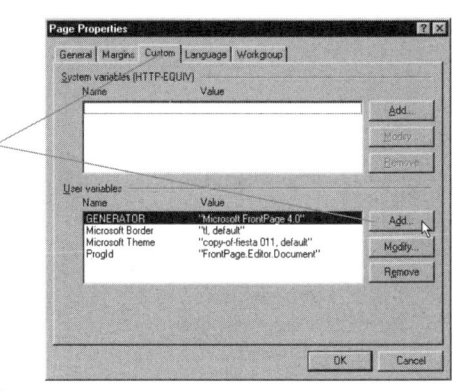

> *Some of the items in the list may have been added automatically by FrontPage, so don't change or delete an item unless you are sure where it came from.*

4 Press the HTML tab in Page view to see the Meta-tags:

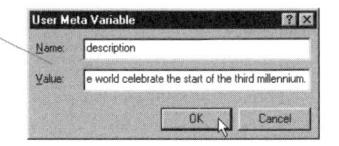

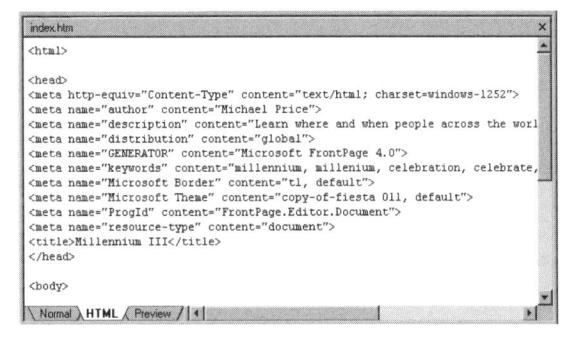

When you have added all the Meta-tags, republish the Web to the Web server.

7. Promoting the Web | 109

Registration services

There are services that will register your Web site on your behalf, for a fee.

While it is easy enough to register your Web site with a few of the main search engines, it can become quite time consuming if you want wider coverage. The answer is a registration service such as WebPromote or Submit It.

To try out the Submit It service using the free trial:

1. Open the www.submitit.com Web site, and select the free trial for one URL registered on ten search sites.

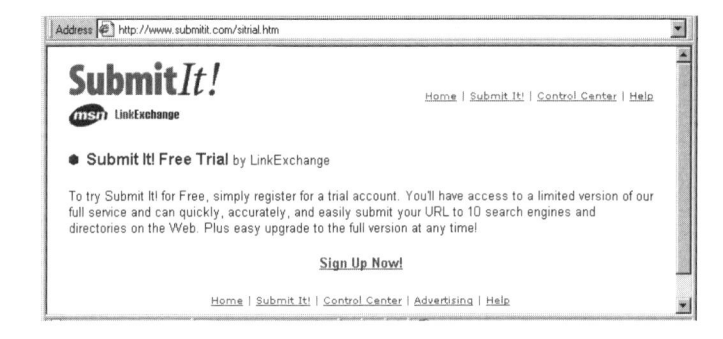

This gives a year's licence for Submit It services. You can upgrade to full function. The minimum cost is $49 p.a. for two URLs.

2. Fill in your personal details. No credit card is asked for. Fill in the Web site master form, describing your Web.

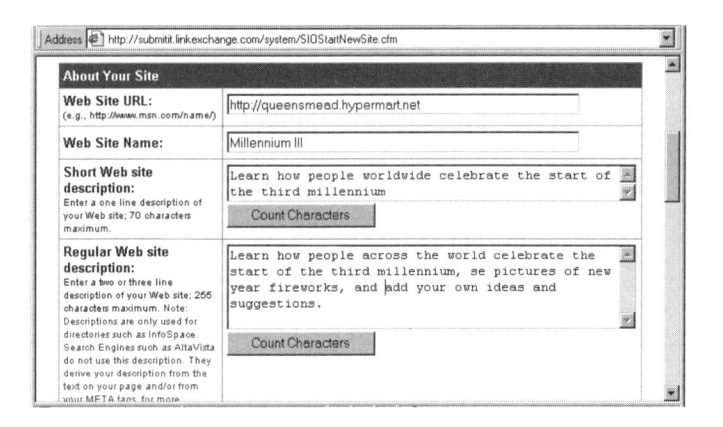

3. Complete the form, adding further data such as keywords. Note that entries are severely restricted in size (255 chars).

...cont'd

Even with help, it still takes time to fill in all the required data, so allow about an hour to complete the sign up with Submit It.

4 Complete the URL and the contact data requested, and Submit It will offer to analyse your Web site.

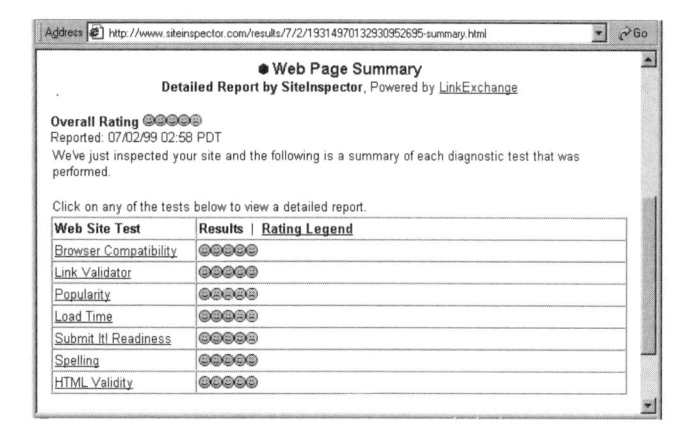

5 Continue on to the final steps, where you confirm the search engines, and add categories or location details.

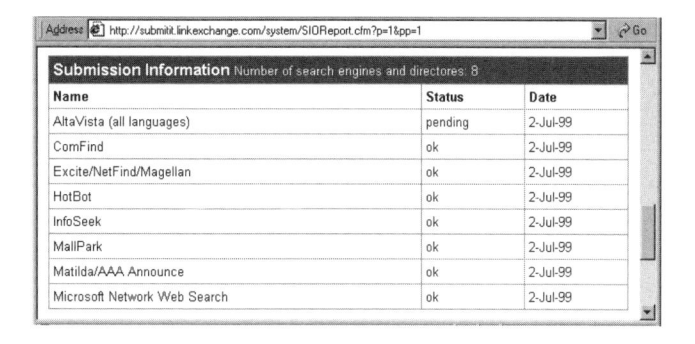

Not all robots honour Meta-tags. Some search sites believe that extracting actual text is more valid.

6 You can Login to the Submit It site at any time, to get an update on the progress of your registrations.

Even when you've registered, it may still take several days or weeks for the search site robots to locate your Web site and collect the additional details from the Meta-tags or from the text within your pages.

Search sites

There are very many different search sites, directories and search engines, general and special purpose.

There are many search sites available on the Internet, and each may offer regional versions such as UK or Europe. These are some of the main search services, based on general popularity and usage.

These and additional links are on the Useful Links page in the Millennium III Web site at http://queensmead.hypermart.net . The links take you directly to the form or instructions for URL registration.

AltaVista	http://www.altavista.com/
Ask Jeeves	http://www.askjeeves.com/
Direct Hit	http://www.directhit.com/
Excite	http://www.excite.com/
Go	http://beta.go.com/
Google	http://www.google.com/
GoTo	http://www.goto.com/
HotBot	http://www.hotbot.com/
Infoseek	http://www.infoseek.com/
Inktomi	http://www.inktomi.com/
LookSmart	http://www.looksmart.com/
Lycos	http://www.lycos.com/
Northern Light	http://www.northernlight.com/
Open Directory	http://dmoz.org/
Planet Search	http://www.planetsearch.com/
RealNames	http://www.realnames.com/
Search.com	http://www.search.com/
Snap	http://www.snap.com/
WebCrawler	http://www.webcrawler.com/
Yahoo!	http://www.yahoo.com/

Rating your Web site

A site that has no rating at all may be excluded by one of these filtering agents, whatever the content, so it is worth getting an official rating for your Web site.

To be sure that your Web site will be allowed past the Internet Explorer content advisor, Net Nanny or other screening applications, you can have a rating for your Web site from the Recreational Software Advisory Council (RSAC), a non-profit organisation which is located at: http://www.rsac.org/

To rate your site:

1 Open the RSAC Web site and click to register your site.

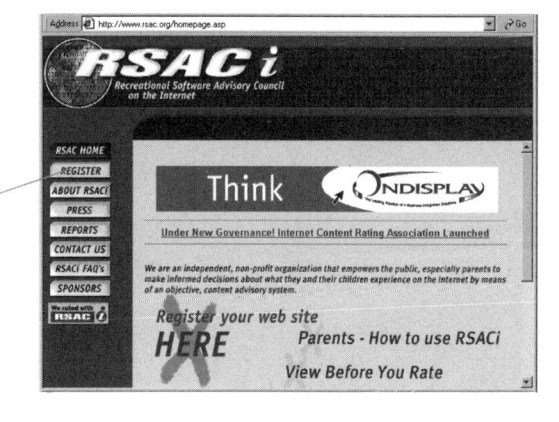

2 You may register a page, a branch or the whole site.

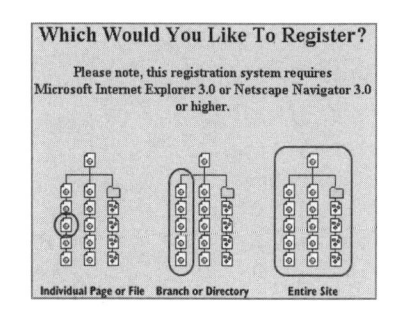

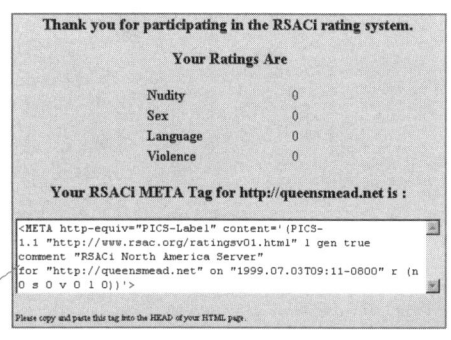

The rating system is based on voluntary self-disclosure, as part of the self-regulation of the Internet.

3 Supply the URL, and your personal details.

4 Fill out the questionnaire to rate your Web site on a series of criteria, and submit the form.

RSAC also sends a follow up e-mail containing the code and instructions for applying it to your site.

5 RSAC confirms your ratings, and supplies the HTML code to add to your home page Index.htm.

7. Promoting the Web | 113

Apply the rating

The HTML code must be added between the <head> and </head> tags in the Index.htm page.

The HTML code provided by the RSAC is in the form of a System Meta-tag. To add this to your Web site:

1. Open the Web, open Index.htm in Page view, and select the HTML tab. Locate the <title> tag.

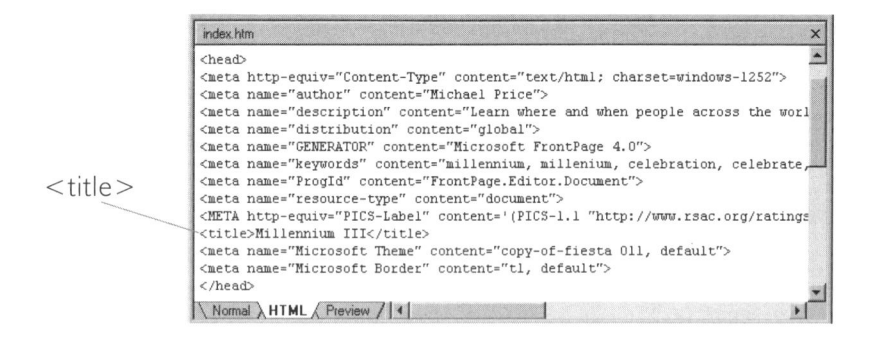

```
index.htm
<head>
<meta http-equiv="Content-Type" content="text/html; charset=windows-1252">
<meta name="author" content="Michael Price">
<meta name="description" content="Learn where and when people across the worl
<meta name="distribution" content="global">
<meta name="GENERATOR" content="Microsoft FrontPage 4.0">
<meta name="keywords" content="millennium, millenium, celebration, celebrate,
<meta name="ProgId" content="FrontPage.Editor.Document">
<meta name="resource-type" content="document">
<META http-equiv="PICS-Label" content='(PICS-1.1 "http://www.rsac.org/ratings
<title>Millennium III</title>
<meta name="Microsoft Theme" content="copy-of-fiesta 011, default">
<meta name="Microsoft Border" content="tl, default">
</head>
Normal  HTML  Preview
```

See page 32 for an example of using a Gif file as a hyperlink button.

2. Insert a blank line before the <title>, and copy the HTML code from the RSAC confirmation page or from the e-mail.

3. From the RSAC home page, copy the Rsaclabel.gif picture button, and insert it onto Index.htm.

4. Make the image into a hyperlink to the RSAC Web site.

5. Save the page and publish the changes to the Web server.

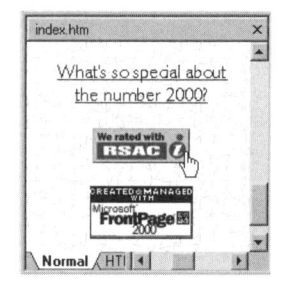

Visitors to your site will now see that you have a rating, and the Web page filtering agents will automatically pick up the rating from the home page, so there will be no unintended barriers to your Web site.

Bells and whistles

When you have published and registered your Web, you can start adding features to make sure that visitors find the site worth revisiting and worth recommending. You'll also need to measure the rate of success that you achieve.

Covers

Counting on success | 116

Add a time stamp | 118

Horizontal lines | 120

Background sound | 121

List effects | 122

Display form results | 124

Using colour | 126

Print a page | 128

Temporary files | 130

Chapter Eight

Counting on success

To show that the search sites are doing their job, you need some means of checking how many visitors you have had to your site.

A hit counter keeps a tally of the number of visits, and shows the current total on the page. You'd usually put the hit counter on your home page, since this is the normal entry point. Displaying the counter means that both you and your site visitors can see how popular the Web site has become.

To add a counter:

1. Open the Web and the Index.htm page, and position the cursor.

2. Select Insert, Component, Hit Counter and select the type of counter you want.

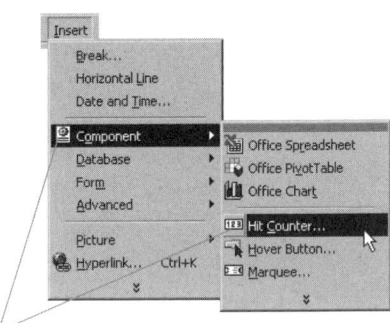

You must use a Web server that supports FrontPage Server Extensions.

3. Click the Reset counter box, and enter the initial number.

4. Set the Fixed number of digits to display with leading zeros.

5. Save the page, and republish the Web to the Web server.

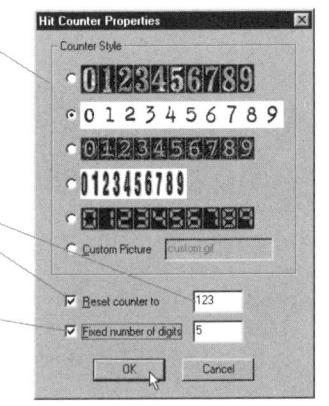

In Page view and the Previews, a placeholder is shown. When the home page is viewed on the Web server, however, the counter displays and is updated on each visit.

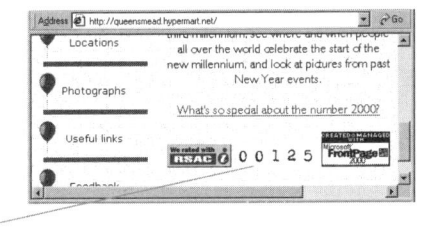

...cont'd

You can reset the counter when you have finished your testing, or if you introduce a new set of topics.

To reset the counter:

1. Open the Web, open Index.htm and double-click [Hit Counter].

2. Click in the Reset box, and enter a new starting point if desired.

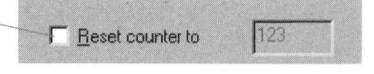

You might wish to add the date when the counter was reset as a comment or as a displayed entry.

FrontPage provides a number of counter styles, but you can supply your own number graphics. Create a picture in Gif format with the numerals 0-9 evenly spaced. You can add borders to the images.

For example, to create a hit counter tripometer style:

3. Create the image, making it for example 200 x 30 pixels, and save as Mycount.gif, in the Images folder for the Web.

You must save the page, and republish to the Web server, to see the effect of any changes.

4. Open the Component Properties, click Custom Picture, and enter the relative path and file name.

5. Save and publish, and the your visitors will see the new counter when they display your home page.

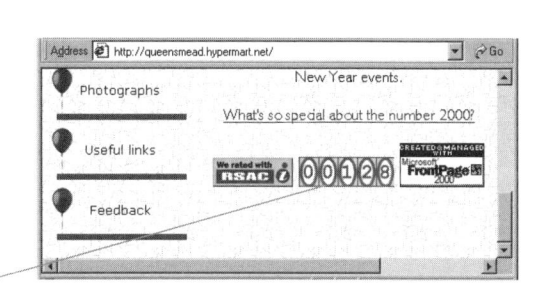

8. Bells and whistles | 117

Add a time stamp

Put the date when your Web site or page was created or last updated.

Add a time stamp to a page to display the date or the time and date that the page was last published. This tells visitors that the site is up to date and active, and encourages them to pay return visits or recommend your site to others.

To add a time stamp:

1. Open the Web and the Home page, select Format, Shared borders, add a bottom border.

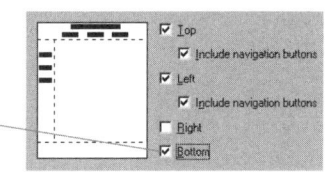

You can stamp one or more pages, or put the stamp in the bottom margin, and a stamp will appear on every page.

2. Click the Comment field, and press Insert, Date and Time.

3. Select your preferred format for date and time. Use the Month, to avoid confusion with USA and UK formats.

4. If you choose a time, use the TZ (time zone) format since the time will be shown in local time at the Web server.

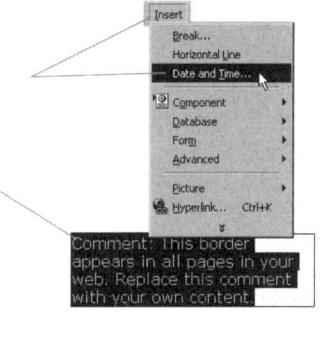

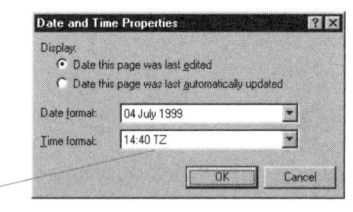

You can choose Date last edited, or the Date last updated by FrontPage.
Note that the time is shown in the local time for the PC.

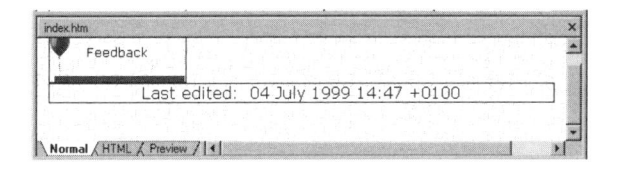

5. Add an expression such as 'Last edited:' to qualify the date and time value.

...cont'd

6 Save and close the page, and republish the Web to the Web server. The home page and borders are transferred, and the borders in all the other pages are updated.

If the Web site is already open in the browser when you publish an update, press Refresh to rebuild the screen.

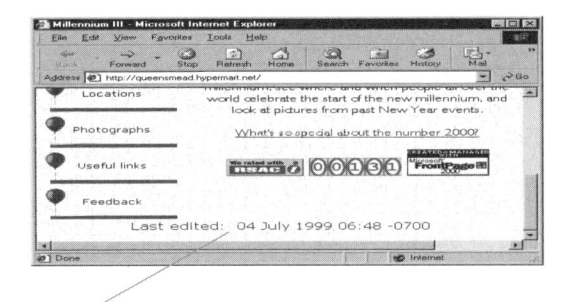

7 The date and time that the page was saved are shown, but in the local time for the server – in this case a West coast USA machine. The time zone differential makes this clear.

8 Click one of the buttons on the Navigation bar to switch to a different page in the Web.

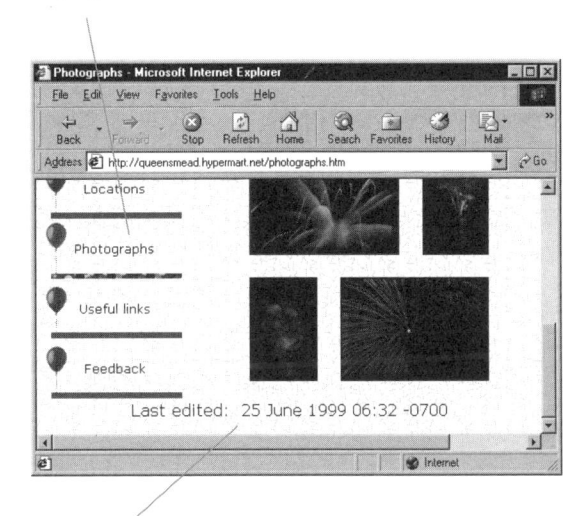

Make a practice of editing the important pages on the Web, or the time stamp will get out of date and spoil the effect of your Web.

9 The bottom border has the time stamp, but the values shown are when this page was last edited.

Horizontal lines

You can add a horizontal line to a page, to separate items or add effect.

To add a line above the timestamp:

1   Position the cursor before the text and select Insert, Horizontal Line.

2   The style of the line is fixed in the Theme you have chosen.

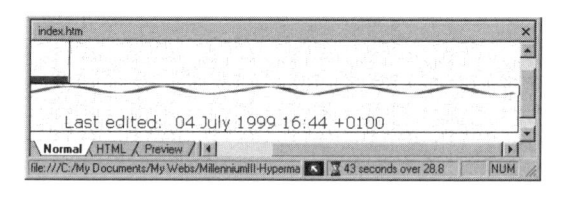

When you add a line to a page without a Theme, it is plain. You can modify its properties to change the effect.

If the current page uses a theme, you can change only the alignment of the line. All other properties are greyed.

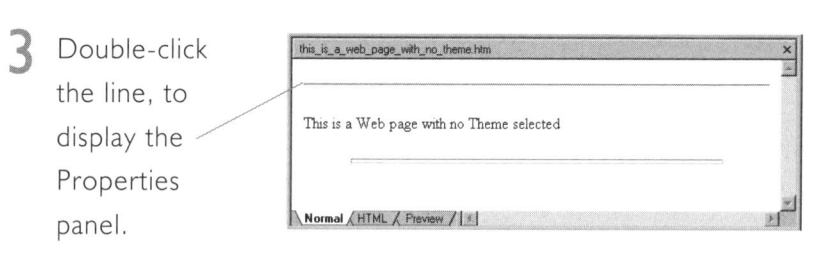

3   Double-click the line, to display the Properties panel.

4   Specify the Width as a percentage of the window Width or as a number of pixels. Enter the Height in pixels. Set the Alignment on the page. The line is shaded unless you select a Colour or click Solid line.

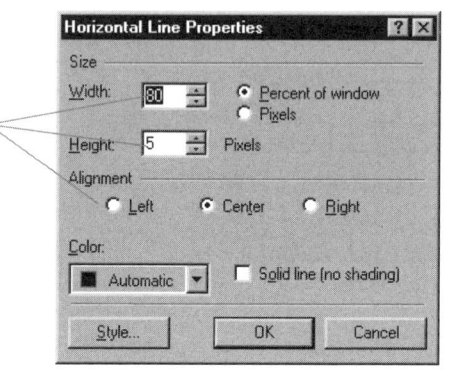

Background sound

BEWARE — *This is not supported by all Web browsers. Remember also that some visitors may be deterred by audio effects.*

You can set a background sound which plays when the visitor opens the page.

To specify the sound:

1. Right-click the page, and select Page Properties and the General tab.

2. In the Background sound Location box, type the sound file you want to play (or click Browse to find the file).

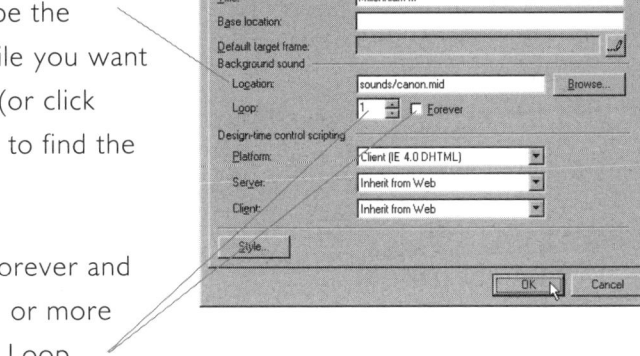

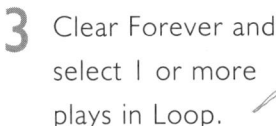

HOT TIP — *You can use Wav files or the compressed MP3 files for short sound extracts, but Midi files are much better for music.*

3. Clear Forever and select 1 or more plays in Loop.

4. Republish the Web, and the sound plays when the home page is accessed. This works with most browsers. Here for example, the page is displayed in Opera 3.6 as the music plays.

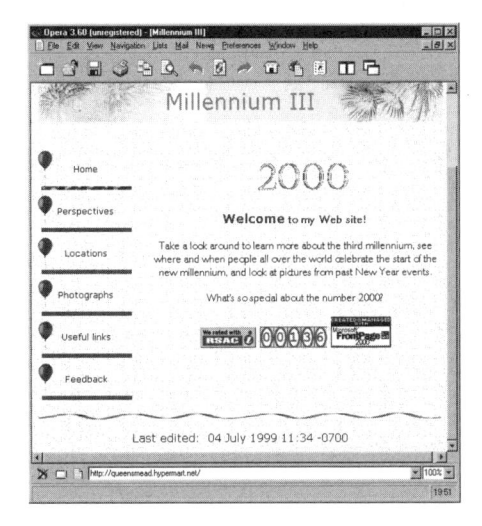

8. Bells and whistles | 121

List effects

Format lists to make the data on the page easier to organise and analyse.

You can create lists of many types, including bulleted, numbered, definition, directory and menu lists. The exact format of the list depends on the browser used by the visitor to the site.

Lists can have nested levels, with different list styles for each level.

1. Open the Useful links page. Organise the links by placing category headings between them.

2. Select the links and headings and click Bullets to create a single level list.

If the page uses a theme, the list can use the styles defined for fonts and picture bullets (see page 123).

3. Select a group of links beneath a heading, and click Increase Indent twice, to introduce a second level list.

4. Repeat for each heading in turn, until all the groups are restructured.

Lists are useful to organise and present information. A particularly valuable feature is the collapsible list. This allows the visitor to show or hide the contents of a level by clicking the relevant heading.

5. Right-click the top level heading and select List Properties from the context menu displayed, and choose the Picture Bullets tab.

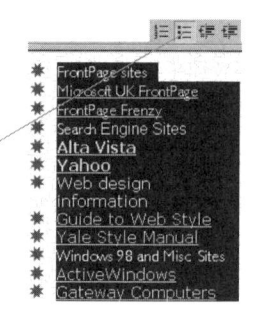

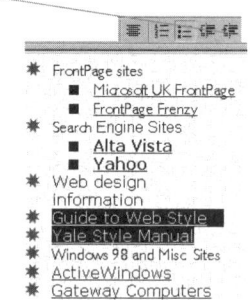

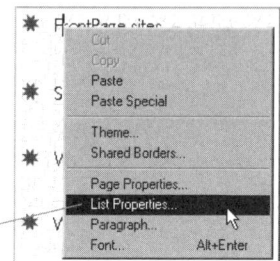

...cont'd

HOT TIP: *Collapsible lists are supported by Microsoft Internet Explorer 4.0 or higher, or other Web browsers that support Dynamic HTML.*

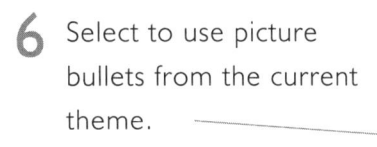

HOT TIP: *This style is very effective when you have long lists of items, since the page size remains manageable, and the visitor can view just the parts that are of interest.*

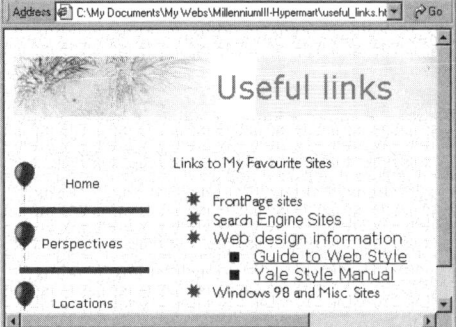

DON'T FORGET: *Add a note on the page to explain to the visitor about the collapsible lists and how to activate them.*

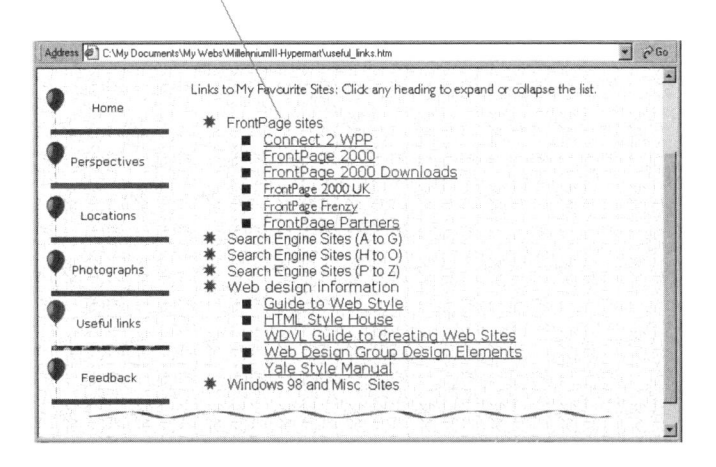

6 Select to use picture bullets from the current theme.

7 Choose Collapsible Outlines, and set them as Initially Collapsed.

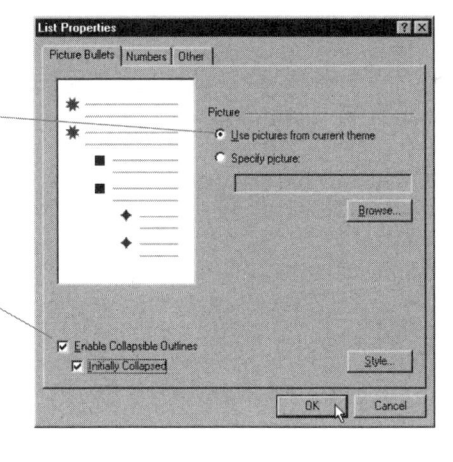

8 Save the changes to the page, and click Preview in Browser to see how the page appears to visitors.

9 The lists are initially hidden. Click on any heading to expand the list. Click again to collapse the list.

8. Bells and whistles | 123

Display form results

You can save the results of a form so that they can be displayed as one of your Web pages.

You can display the feedback from your visitors, so that other visitors can share the comments. To do this, you need to save the results to an HTML file.

1. In the Feedback page, right-click the form, and select Form Properties.

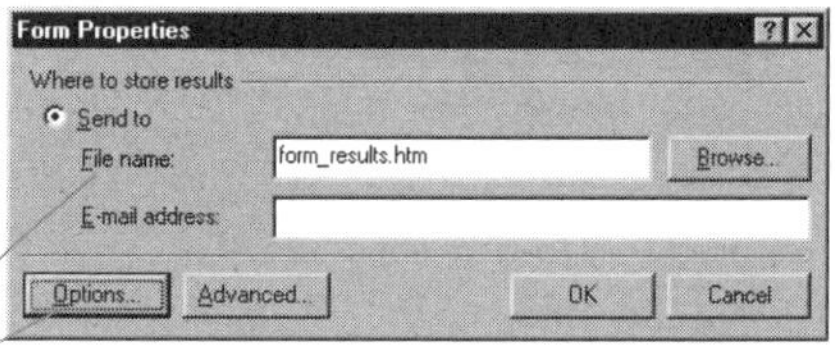

You can save the form results to two files. One could have all the data, for your records, and one could be a subset for display.

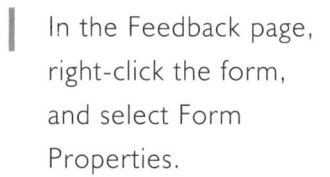

2. Change the file location to the root of the Web, set the extension to Htm, and then select Options.

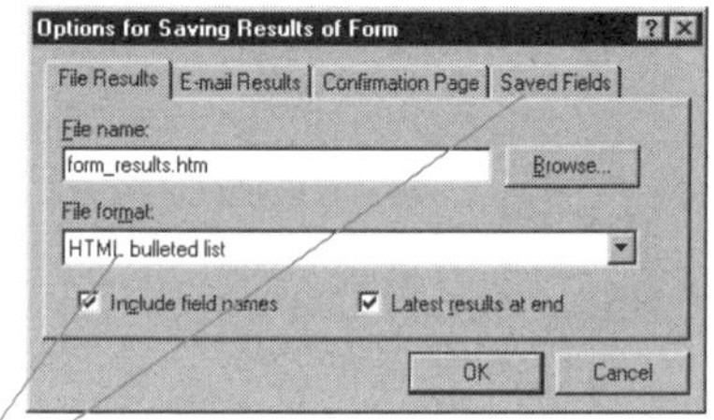

3. Select an HTML type such as bulleted list, and click the Saved Fields tab.

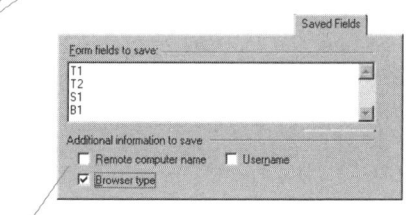

4. Choose which of the fields to show on the results. For example, you may decide not to display T2, the e-mail address. In any event, you won't want to show B1, the button field, which has no associated data value.

You can collect extra data, such as the type of browser used by the visitors (but only if they leave feedback).

5. Add a hyperlink to the page, targeted at the results file, with an appropriate text message.

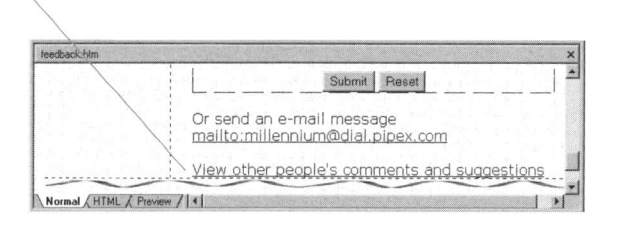

124 | FrontPage 2000 in easy steps

...cont'd

Save the changes to the feedback page, and republish the Web to the Web server. Now you and your visitors can see the comments left by other visitors.

6 Connect to the Internet, open the Web site, switch to the Feedback page, and click the link to the form results.

The Forms wizard can help create forms that save their results in HTML format. When you create a new page in your Web, you can also choose a template that will generate a Guest Book.

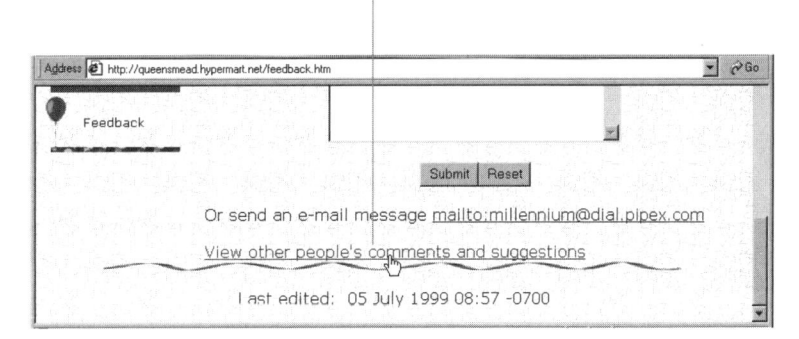

7 The results are displayed as an HTML page. Press the Back button to return to the Web page.

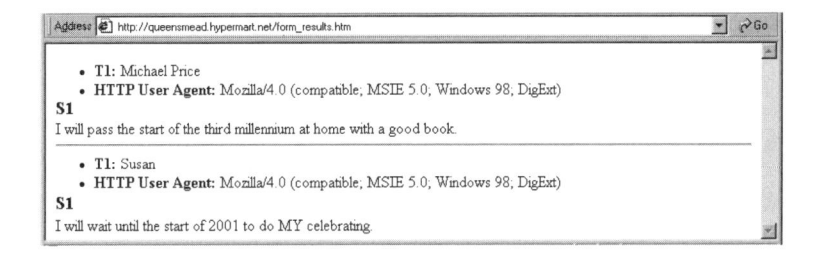

If you are using a Web space provider such as Hypermart, with a requirement for a banner on every page, you may need to amend the results file.

8 Save the results file to your hard drive. Insert the required HTML code (see page 97). Republish the Web to update the Web server copy.

8. Bells and whistles | 125

Using colour

See your Web pages as others see them, and avoid colour effects that may miss the mark in the visitor's eyes.

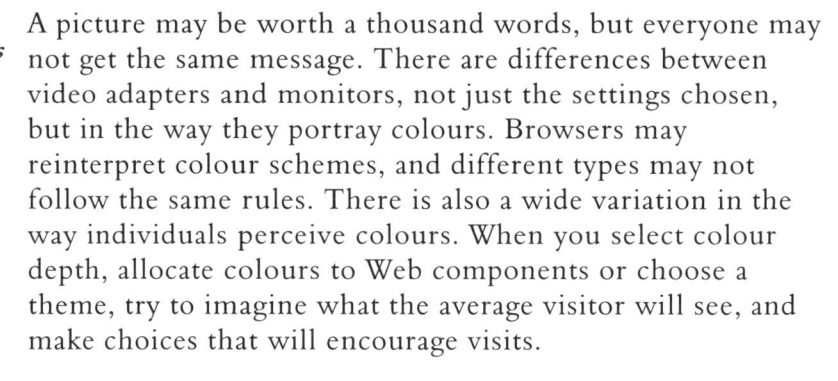

A picture may be worth a thousand words, but everyone may not get the same message. There are differences between video adapters and monitors, not just the settings chosen, but in the way they portray colours. Browsers may reinterpret colour schemes, and different types may not follow the same rules. There is also a wide variation in the way individuals perceive colours. When you select colour depth, allocate colours to Web components or choose a theme, try to imagine what the average visitor will see, and make choices that will encourage visits.

PCs can display colours selected from over 16 million combinations, using the true colour 32-bit setting. In practice many users will restrict their display to the de facto standard for Windows and the Internet, choosing the 8-bit, 256 colour setting.

GIF image files can use 256 colours only, but it could be a different set of 256 for each image.

The GIF file image format uses 256 colours, so when you save an image to GIF, the graphics program may use dithering. This mixes some of the available colours in a mottled or checkerboard effect, to approximate other colours. Also, if the PC is set for 256 colours, the browser will use a fixed 256 colour palette and may simulate missing colours by dithering. These changes may degrade the image, especially with large blocks of single colours.

The easiest way to get a Web-friendly palette is to capture a screen shot of the browser displaying an image, and save the palette from that screenshot.

To avoid the effect, create or modify the image to use the same 256 colour palette as one of the main browsers. Netscape uses six shade levels of red, green and blue (0, 51, 102, 153, 204 and 255) to give 216 colours, the rest being standard Windows colours. Unfortunately, other browsers may use a different fixed palette, or may select the nearest matching colour, so the Web-friendly palette is not a universal solution.

...cont'd

To enhance the effect of graphics images you can use transparency. A transparent colour around an irregular image makes it stand out, especially when your page has a background picture or pattern.

To choose a transparent colour:

1. Open the page, and click the image to display the Picture toolbar.

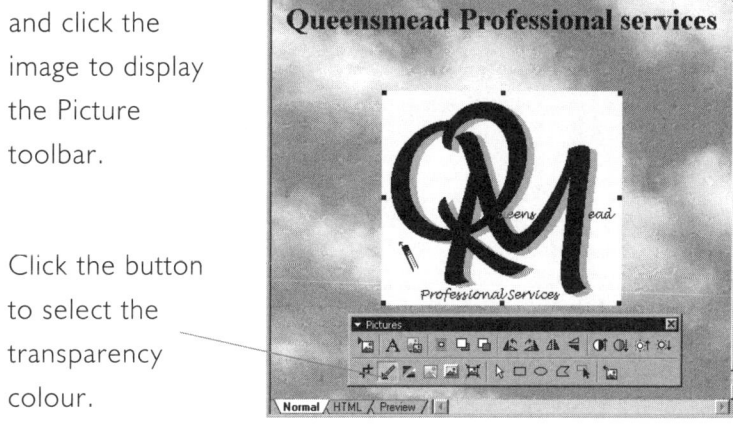

You can choose any suitable colour, it does not have to be white. You should choose a colour that is not used in the image as such.

2. Click the button to select the transparency colour.

3. Move the pointer to the colour you want, and click to select it. The image appears superimposed on the page.

4. Save the page, and republish the Web when your changes are complete.

You can also use the transparency colour to create a background, partially transparent image as a watermark for the page, and overlay it with text or other images.

8. Bells and whistles | 127

Print a page

You have several ways of printing your Web pages from FrontPage, depending on the type of information you need.

You can print the current page to the Windows printer, and it will show the hyperlinks and the images and pictures as they appear in the Normal view.

1. In Page view, click the Normal tab and select File, to see the usual Windows Print and Print Preview.

2. Select Print, and choose the printer and options, including pages and copies needed.

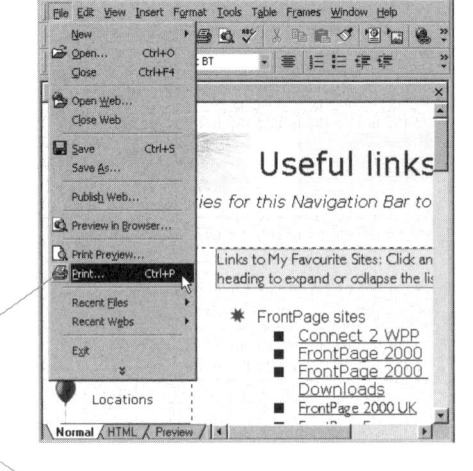

3. Click OK to send the data to the printer or to a file if required.

You can print any FrontPage HTML file from Page view, including the results of forms that have been saved in HTML format.

Unlike the print from the browser, this print is paginated and page numbers are appended.

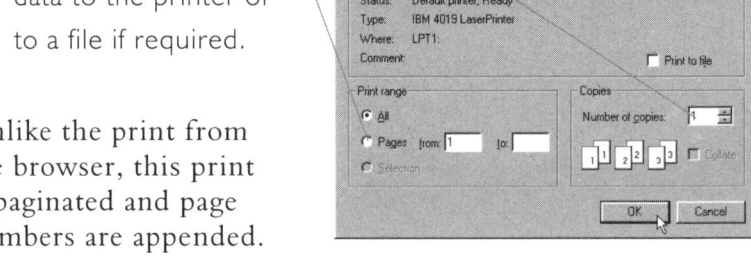

4. Select the Print or Print Preview command from the HTML view.

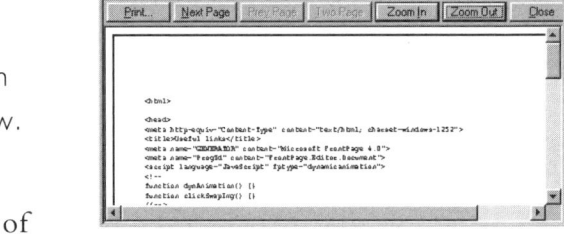

The print will be of the actual HTML code that generates the Web page.

...cont'd

With collapsible lists, the page will appear in the state of expansion chosen by the visitor.

To print the page as visitors see it, you must use your Web browser.

5 Select File, Preview in Browser, and then select File, Print.

6 The browser does not paginate. There is one logical page. You can select page frames (see page 138) if relevant.

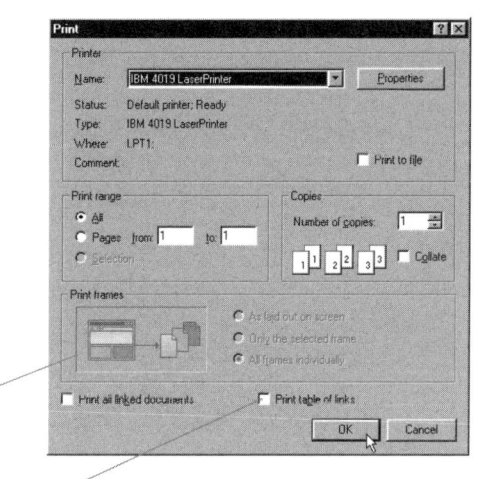

7 Click here to add a table of the names and URLs for all the links on the Web page.

The Print and Print Preview commands are greyed and unavailable in the Preview Page view, or in any of the other Views except for Navigation.

You can print the navigation structure of the current Web as it is displayed in Navigation view:

8 Right-click the Navigation view and select Rotate to change the orientation if desired.

9 Select the Print Preview command to view the navigation structure, or Print to select the print options and print out the structure.

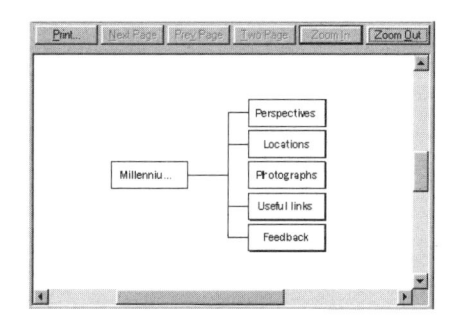

Temporary files

FrontPage uses some temporary files on your hard disk to store data about the Web. This speeds up the process of opening a large Web.

When you initially open or create a Web on a server, FrontPage creates temporary files, located on your local hard drive, that contain information about the files in the Web. The next time you open the Web, FrontPage reads the local temporary files for information about the Web, instead of downloading the information from the Web server.

If you are developing your Web as a group, you may have several authors adding, removing, editing and renaming files in the same Web. Your temporary files may get out of sync with the Web server.

To rectify this and re-synchronise the local information:

Apply the steps in turn, until you reach the position where your reports show full and correct information about the Web.

1. To refresh a page or view, click the Refresh button on the toolbar.

2. Select Tools, and click Recalculate Hyperlinks. For large Webs with many hyperlinks, this process may be time-consuming.

3. On the Tools menu, click Web Settings, click the Advanced tab, and then click Delete Files.

The next time you open the Web on the server, it may taker longer, since FrontPage must copy the Web information from the server to recreate your local temporary files.

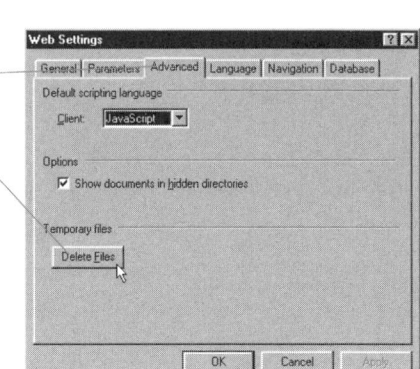

Upgrading Webs

If you have an existing Web, it can take advantage of FrontPage 2000 design and publishing features, even if it was created in a previous version of FrontPage, or in a totally different HTML editor. If your Web server has the FrontPage extension, you can upgrade the Web to exploit them.

Covers

Import the Web | 132

Analyse the Web | 134

Upgrade the Web | 136

Frames page | 138

The main page | 140

No frames | 142

Guest book | 143

Chapter Nine

Import the Web

If you have an existing Web you can import it into FrontPage 2000. You can import the original source files and folders from the hard disk, or you can import the Web pages and components from the Web server on your network or on the Internet and store them in a FrontPage 2000 Web.

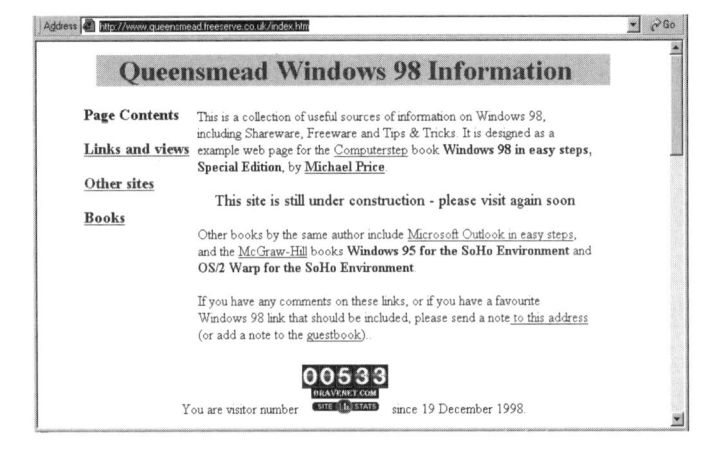

You can import pages from any Web, even though you don't own or manage the site.

To import an existing Web site:

1 Start FrontPage, close any open Webs, select File from the menu bar and then click Import.

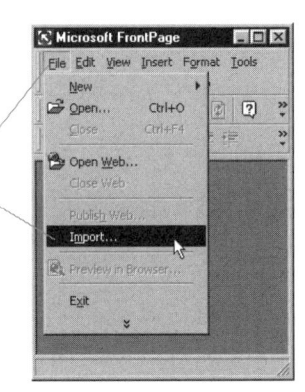

If you are already editing a Web in FrontPage, the Import panel displays and you click the From Web button.

2 The New Web panel displays, with Import Web Wizard already selected. Specify the location for the new Web you will create from the Web site you import, and click OK.

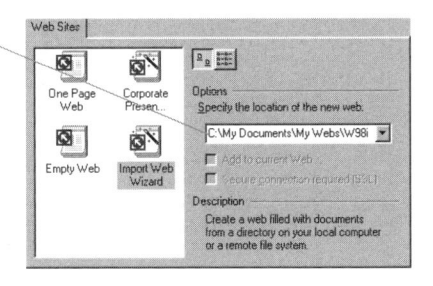

132 | FrontPage 2000 in easy steps

...cont'd

For a source directory, specify the folder on your hard disk or network drive. For a Web on the Internet, specify the full URL.

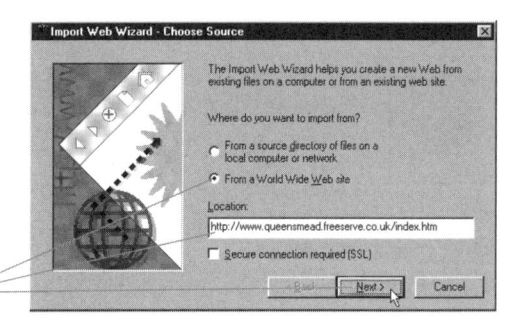

3 When the Import Web Wizard starts, select the location, and enter the path for the Web you want to import.

The starting page can be any page in the Web, not just the home page.

4 Specify how many levels below the starting page, place a limit on how much disk space to use. Choose to import text and images only, or all files referenced on the pages selected.

5 Click Finish, and the selected files and folders of the Web site are copied to the hard disk as a new Web.

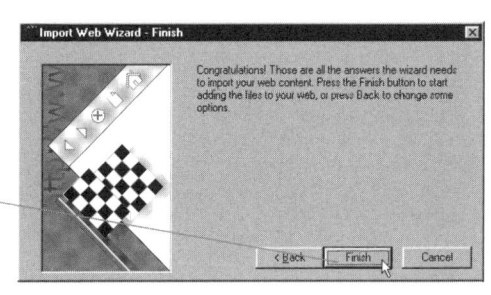

6 The new Web will be shown in FrontPage, ready for you to view and edit as required.

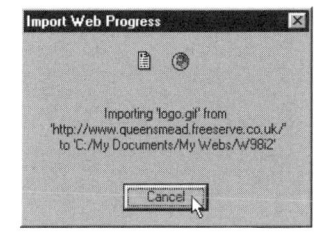

9. Upgrading Webs | 133

Analyse the Web

> **HOT TIP**: Review the style and structure on the Web, to decide what changes are appropriate to bring it up to the FrontPage 2000 level.

The downloaded Web has been given a FrontPage 2000 folder setup, but all of the files are in the root. It has three image files and three pages. There is no navigation structure defined – only the home page shows.

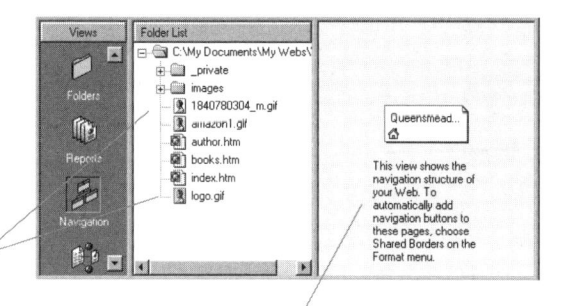

This is typical of the simpler Web designs. It uses tables to organise and position text, graphics and links.

One table contains a simulated Navigation bar, linking to pages and bookmarks in the Web.

> **HOT TIP**: Both of these facilities are maintained and managed by external Web sites.

There are links to a hit counter and a guest book.

The graphical image is positioned within a cell of the table, to control its relative placing.

The text tables give the effect of a magazine by simulating columns on the page.

The page is long, so when you scroll down, the navigation table disappears. To make up for this, more scrolling links are provided at the foot of the page. Note that FrontPage can update the edit date.

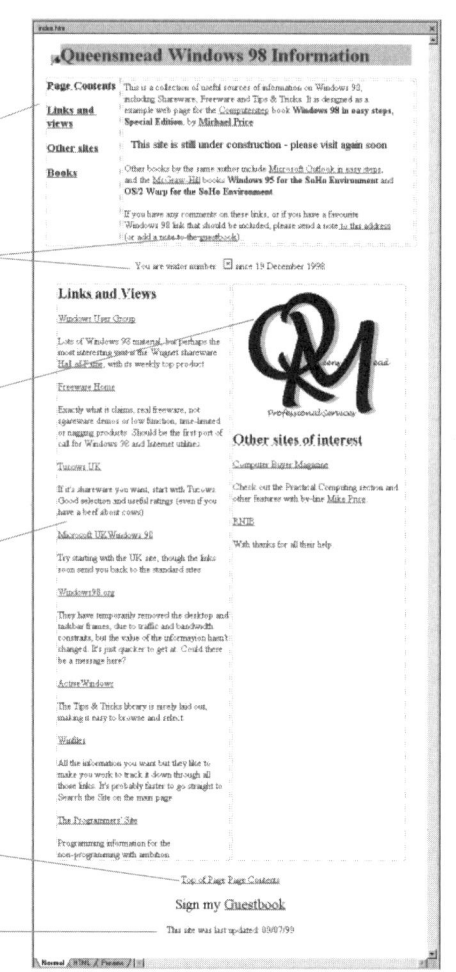

...cont'd

Your Web could use tables, shared borders, frames, or two-dimensional positioning to lay out Web pages. Each method has its own pros and cons.

Web designs take several forms, and you have the opportunity to revise the design when you import a Web.

Table structure

This is the simplest and most universal design. Tables provide an easy way to get columns, and align graphics with text. Your visitors don't even see the table because you can hide its borders. With tables used to organise the text and graphics on the page, virtually all Web browsers will support your Web site.

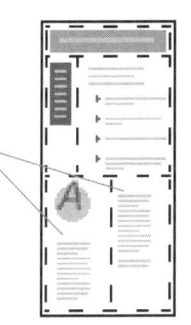

Shared borders

Shared borders are useful when you want the same items to appear on each page, for example, a company logo or a page banner. They also support navigation bars, as described for the Millennium Web, where FrontPage creates and maintains links between the pages. However, they are not very flexible when you want something different from the standard layout.

Visitors who use non-graphical browsers or screen readers may have difficulty with tables or with positioning, since it is impossible to present the page contents in sequence.

Frames

Frames allow you to display multiple pages dynamically on one page. They let you display some information continually, such as a list of hyperlinks, and to display a large amount of information that can be scrolled without interfering with other components on the page.

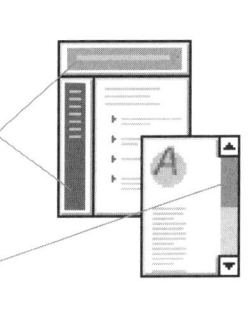

Requires CSS 2.0, so older browsers do not support positioning and will not display the page correctly.

Positioning

Relative and absolute positioning allow you to place text/graphics elements anywhere on a page, independent of paragraph marks, specify layers so that you can overlap text and graphics, and group elements to treat them as a unit. It is the most flexible, can match any requirement but is the hardest to maintain.

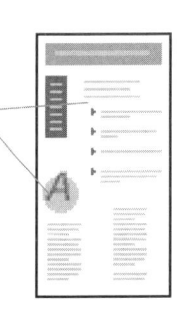

Upgrade the Web

FrontPage manages Webs you import, without needing changes to their structure.

You do not need to make any significant changes to the imported Web, in order to upgrade it to FrontPage 2000. In fact, just saving the pages is sufficient. It will support the original design, whether table or frame, and you can use the FrontPage 2000 facilities to manage the Web, make editorial changes to the contents as needed, and publish the Web back to the Web server.

Check the Web to see if there are any changes that would make Web organisation more standard.

1 With the imported Web open, select Reports from the Views bar, and check the status of the Web.

You may need to move files to a more suitable folder, e.g. the image files to the Image folder.

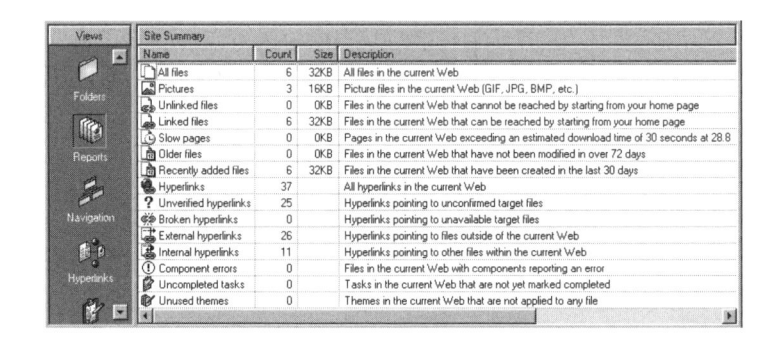

2 With the imported Web open, select Folders from the Views bar, and click the root folder of the Web.

Click the Type header to sort the files, to make it easier to select all the image files.

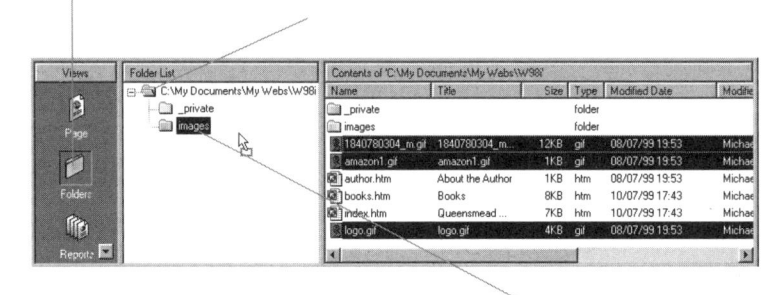

3 Press Ctrl and select all the image files. Drag them, and drop them into the Image folder.

...cont'd

Some changes will be required, if you want to convert to shared borders.

4 Right-click a file name, select Properties and check the page title. A shorter title is better for navigation bars.

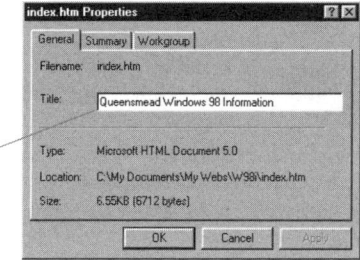

5 Select the Navigation view, click the home page, and drag the second level page files to the appropriate position in the navigation structure.

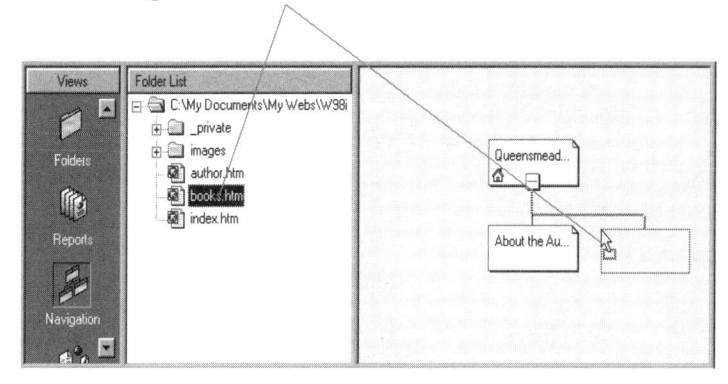

Avoid the use of navigation bars if you are planning to use frames, since the combination creates confusion in navigating the Web.

6 Add shared borders and navigation bars, as described on page 61, and remove the navigation table from the page.

7 To use a frame page instead, first rename the Index.htm file to main.htm, since the frame page will become the new home page.

You must rename the home page if you want to have a frames version.

9. Upgrading Webs | 137

Frames page

> **HOT TIP:** A frames page is a special kind of HTML page that divides the browser window into different areas called *frames*, each of which can display a different HTML file.

The frames page itself contains no visible content. It is merely a container that specifies which other pages to display and how to display them. You click a hyperlink on a page in one frame, and the linked page is displayed in another frame, the *target* frame.

You create a frames page using one of the frames page templates provided in FrontPage. These have the navigation between frames already set up. The Banner and Contents frames page template, for example, would provide an alternative structure for the imported Web.

To create a Frames page:

1. Select Page view and click File, New, Page.

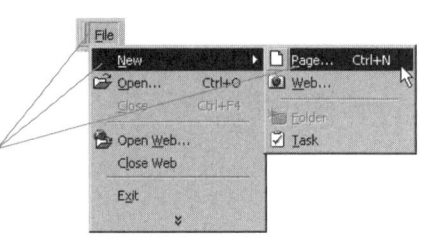

> **BEWARE:** When you use frames avoid the use of navigation bars, since this would create problems in navigating the Web.

2. Click the Frames Pages tab, and preview the templates. It gives a description and preview when you click on any of the templates.

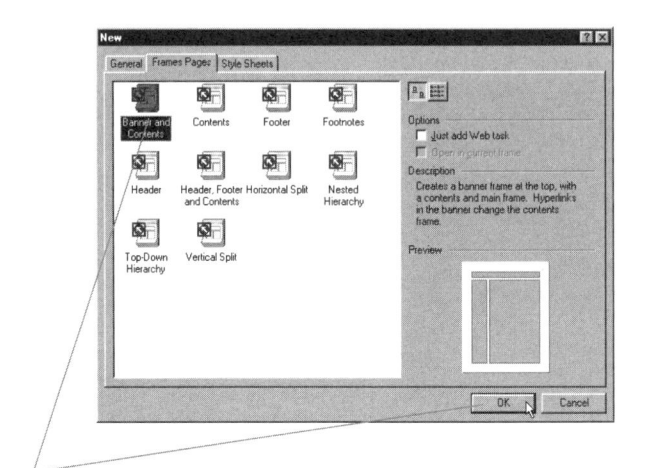

3. Select the Banner and Contents template and click OK.

138 | FrontPage 2000 in easy steps

...cont'd

Select or create the pages to display initially in each of the frames.

This will create a frames page with three frames, ready for you to set the initial page, or define a new page.

4 Save the frames page as Index.htm, and select New Page for the top banner frame.

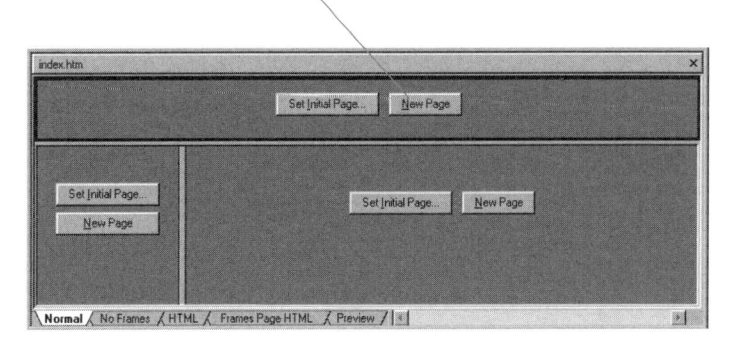

5 Enter the banner title for the Web site, format the text as Heading 1 and Centre, and save the page as Banner.htm.

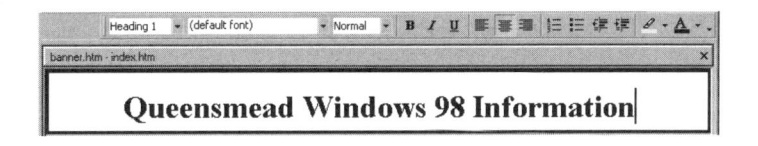

Queensmead Windows 98 Information

You must specify the starting page for the TOC, and the rules e.g. don't show unlinked pages, and recalculate table when the pages are edited.

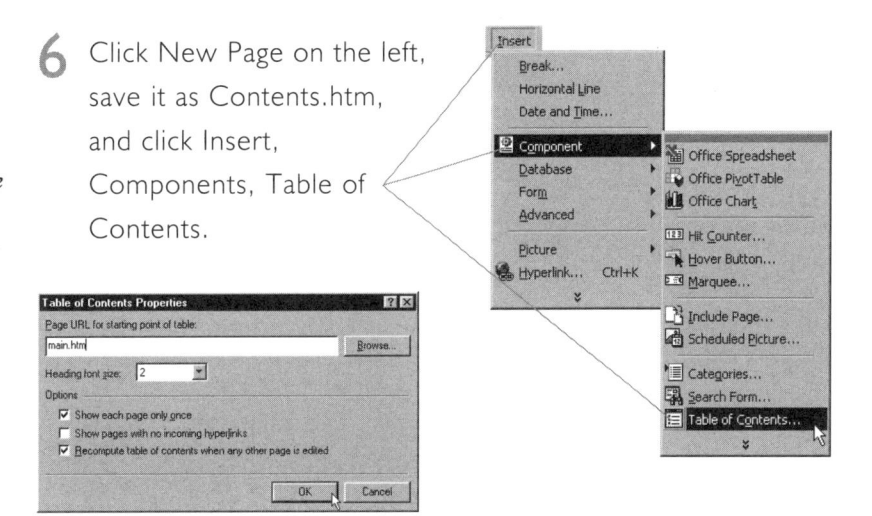

6 Click New Page on the left, save it as Contents.htm, and click Insert, Components, Table of Contents.

9. Upgrading Webs | 139

The main page

HOT TIP: *The main page and any other pages in your Web will be displayed in the right hand frame.*

1. Click Set Initial Page in the right hand frame, and specify the page file Main.htm.

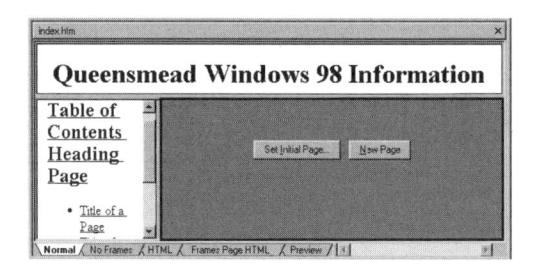

2. Edit the page, Remove the components no longer required, and create new pages with parts of the text, taking advantage of frames facilities.

HOT TIP: *The changes needed will vary from Web to Web, but you need to apply changes to remove such items as contents links which are handled by other frames. You also need to rearrange the text to work with frames.*

3. Remove banner heading.

4. Remove contents table.

5. Create separate pages for Links and Other Sites.

6. Relocate the graphic image on Main.htm.

7. Select each table, and click Table, Convert, Table to Text to remove the table and leave the text freestanding.

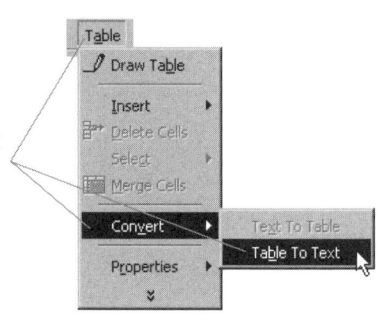

140 | FrontPage 2000 in easy steps

...cont'd

This does not add the pages to the Table of Contents. Pages must be linked, directly or indirectly, from the starting page.

8 Add the new pages in Navigation view, to show where they fit in the Web structure.

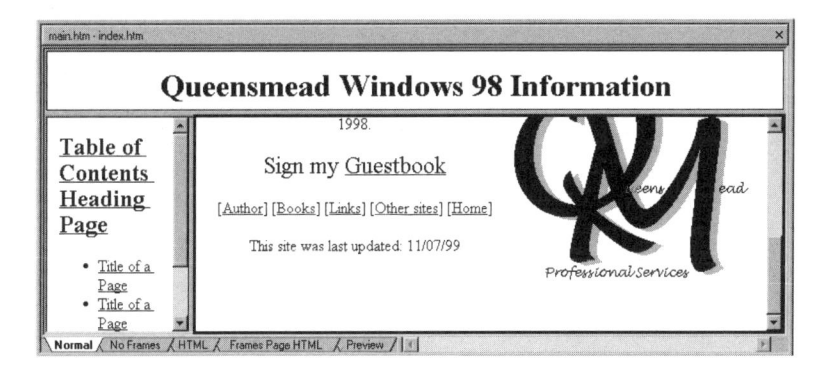

You might wish to copy these links onto all the pages, to help visitors with older browsers (see page 75).

9 Add links to all the pages at the foot of the Main page. Save the changes, and press Preview in Browser.

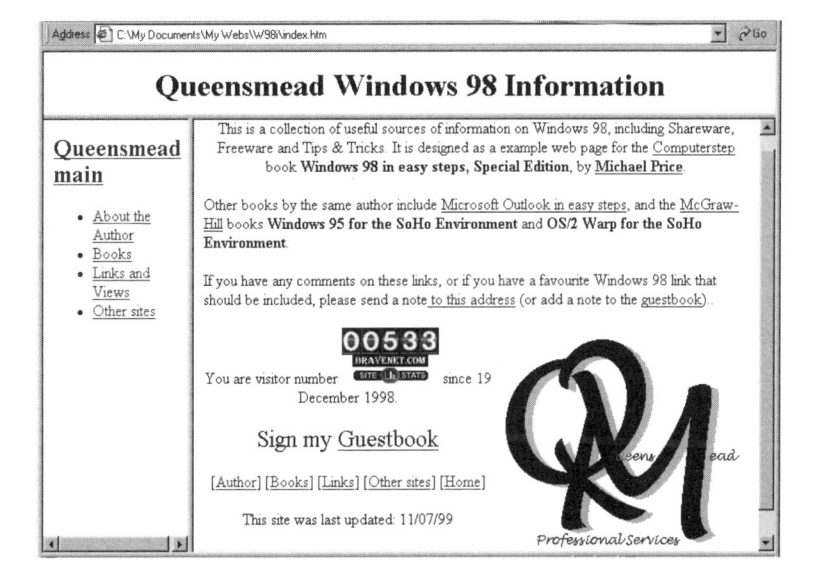

Linked pages are listed in the Table of Contents as well as at the foot of the page.

9. Upgrading Webs | 141

No frames

Some visitors are unable to view Web pages that use frames, due to older browsers or to the use of Web TV to access the Internet.

Older browsers such as Internet Explorer 2 and Netscape 2 do not support Frames pages. The lack of support in Web TV is perhaps a more serious restriction. This means that your site may get visitors who are unable to display even the initial home page. FrontPage handles this situation by displaying a simple message to warn the visitor of the problem.

To display the default No Frames message:

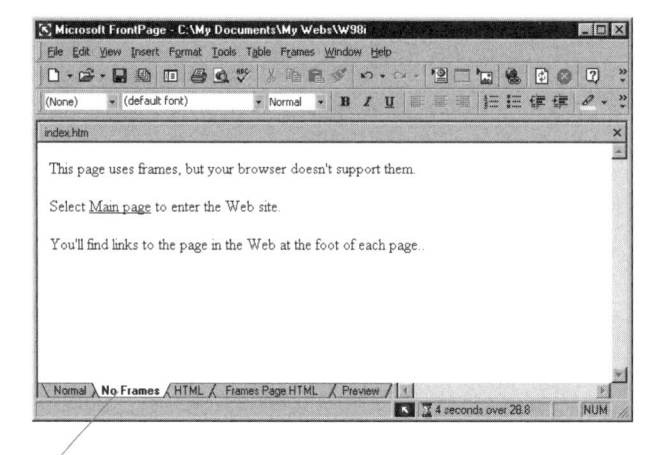

With links on the pages of the Web site, even visitors without frames support can view the site, though they won't have the full benefit of all the facilities.

1. Open the Index.htm frames page and click the No Frames tab at the bottom of the display.

2. The first line shows the default message, which provides no alternatives for the visitor.

3. You can add a text message with a hyperlink to a non-frames page. This could be the same Main.htm used for the normal Frames display.

4. If you have added links to the pages (see page 141), the visitor will be able to view the contents of your Web site.

Guest book

The Server Extensions allow you to replace the facilities used for hit counter and guest book.

In the example Web site, the guest book is hosted at http://www.guestbook.de. If you have the server extensions installed on the Web server, you can use the FrontPage guest book instead.

To add a guest book:

1. Select Page view, click File, New, Page, and select Guest Book.

2. Click OK to create the page. Save it as Guestbook.htm.

You use this page to collect the reactions of visitors to your Web site. The comments are sent to Guestlog.htm which is then included below the form.

To see the comments:

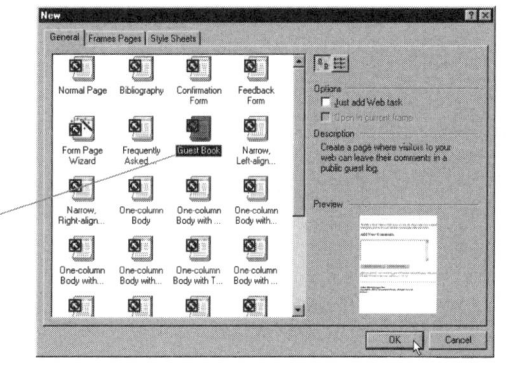

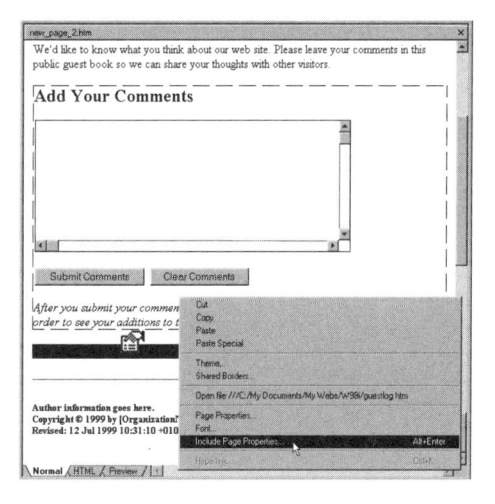

3. Locate the Include component, select it, right-click and choose Include Page Properties. This will include the collected comments at the foot of the visitor form.

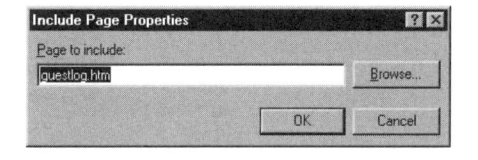

9. Upgrading Webs | 143

...cont'd

To add the guest book to the Web:

4 Edit the Guest Book hyperlink on Main.htm, and change it to the address of the Guest book results file: Guestlog.htm.

After the visitor has submitted comments, it may be necessary to reload (refresh) the page to see the additions to the log.

5 Save the changes and publish the Web to the Web server supporting the FrontPage Server Extensions.

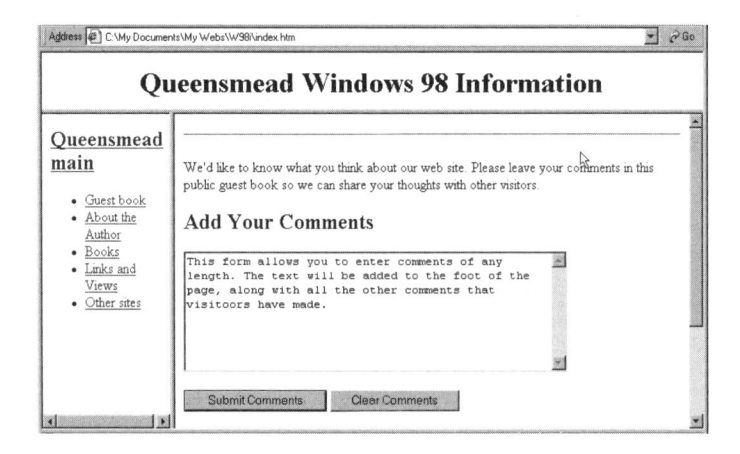

6 When a visitor enters comments and presses Submit, the text is added to the log file and displayed on the form page.

You can replace the hit counter, from www.bravenet.com, using a similar process, discussed on page 116.

Web designs

You may want several Webs at the same ISP, for personal and business use, or for different members of the family, or to suit different browsers. Subwebs make it easy to manage such varying needs.

Covers

Web page size | 146

Web structures | 148

Create the parent | 149

Create subwebs | 150

Set up the parent Web | 151

Preview the Webs | 152

Publish the Webs | 153

Visiting subwebs | 154

Edit the Web server | 156

Switching sites | 158

Web page size

> **HOT TIP**: Short pages are easier to scan, and you can update sections of data at a time. Long pages are better for concentrated research, and you have fewer files and links to maintain.

Your Web site could have just one page or many pages. It depends on how much information you have, and how much you put in each document.

There's no maximum size as such for a page, but you can only display a screenfull at a time. If you have a lot of reference material, you should help the visitor to find the main items on the page.

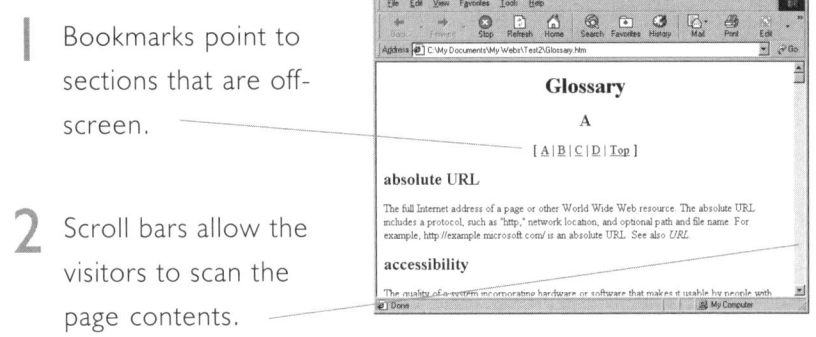

1. Bookmarks point to sections that are off-screen.

2. Scroll bars allow the visitors to scan the page contents.

> **HOT TIP**: The size of the scroll bar section indicates the amount of data that is off the screen.

However, long documents take more time to download, and visitors may fail to spot items that would interest them. This is especially true when casually browsing or surfing the Internet.

You can split the page up into a number of smaller pages, each providing a screen of information, with little or no scrolling needed.

3. Each page needs links to all the other pages, or to the next and previous pages.

4. An overall index page will put the pages into context.

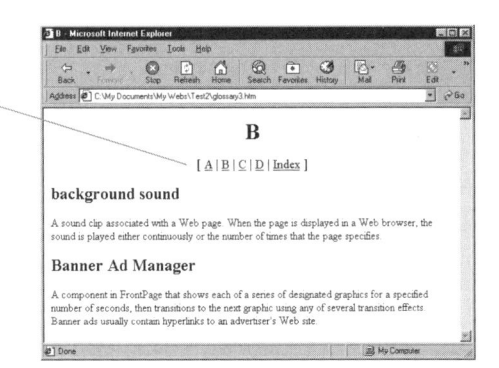

146 | FrontPage 2000 in easy steps

...cont'd

You can arrange the links in navigation bars or tables of contents, if you use shared borders (see page 61) or frames (see page 138).

Choose the page size and style based on the type of information and the type of visitor you expect. There is no single right answer, but there are some guidelines you can consider:

The default screen size is normally assumed to be 800 x 600 pixels.

- For overviews and presentations, don't make the page longer than the default window size.

- Use scrollable screens for longer pages, with text or reference lists.

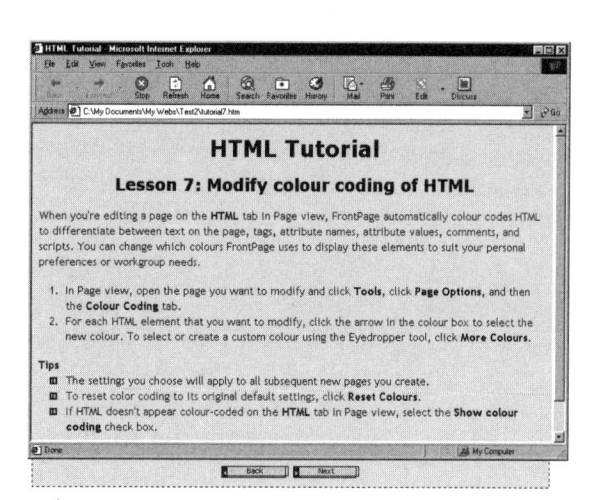

Some users need screen reader software which may need to rearrange the screen content to present it in a logical sequence.

- For general purpose pages, keep the size around one or two screens, and don't hide important features like Continue buttons below the edge of the initial display.

- Consider preparing a separate, single page version of your Web site for printing or downloading, or for non-graphical browsers.

- If your Web site uses frames, consider a separate entry point for users without frames support (or with an aversion to frames).

10. Web designs | 147

Web structures

Web space providers and ISPs cater for the standard Web structure which has a home page and optionally one or more levels of child page.

For example:

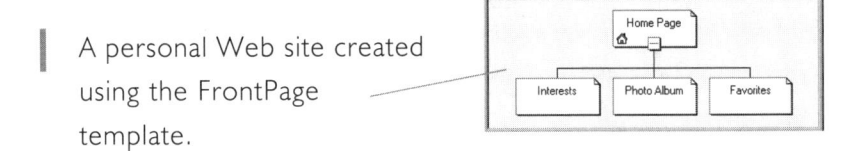

> A personal Web site created using the FrontPage template.

If you are sharing the Web space with family or business colleagues, you might want a Web site structure that gives each of you some independence:

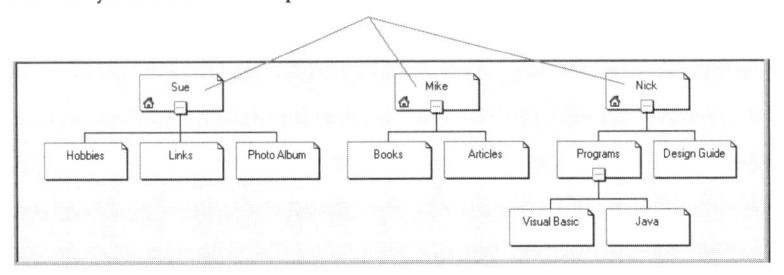

FrontPage can't give you quite that much independence, but you can create a master or parent Web, and create independent subwebs within it. Each subweb can have its own settings and themes, and be separately edited. The set of Web pages can be published and maintained as a group, to a single ISP or WPP account, giving you in effect a structure of the form:

This is the conceptual view. When you add the subwebs, they don't show in the Navigation view.

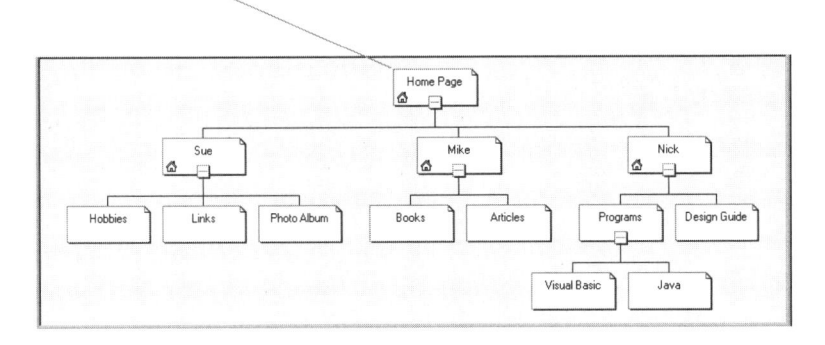

Create the parent

Hot Tip: Create a Web to act as the entry to the subwebs that you want to create.

1 Start FrontPage, close any open Webs and select File, New, Web.

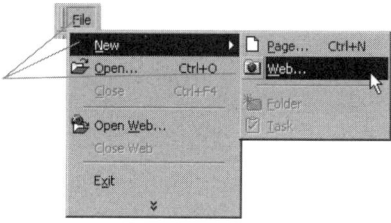

2 Select the One Page Web template, specify the location and name for the Web, and click OK.

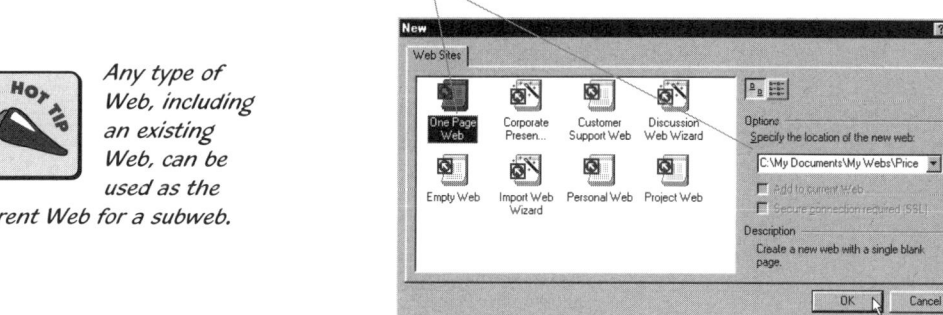

Hot Tip: Any type of Web, including an existing Web, can be used as the parent Web for a subweb.

The Web is generated with a single blank Web page named Index.htm, plus the necessary FrontPage folder structure.

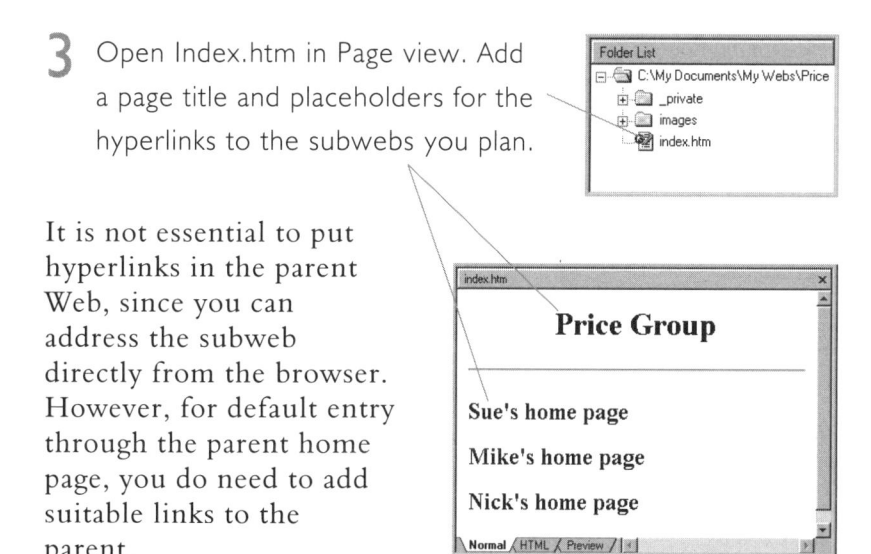

3 Open Index.htm in Page view. Add a page title and placeholders for the hyperlinks to the subwebs you plan.

It is not essential to put hyperlinks in the parent Web, since you can address the subweb directly from the browser. However, for default entry through the parent home page, you do need to add suitable links to the parent.

10. Web designs | 149

Create subwebs

1. Open the parent Web. Select File, New, Web, choose the template (e.g. Personal Web), and specify the location as the parent Web folder. Add the subweb name.

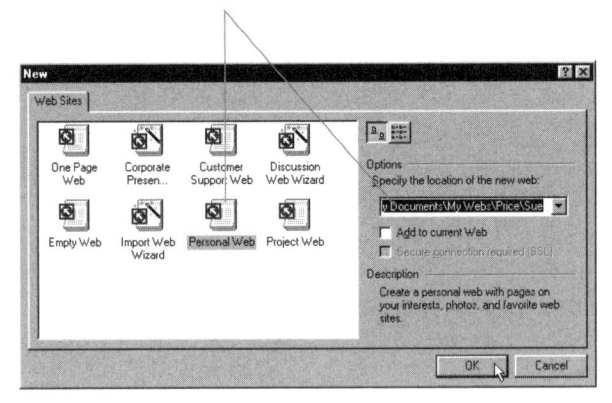

The subweb is created within the parent Web, and starter versions of the pages are created.

If you update the Web this way, the Web settings from the original Web will be retained, so you'll have to reapply shared borders and themes.

2. If you want to apply a template to an existing Web, open that Web, select File, New, Web and choose the required template. Select Add to current Web, and the files & folders are inserted.

If there is already a file of the same name, you are given the option to replace it, or retain the existing version.

3. Repeat the process to create the remaining subwebs inside the parent Web folder.

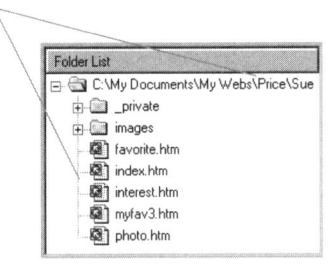

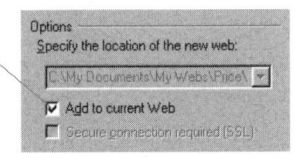

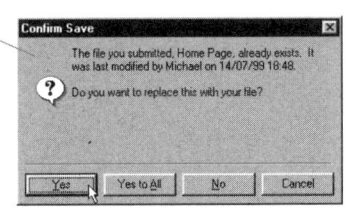

150 | FrontPage 2000 in easy steps

Set up the parent Web

1 Open the parent Web, edit the home page Index.htm, and highlight one of the subweb hyperlink placeholders.

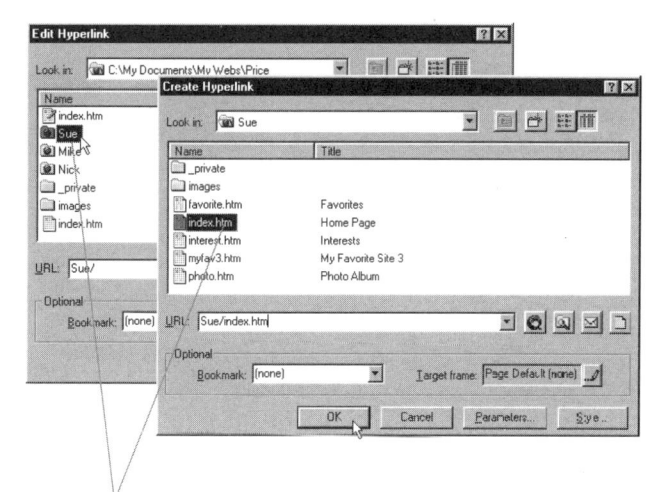

You can specify the full URL for the home page, or just the subweb. See page 152 for the effect on browser previews.

2 Select the subweb, double-click to open it, and click the home page Index.htm, to add it to the URL.

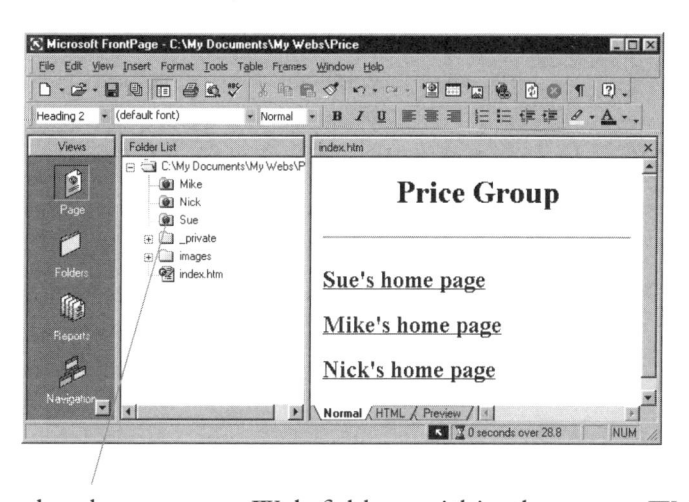

The subwebs appear as Web folders within the parent Web folder. You can open the subweb by double-clicking the folder. A new instance of FrontPage will be launched for the subweb; you can edit the files or review the reports, as with any Web.

10. Web designs | 151

Preview the Webs

1. Open the parent Web, open the home page and press the Preview in Browser button.

2. The home page for the parent Web is displayed. Click one of the subweb hyperlinks.

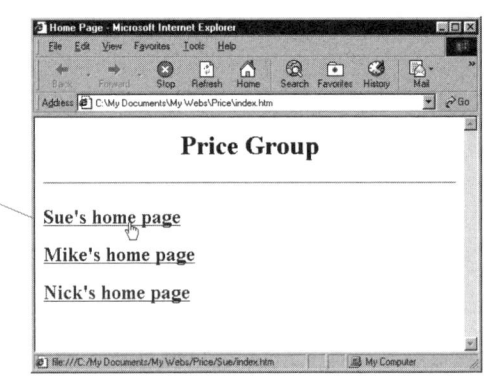

If you specify just the subweb URL, Preview in browser will open the folder rather than the Web. When you are online, specifying the Web URL with or without the home page will open the Web just the same.

3. The home page displays, if the full URL is defined in the hyperlink.

4. The Web folder is displayed in the Windows Explorer style, if the hyperlink contains the Web URL without the page name.

5. Double-click the icon for the home page to open the subweb in the normal Internet Explorer manner.

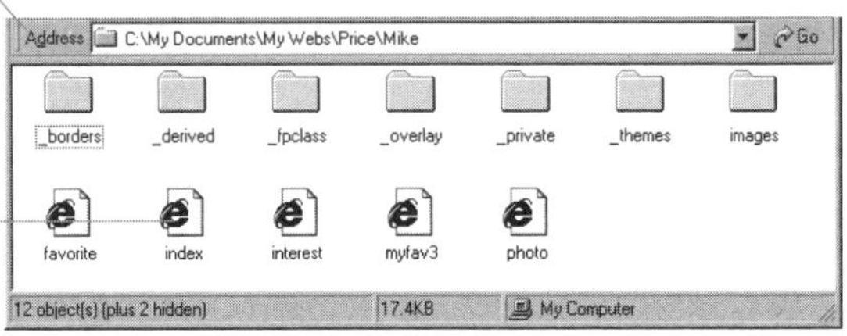

Publish the Webs

1 Open the parent Web, and select File, Publish Web.

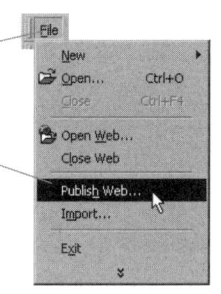

The only difference when you publish a Web with subwebs, is the tick in the box.

2 Enter the URL specifying the location of your Web server. Choose to Publish all pages, and to Include subwebs. Click the Publish button.

3 The files and folders in the parent Web and in the subwebs are copied to the Web server.

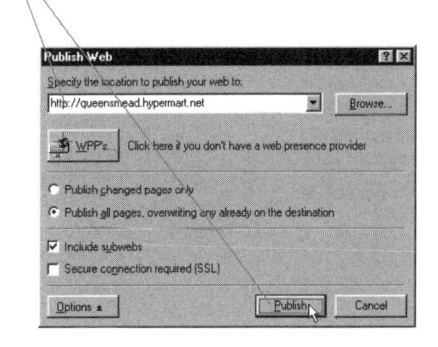

4 FrontPage detects conflicts between the existing contents at the Web site and the new Web. If you are replacing an existing Web site, replace the structure. If the Web is being maintained by several authors, let FrontPage manage and synchronise changes.

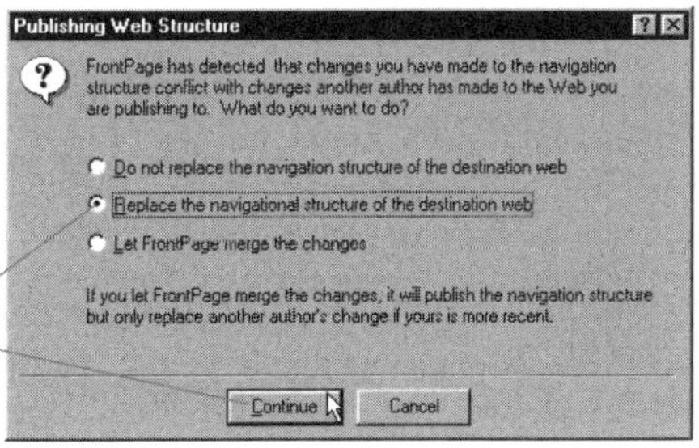

FrontPage replaces files and folders with matching names, but it won't delete files and folders no longer being referenced.

5 When the transfer completes, the new Web site is ready to use. Click the link to view the site on the Internet.

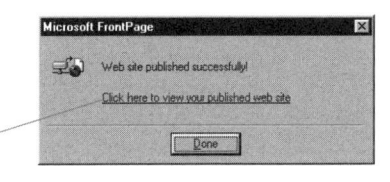

10. Web designs | 153

Visiting subwebs

1. Select the Web site in your browser while connected to the Internet, to display the parent home page.

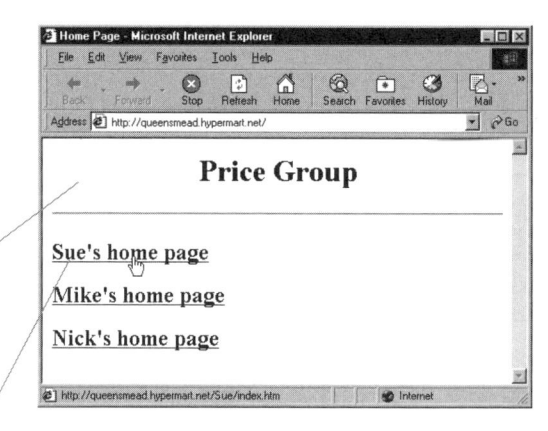

When you provide a URL without a page name, the browser tries the standard names for home pages, and displays the first match it finds, in this case 'Index.htm'.

2. Click on the hyperlink to display the subweb at the home page.

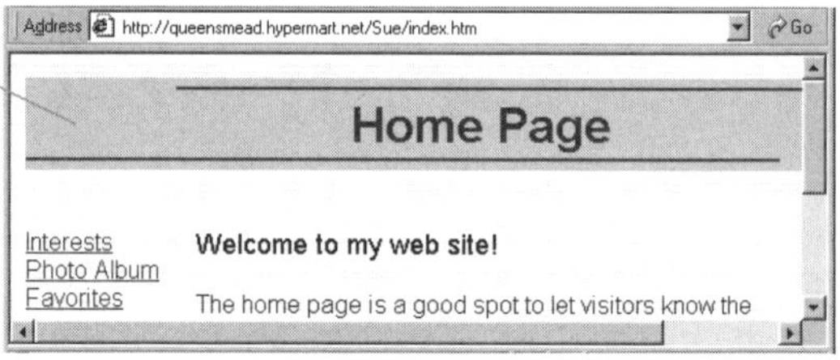

3. You'll get the home page even if the link has no page name. However, you must specify the proper case. Unlike Windows, the Web servers are case sensitive.

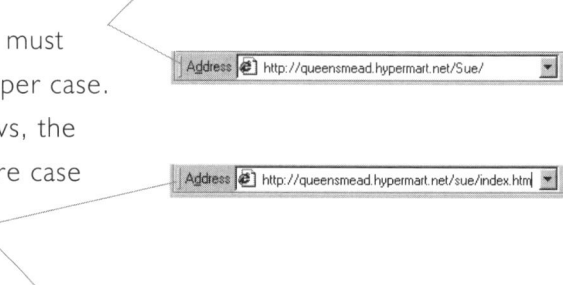

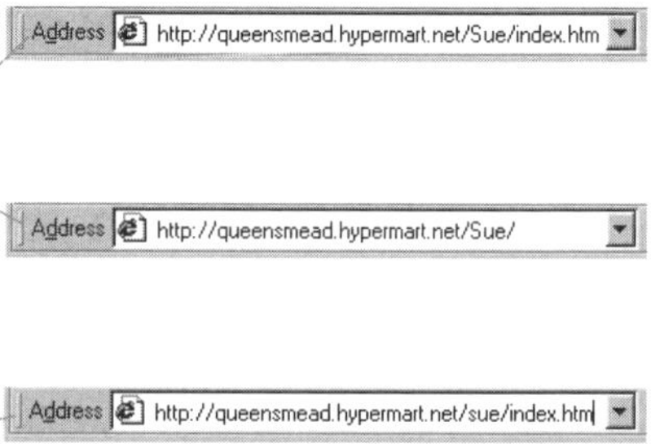

The Web folder name usually doesn't matter because it is not published. However, when a Web becomes a subweb, the name and its case become an issue.

You will need to tell your contacts what capitalisation to use, or you can rename the Web folders with lower case names.

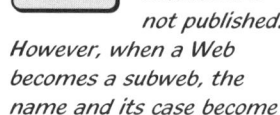

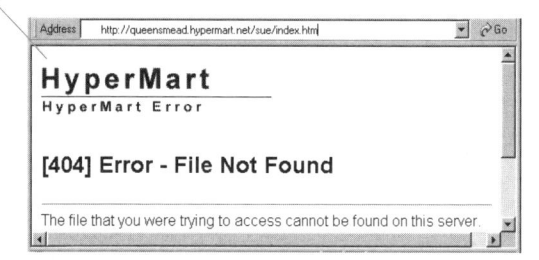

...cont'd

> **HOT TIP**
> *View and edit the contents of the Web folders, at the Web server, when you have the FrontPage Server Extensions.*

If the Web server supports FrontPage server extensions, you can view the Web folders and make immediate changes to the contents:

To open a Web page:

4 Use your browser to view the page to be changed, and select File, Edit with Microsoft FrontPage.

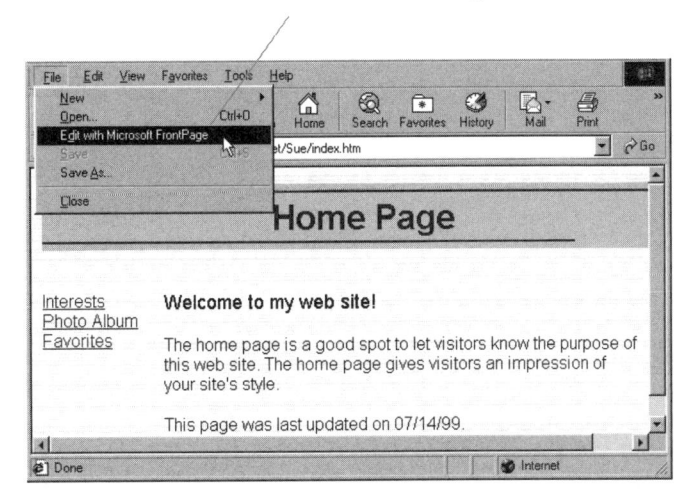

> **DON'T FORGET**
> *Type the folder and file names exactly as they appear in the Web folder, using the correct case.*

5 Alternatively, select File, Open, specify the Web site URL and choose to Open as Web Folder.

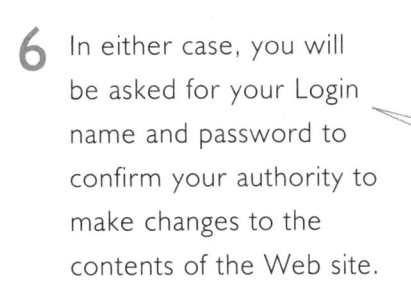

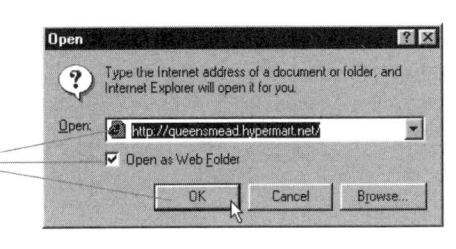

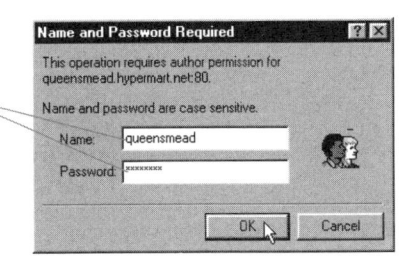

6 In either case, you will be asked for your Login name and password to confirm your authority to make changes to the contents of the Web site.

10. Web designs | 155

Edit the Web server

You can open folders and subwebs within the Web folder to find the pages or image files that you wish to revise.

1 Explore the Web folders to locate the Web and the Web page to be modified.

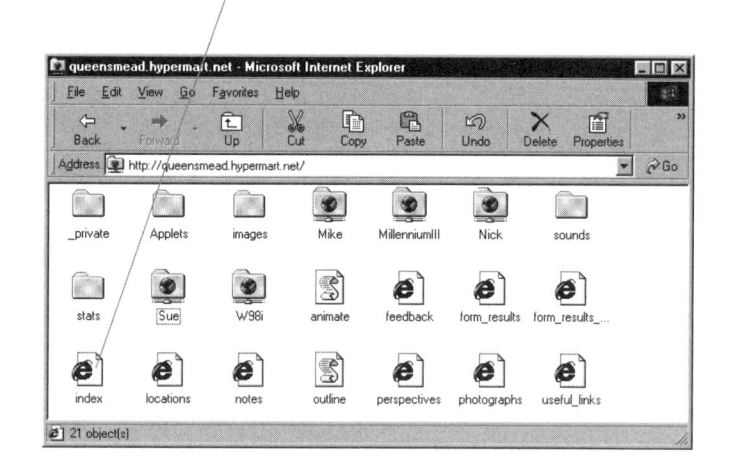

Working with the Web server is very useful when you have two or more people in your group who are allowed to apply changes.

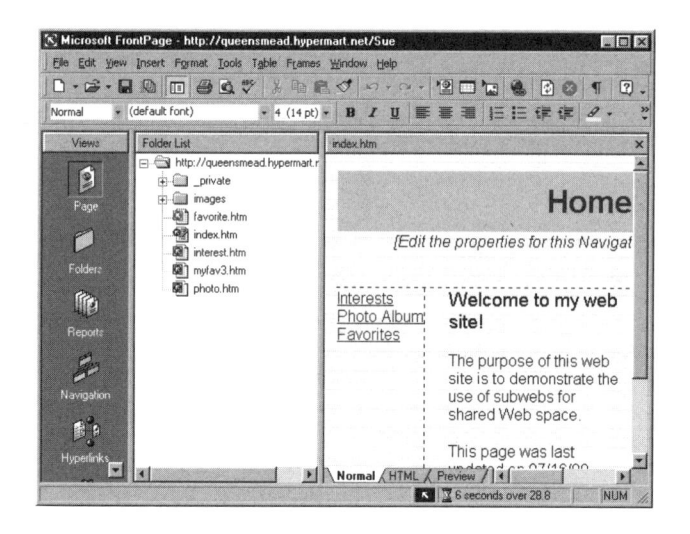

2 Make changes to the Web page, Save the file and Close the Web. The copy at the Web server is updated.

3 If necessary, press the Reload or Refresh button in your browser to display the updated version of the page.

...cont'd

The Web page shows the new content and date of modification.

The page is displayed with the updated contents and a new date last revised is inserted.

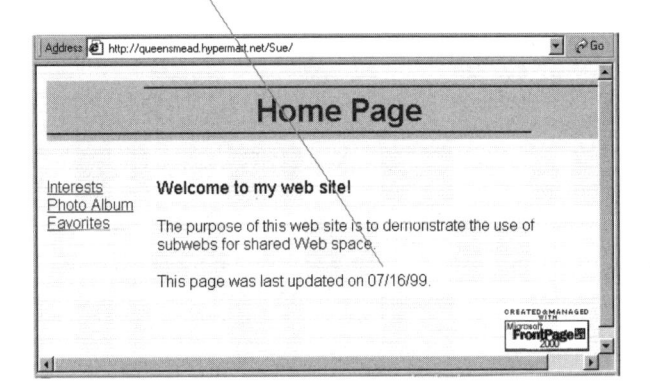

The original copy on your hard disk will not be updated. You can Publish the Web from the Web server to your hard disk to refresh your copy.

If you build a Web site on a Web server that does not support server extensions, you will not be able to view the Web folders or edit the files at the Web server.

Changes must be made locally on disk and published by FTP to the Web server.

4 Select File, Open, specify a Web file name. Open as Web Folder.

5 You'll see a message saying default view only allowed.

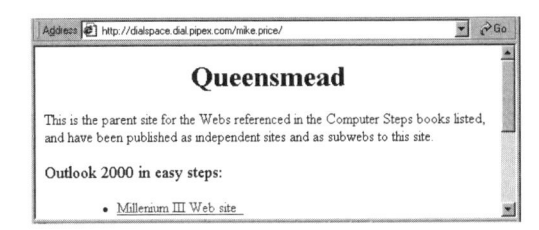

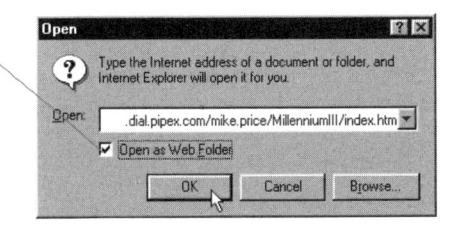

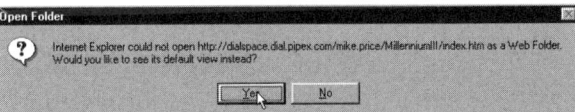

10. Web designs | 157

Switching sites

When you move your Web site to a new Web server, e.g. to get support for Server Extensions, redirect visitors to the new location.

1 Create a new home page for the old location, with a suitable message, and a hyperlink to the new location. Remind the visitor to update any bookmarks.

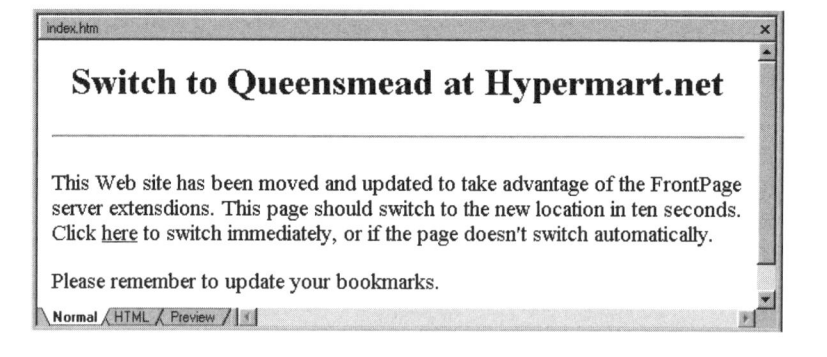

> **Switch to Queensmead at Hypermart.net**
>
> This Web site has been moved and updated to take advantage of the FrontPage server extensdions. This page should switch to the new location in ten seconds. Click here to switch immediately, or if the page doesn't switch automatically.
>
> Please remember to update your bookmarks.

See page 108 for more details on meta-variables.

2 Right-click the page, select Page Properties, Custom, and Add a system meta-variable to Refresh the page after ten seconds, with the URL for the new location.

Visitors could bookmark any page on your site, so use Refresh, when you remove or replace a page, to give an explanation and a redirection within the Web.

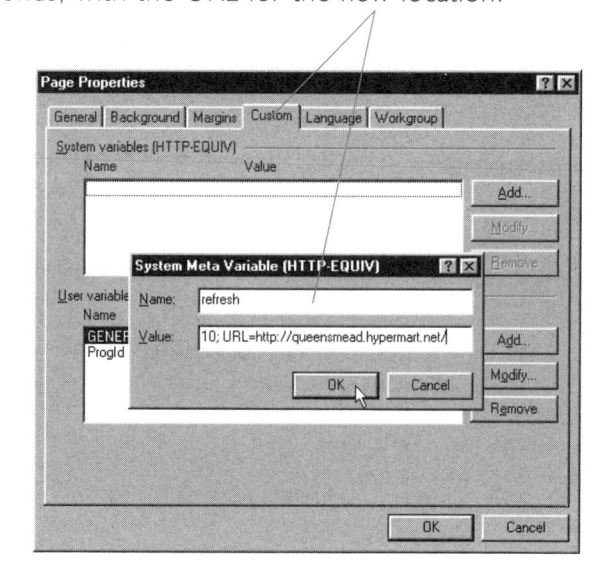

When the visitor next visits your old site, there will be a message and an automatic transfer from the old Web site to the new. Leave the Refresh in place as long as possible.

158 | FrontPage 2000 in easy steps

Tables, images and forms

A more detailed look at features of FrontPage, including the use of tables, the design of image maps and the creation of discussion group Webs using interactive forms.

Covers

Creating tables | 160

Draw a table | 162

Convert text to table | 163

Tables within tables | 164

Image maps | 165

Hotspots | 166

Set up a discussion group | 168

Discussion group Web | 170

Web conversations | 172

Chapter Eleven

Creating tables

Tables are used in Web pages for two different purposes. They are used as a method for arranging text and graphics, as discussed on page 135, and they have their more usual function of presenting text and numeric data.

FrontPage provides several ways of creating tables. You can create a simple table by specifying the number of rows and columns. To create the table, in Page view, select the insertion point and:

1 Click the Insert Table button to display the table selector.

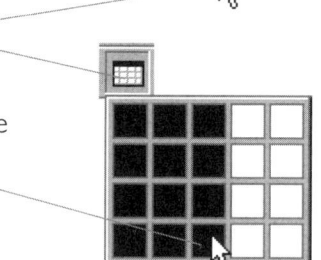

2 Drag down and across until you've selected the required number of rows and columns. The selector expands as needed.

3 Release the mouse button to generate the table with default property values set.

You can modify the properties of the table after creating it. See opposite for examples of layout properties.

4 Right-click the table and choose Table Properties to adjust table settings such as Alignment, Padding, Spacing or Color.

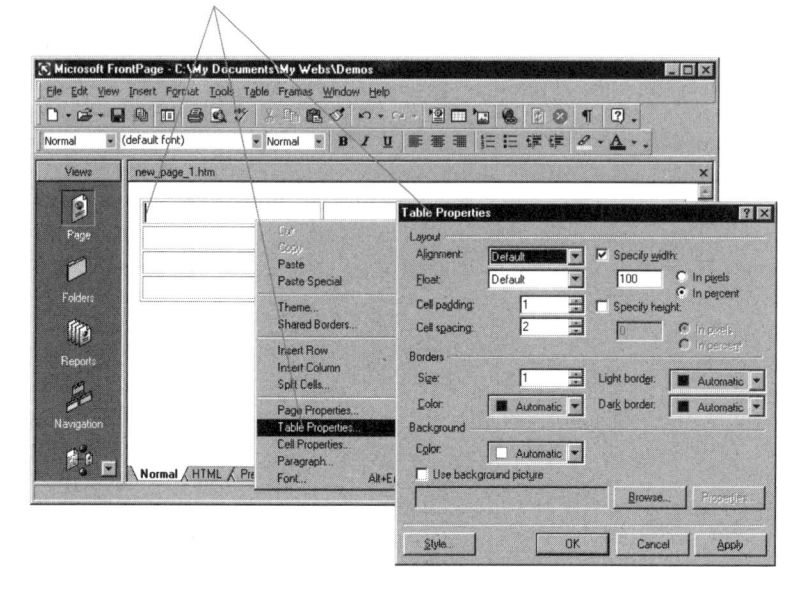

160 | FrontPage 2000 in easy steps

...cont'd

You can specify properties, for the table as you are creating it.

1. Select Table from the menu bar and click Insert, Table.

2. Type the number of rows and the number columns that you want.

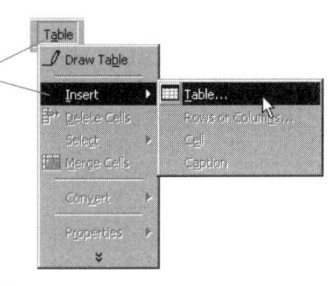

3. Set the Alignment on the page (Left, Right, Centre or Justify).

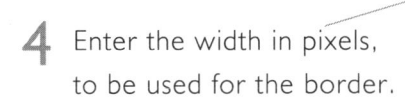

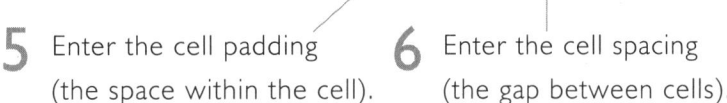

4. Enter the width in pixels, to be used for the border.

5. Enter the cell padding (the space within the cell).

6. Enter the cell spacing (the gap between cells).

Layout Properties that you specify for the table will be used as the default properties the next time you create a table.

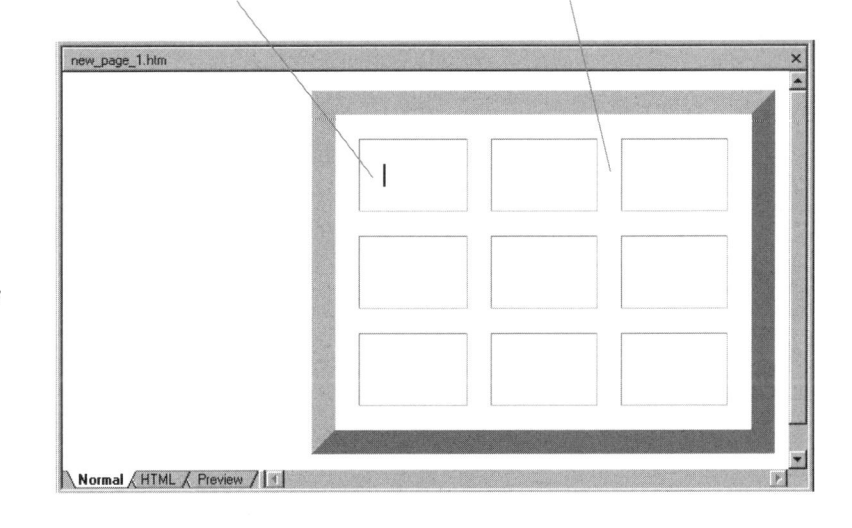

7. Specify the width of the table in pixels or as a percentage of the screen or Frame width.

11. Tables, images and forms | 161

Draw a table

If you want a complex table, with different sizes of cells and varying numbers of columns and rows, you can draw it the way you want, no matter how irregular.

1. In Page view, select Table and click Draw Table. FrontPage opens the Tables toolbar with Draw Table selected.

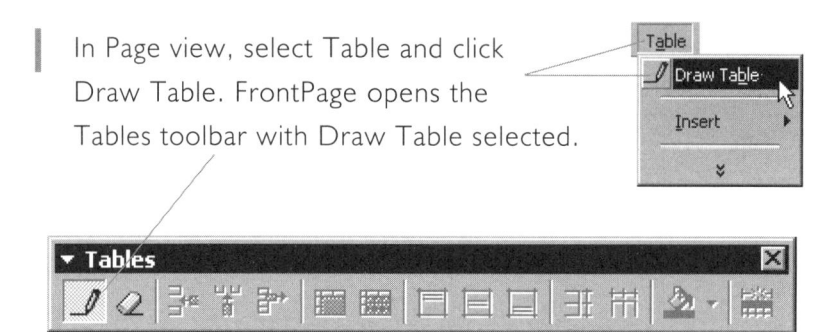

2. Draw the outside border of the table by dragging from the upper-left corner to the lower-right corner of the table.

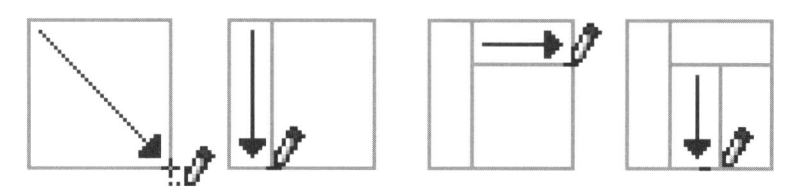

3. Draw vertical and horizontal lines, to create columns and rows in the table, and nested within cells.

Click Draw Table on the Tables toolbar, to deselect the button and end table drawing.

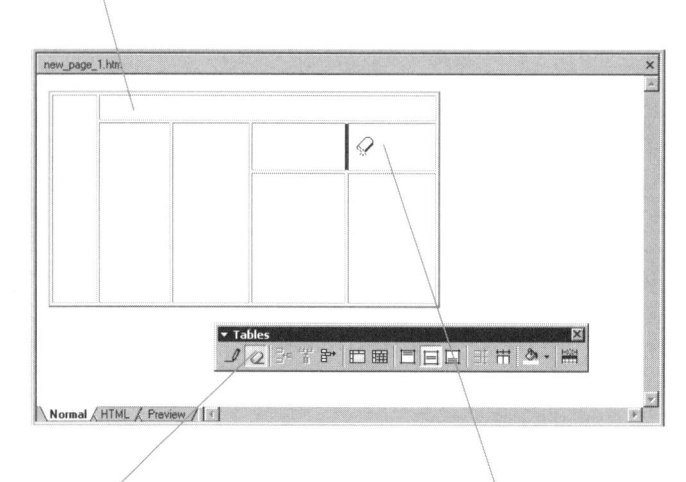

4. Click Eraser on the toolbar, and drag across an unwanted line. When the line turns red, release the mouse button.

Convert text to table

You can convert text into a table if it has been delimited – separated into rows and columns.

HTML does not directly support tab characters, so avoid using tab characters as your text delimiter.

1 Open the Web and open the page in Page view.

2 Type or copy the text onto the page, using a separator character such as a comma to mark the column boundaries, and the end of line (paragraph marker) to indicate the end of each row.

3 Highlight the text (excluding the title) and select Table, Convert, Text to Table.

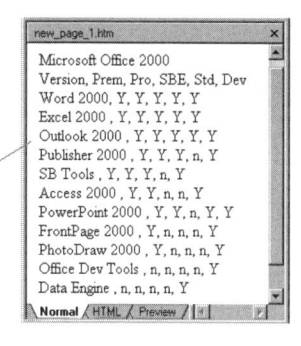

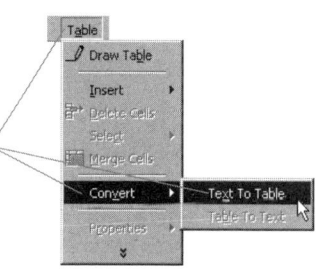

4 Specify the separator character that you have used and click OK.

If you select None, all the text will be placed in a single cell table, for example to keep all selected text together when you use tables for page layout.

If you do specify a separator character, the table will be created with the number of columns defined on the row with the most separator characters.

You can change properties, and resize the cells and the columns.

The current default values will be used for borders and spacing.

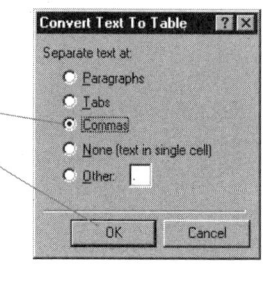

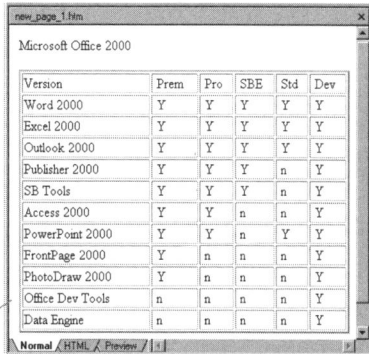

11. Tables, images and forms | 163

Tables within tables

> **HOT TIP**
> You can remove lines to combine cells, or split a cell into several rows or columns, or insert a whole table within a cell.

Add extra table entries e.g. title and product prices:

1. Click in the first row and select Table, Insert, Rows or Columns.

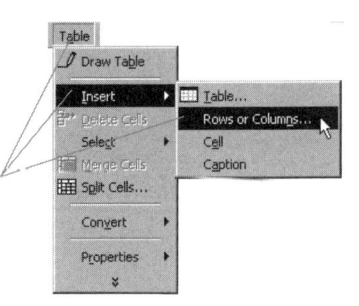

2. Click to add one row above the selected row.

3. Repeat the Insert, but this time add one row below the selection.

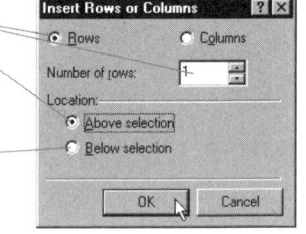

> **HOT TIP**
> You can also split selected cells by clicking Split Cells on the Tables toolbar.

4. Select the first new row and click Table, Merge Cells, to combine them.

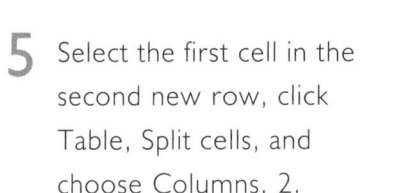

5. Select the first cell in the second new row, click Table, Split cells, and choose Columns, 2.

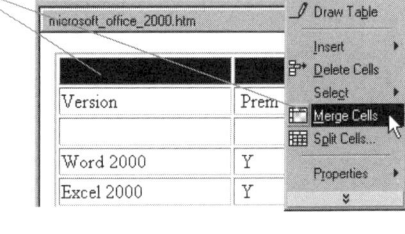

6. Select all except the first cell in the second new row, click Table, Split cells, and Rows, 2.

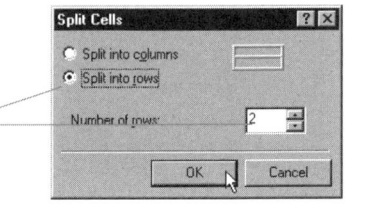

7. Enter the title, centre it, and enter the subtitles and data values.

	Microsoft Office 2000					
Version		Prem	Pro	SBE	Std	Dev
Prices	Full	£490	£418	£324	£321	£589
	Upgrade	£255	£204	£147	£148	£370
Word 2000		Y	Y	Y	Y	Y
Excel 2000		Y	Y	Y	Y	Y

Image maps

You can associate several URL links with parts of an image, and so create an image map.

You can define a hyperlink for a graphic, to create an image button. When you click anywhere on the image, it switches you to the specified URL. If the image has several distinct elements or sections, you may want a different hyperlink for each. When a hyperlink is associated with a part of an image, you have a hotspot. You can define a number of hotspots on the image, making it an image map, with each region on the map pointing to a different URL or bookmark.

1. Select Insert, Picture, From File, to add the image onto the page.

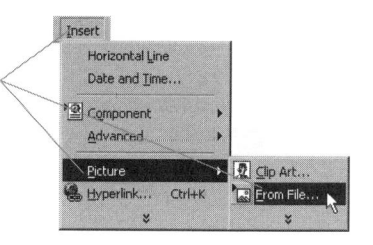

See page 32 for details about creating the hyperlinks and bookmarks.

2. Click the image to select it, showing the picture handles.

3. Right-click the image and select Hyperlink from the menu.

4. The Create Hyperlink screen is displayed.

If you are using frames, you can set the destination of the hyperlink to a specific frame.

5. Define the URL for a Web page or bookmark.

This link will be the default for the image, and will be associated with any area of the picture not separately defined as a hotspot.

11. Tables, images and forms | 165

Hotspots

To add hotspots to the image:

1. Click the picture. If the Picture toolbar does not appear, click View, Toolbars and select it.

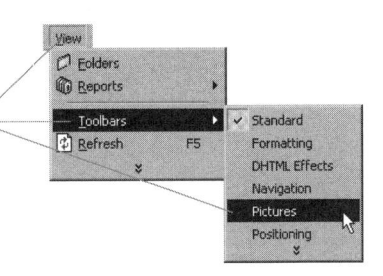

You can define a close fitting polygon of any shape, by taking small steps, or you can allow a loose fit for ease of selection.

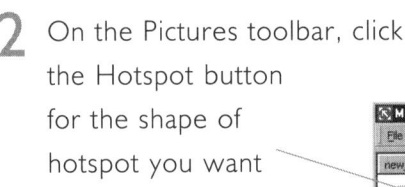

2. On the Pictures toolbar, click the Hotspot button for the shape of hotspot you want (Polygon, Circular or Rectangular).

3. Draw the shape onto the image. For a polygon, click the corners in turn. Double-click to finish.

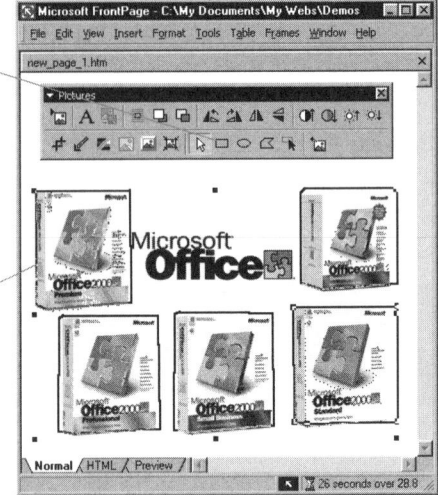

Any parts of the image not covered by a hotspot will take on the default hyperlink address.

4. When you release the mouse button, the Create Hyperlink screen appears. Enter the URL for the target Web page or select a bookmark for the hotspot.

Repeat the drawing and hyperlink definition for each hotspot region, until the map is complete.

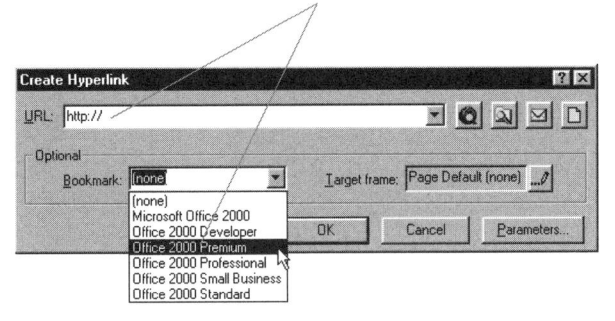

166 | FrontPage 2000 in easy steps

...cont'd

> **A text hotspot is a string of text that you place on the image and assign a hyperlink.**

You can add a text hotspot to the image:

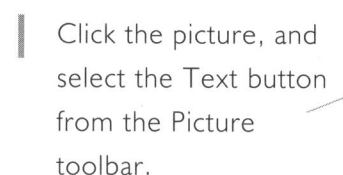

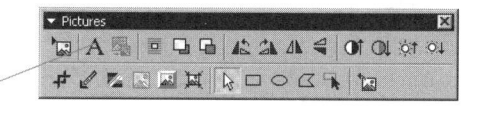

1. Click the picture, and select the Text button from the Picture toolbar.

2. If the image type is a different format, a GIF format version will be created.

> **Move or resize the text box as necessary to fit it onto the right part of the image.**

3. Type the desired entry in the text box.

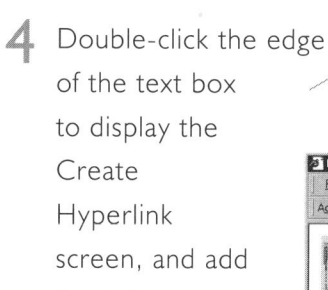

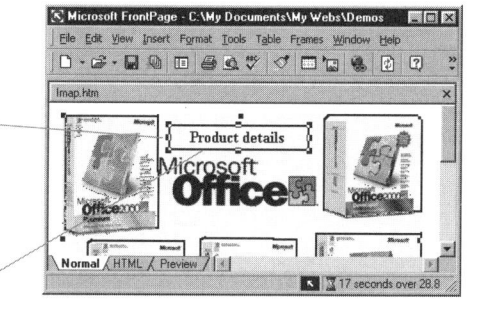

4. Double-click the edge of the text box to display the Create Hyperlink screen, and add the link.

> **In this example, the image hotspots link to bookmarks in a collapsible list.**

5. View the image map in the browser. The hotspots are hidden until the mouse pointer moves over them.

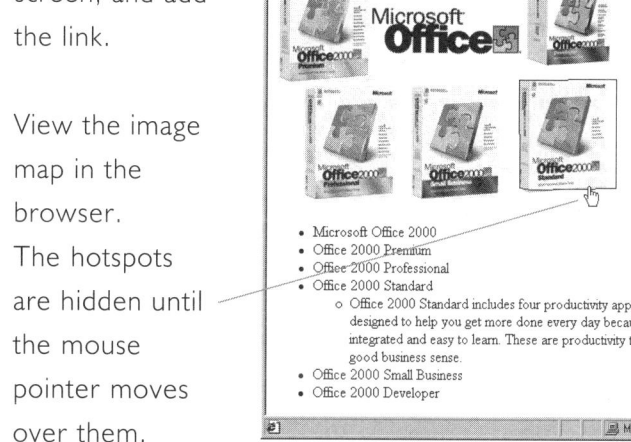

11. Tables, images and forms | 167

Set up a discussion group

You can use the Discussion Web wizard to create a Web with the features you want.

As well as exchanging information with your visitors, you can set up an environment for them to communicate with each other. This is known as a discussion group, and it allows visitors to post or reply to messages stored at the site.

1. Select File, New, Web and the Discussion Web wizard.

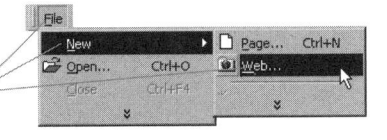

You don't have to create a subweb, since you can add the new pages as an extension to your current Web.

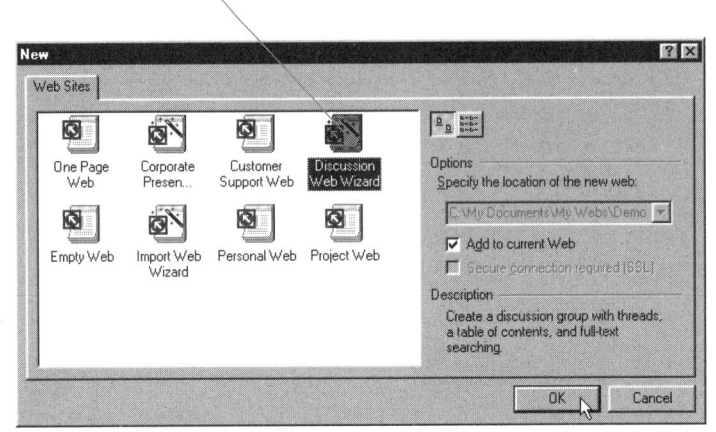

You'll get all the pages needed, including forms for submissions, searches and replies, plus a table of contents.

2. The wizard guides you through, suggesting the forms and pages that you may need. If in doubt, simply click Next to accept the defaults provided.

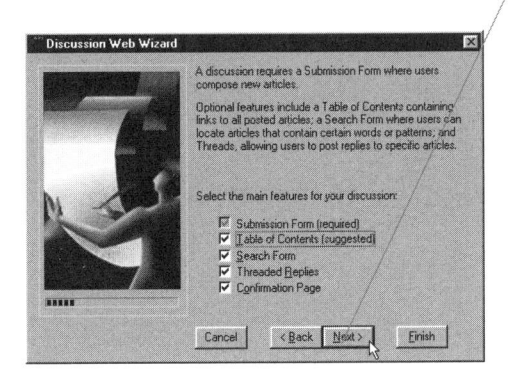

...cont'd

You'll get a full function discussion site by accepting the suggested formats and forms.

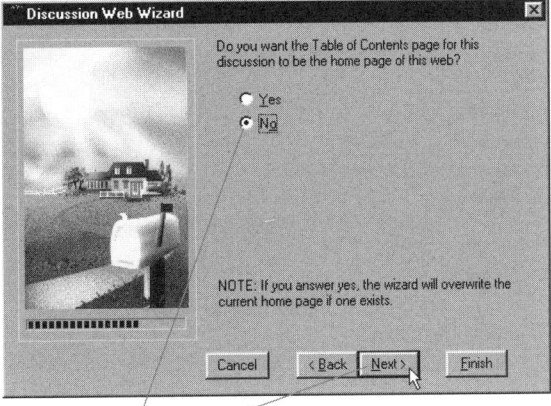

3 Enter the title, choose the input fields and decide the sequence for the contents (newest to oldest is best).

You must add a link to the Contents page on your current home page, so visitors can join in the discussion.

4 If you are adding pages to an existing Web, avoid setting the discussion Contents as the home page.

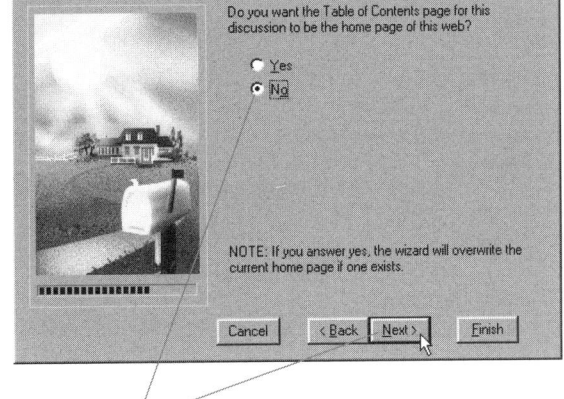

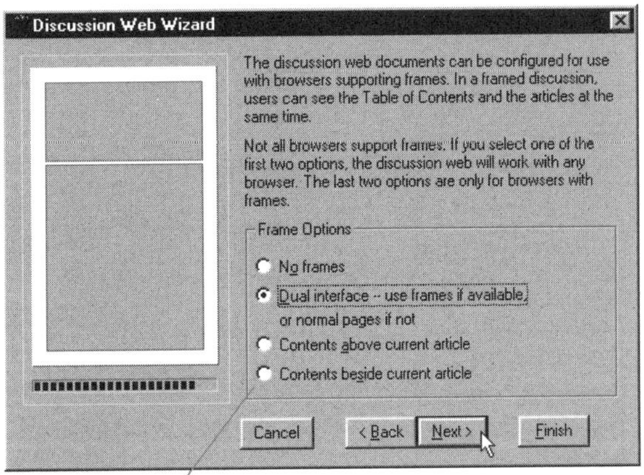

Try to choose the style that best complements your existing Web site.

5 You can select from several page styles, with or without frames, or choose a dual format.

6 Continue through the wizard screens, until the discussion group specification is complete.

Discussion group Web

When the wizard ends, you can review the pages added.

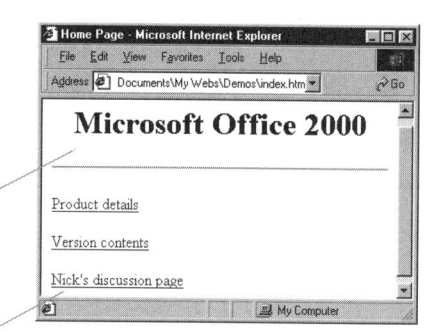

You can edit and delete articles posted to the discussion group by selecting the option to show documents in hidden directories, in Advanced Web settings.

1. Select View in browser to open the Web with your discussion group.

2. The Home page should link to the Contents page for the discussion group.

3. Each page in the group will have a standard heading section, with navigation links.

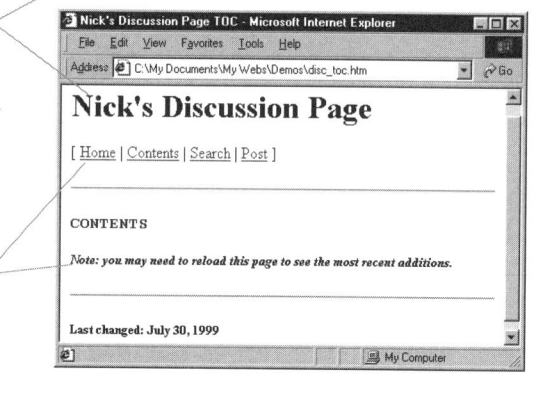

4. The Contents page will list the posted articles, in the sequence that you selected.

The results of a search include the subject, size and date for matching articles, plus a score that measures the relevance based on the search terms.

5. The Search page will allow visitors to locate articles based on particular words or patterns.

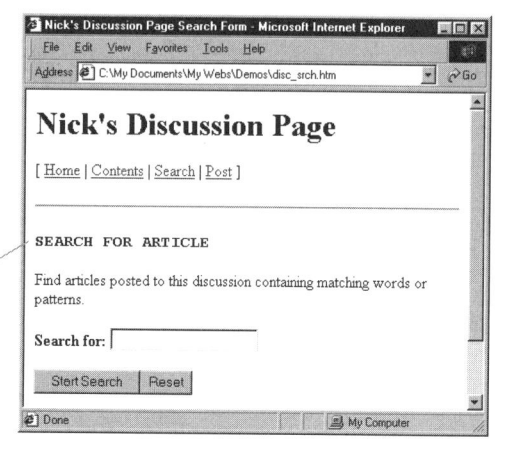

170 | FrontPage 2000 in easy steps

...cont'd

> **HOT TIP**
> *Visitors can reply to previous articles in the discussion, creating conversation threads.*

6 The Post page allows a visitor to create a message or article that will be stored at your Web site, entering:

Subject

Visitor's name

Comment text

Submit button

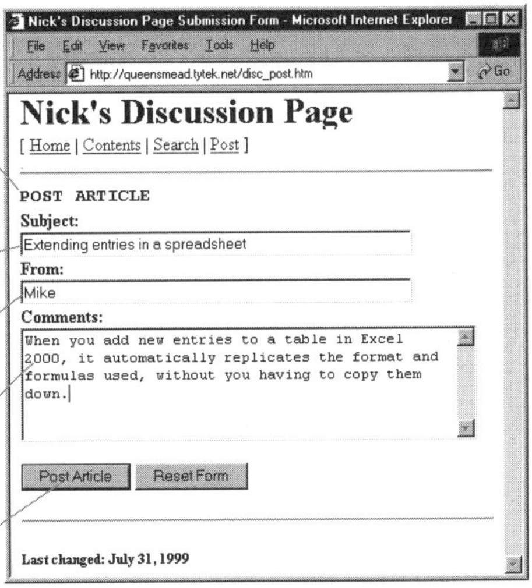

> **DON'T FORGET**
> *You must publish the Web to a Web server with the FrontPage Server Extensions before you can operate with the forms.*

7 Like other FrontPage forms, the discussion group requires the Server Extensions.

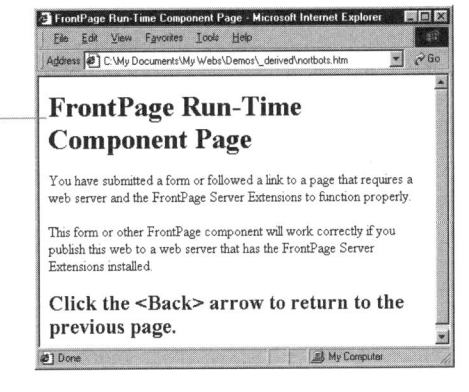

> **BEWARE**
> *Windows NT security and Microsoft Internet Information Services (IIS) do not allow registration through a Web browser.*

You can monitor access to the Web by using the User Registration page template to create a login form for visitor name and password.

If you want a protected Web, you can add a password field to the registration form, and you can specify the list of user names that will be allowed to participate in the discussion. This can be used to create a discussion group for a private topic such as a business topic, even though the users connect through the public Internet.

11. Tables, images and forms | 171

Web conversations

HOT TIP — *When you have published the Web, you and your visitors can take part in discussions, as long as the Web server supports the Server Extensions.*

1 At the Web server, your visitors can view or post messages for the group.

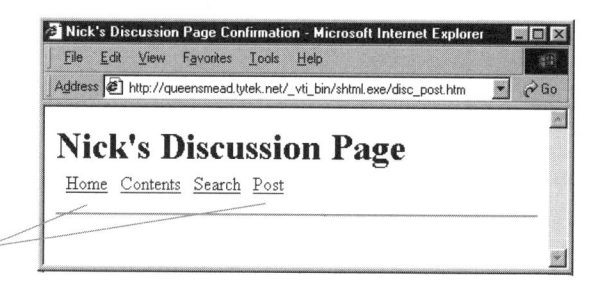

   Nick's Discussion Page
   Home Contents Search Post

2 On the Contents page they'll see the list of messages, with:

   Date
   Author
   Subject
   Conversation thread

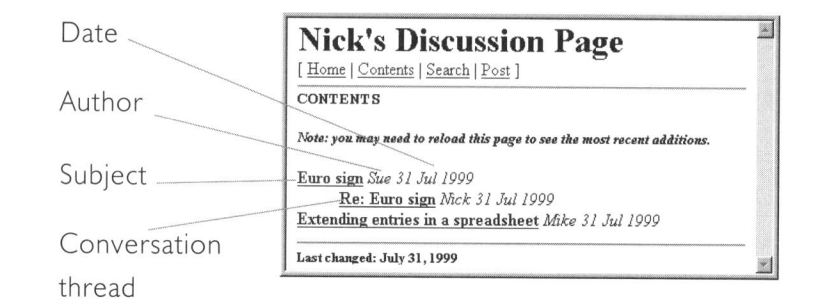

   Nick's Discussion Page
   [Home | Contents | Search | Post]
   CONTENTS
   Note: you may need to reload this page to see the most recent additions.
   Euro sign *Sue 31 Jul 1999*
      Re: Euro sign *Nick 31 Jul 1999*
   Extending entries in a spreadsheet *Mike 31 Jul 1999*
   Last changed: July 31, 1999

DON'T FORGET — *You can change the stored articles, to correct errors, delete old data or remove off-topic entries. Be warned that some visitors may take advantage of your discussion group and post advertisements or other inappropriate entries.*

3 Click on a message to display it, and Reply direct to it, or Post a new item, or view Next or Previous.

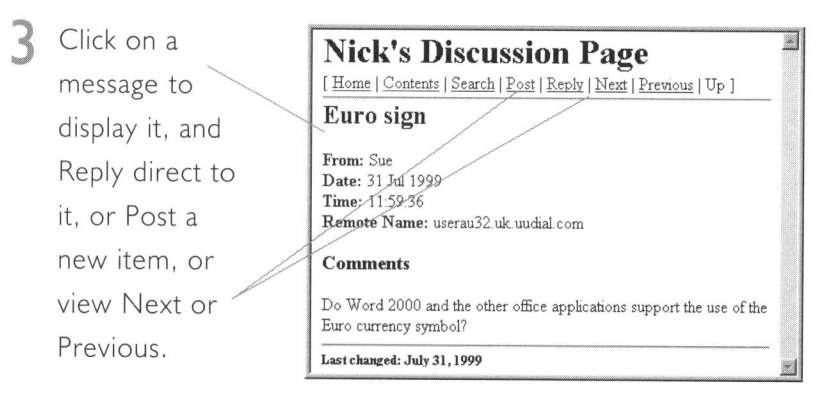

   Nick's Discussion Page
   [Home | Contents | Search | Post | Reply | Next | Previous | Up]
   Euro sign
   From: Sue
   Date: 31 Jul 1999
   Time: 11:59:36
   Remote Name: userau32.uk.uudial.com
   Comments
   Do Word 2000 and the other office applications support the use of the Euro currency symbol?
   Last changed: July 31, 1999

4 Select the Search page to look for specific notes by keyword or word patterns.

172 | FrontPage 2000 in easy steps

Sources of help

There is a wealth of information about Web design on the Internet, from Microsoft, from other hardware and software suppliers and from interested groups such as universities. You'll find free, demo or trial add-ins for FrontPage that make the design task easier. You can even write your own functions.

Covers

Local help | 174

Web help | 175

The Download Catalogue | 176

Install an add-in | 177

Using J-Bots | 178

More info from MS | 179

FrontPage Bulletin | 180

FrontPage Frenzy | 182

Design guides | 183

VBA macros | 184

Web Workshop | 186

Chapter Twelve

Local help

The first and primary source of help and information is provided as part of FrontPage.

1 Select Help, Microsoft FrontPage Help (or click the Help button on the toolbar).

2 Webs

Click [+] to open sections, and [-] to collapse them.

Pages

Publish

Example

Glossary

There are sections in the Help to cover all the aspects of designing, enhancing and publishing a Web site.

You can copy an item such as a table or a form field from the Help example to paste it into one of your own pages in Page view.

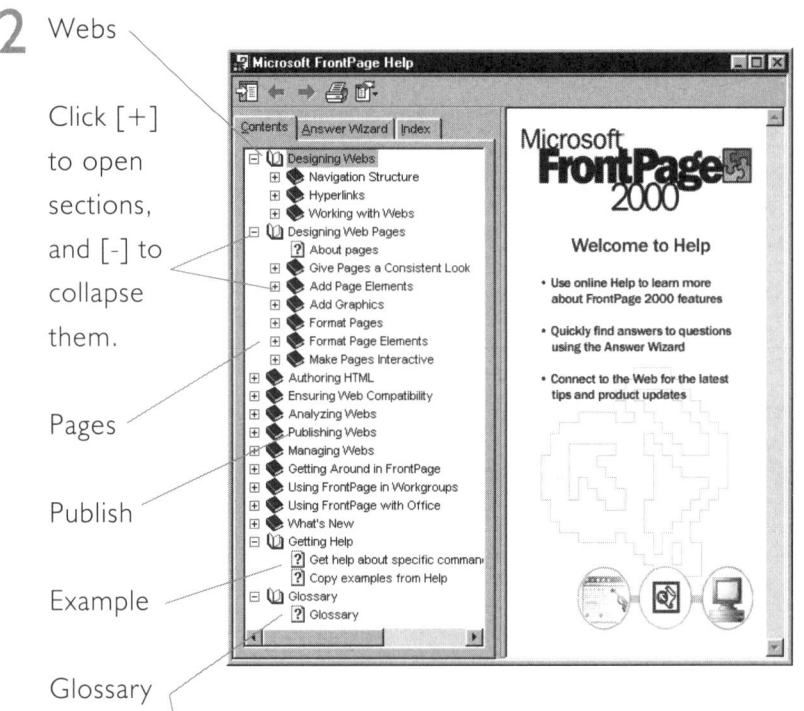

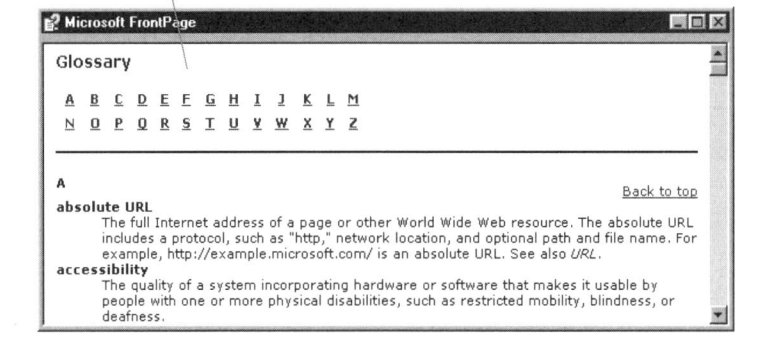

174 | FrontPage 2000 in easy steps

Web help

There is also a link to help on the Internet, via the Office 2000 Update facility.

1 Select Help, Office on the Web. This starts your Internet connection and displays the Office Update Welcome page for FrontPage 2000 data and updates.

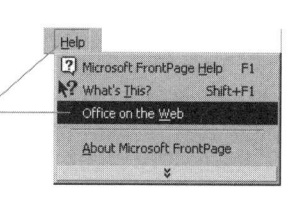

These pages change on a regular basis, so the page contents you see will be different.

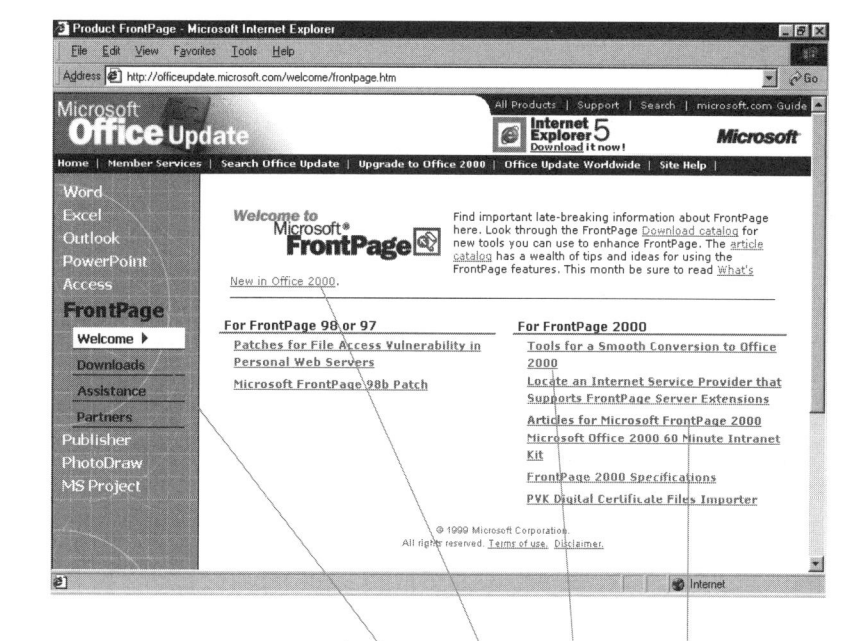

This site will be the source for fixes and enhancements to FrontPage 2000.

2 From this page you can:
Access the Download Catalogue.
Get the latest news about FrontPage.
Get assistance with installing or connecting.
Read articles and information about FrontPage 2000.

This Web site also links you to similar details for the other applications in Office 2000, such as Word and Excel, and to information related to the previous versions of FrontPage.

12. Sources of help | 175

The Download Catalogue

There are downloads for older previous FrontPage versions as well, and some downloads apply to many of the Office 2000 programs.

1 Click the Downloads hyperlink, and select to display FrontPage 2000 downloads.

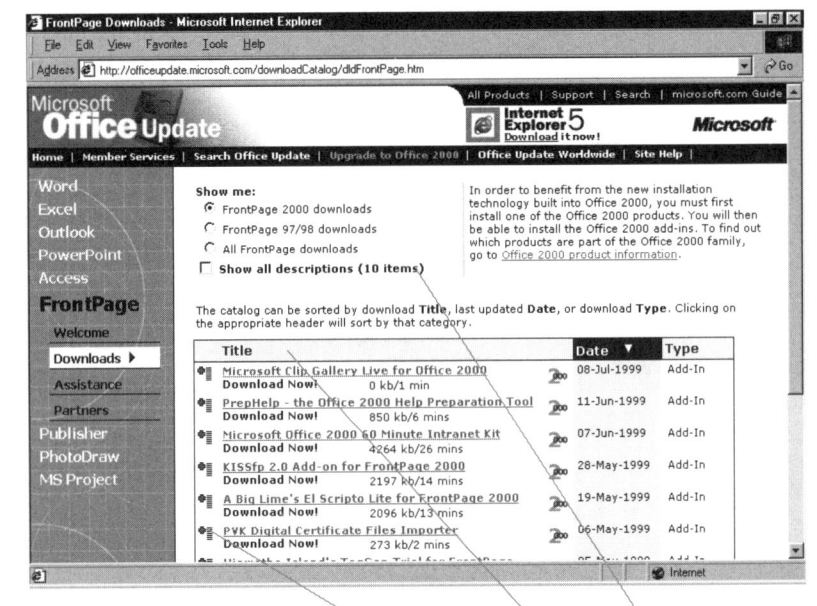

Click Read this first for details of the add-in functions, setup and use.

2 Expand or collapse individual entries.

Click the header to sort by title, date or type.

Expand descriptions for all the update items in the list.

When you select Download Now, the required files are transferred to your hard disk, ready for you to install the add-on or update.

The actual products and options will vary from time to time, but you should expect to find trial versions of third party add-in applications, such as the J-Bots Plus 2000.

Install an add-in

> **HOT TIP**
> An add-in extends FrontPage by adding custom commands or specialised functions. You can obtain add-ins from independent software vendors, or you can create your own (see page 184).

To install an add-in:

1 Find the downloaded module and double-click to run the install program.

2 Select Tools, Add-Ins to start the Add-In Manager.

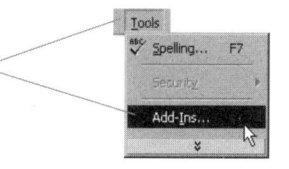

3 Select the box to load, or clear the box to unload an add-in.

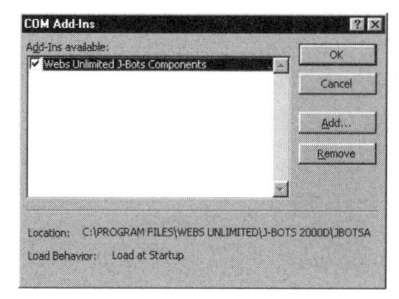

> **HOT TIP**
> The add-ins at the Office Update site are usually trial, demo or lite (limited function) versions, meant to help you decide whether to buy a full version.

When you load an add-in, it remains loaded until you close or exit FrontPage.

Some add-ins may not be registered in the Add-in Manager, but will insert entries into the menu bar.

An example:

4 To start El Scripto Lite after installation, click the entry added directly to the menu bar, and choose one of the menu items.

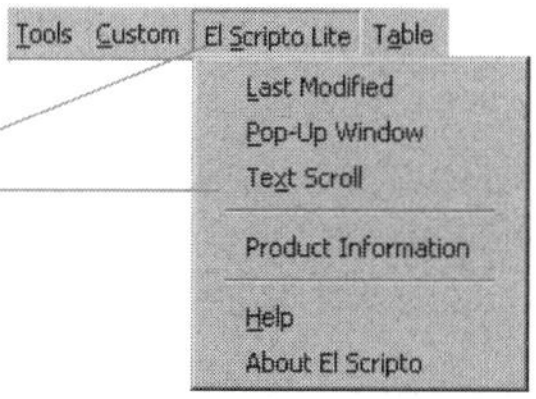

5 Select Custom from the menu bar and click Run TagGen – The Meta Data Composer.

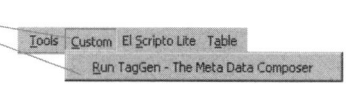

12. Sources of help | 177

Using J-Bots

The J-Bots add-in is a 14 day trial version with just a small number of components. You can upgrade to a full version of 25 or 50 components.

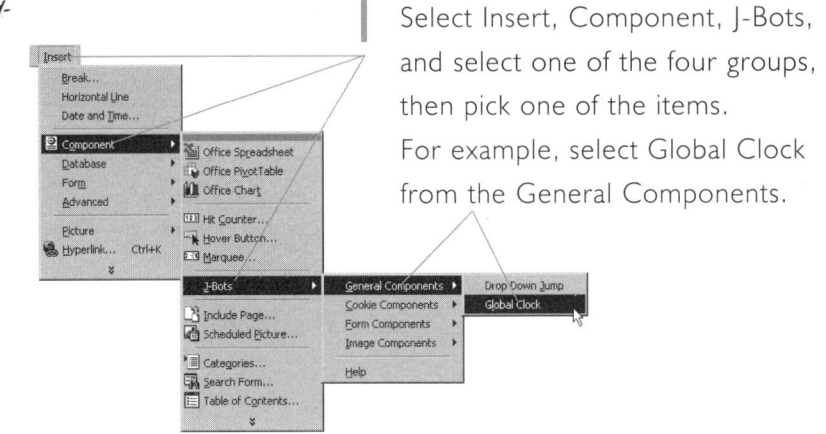

1. Select Insert, Component, J-Bots, and select one of the four groups, then pick one of the items. For example, select Global Clock from the General Components.

Perhaps not the best item to include as a sample, since the Global Clock does not seem to understand British summer time.

2. Enter the time format codes and any text needed, and choose the time zone.

3. Click Generate to enter the required code into the page.

4. You can generate several different entries, if you want to show the time in various places.

5. Preview in Browser, to see the results with the actual times displayed.

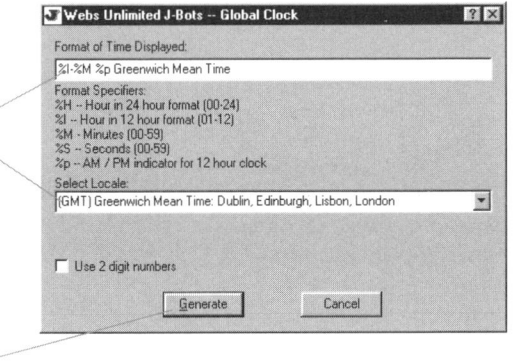

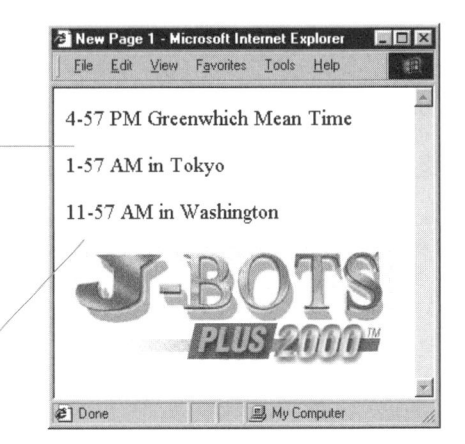

178 | FrontPage 2000 in easy steps

More info from MS

There's a lot more detail on FrontPage offered from the main Microsoft Web sites.

You will find many Web pages devoted to FrontPage at various Microsoft Web sites. The main information is on USA sites. To get started:

1. For product information, visit the US product Web page at http://www.microsoft.com/frontpage

There are links to support pages and related products, and also a link to Office Update (see page 175).

2. For UK based information, visit the Microsoft UK Web pages at http://www.microsoft.com/uk/office/frontpage

From here you can subscribe to various free Office newsletters, including the monthly FrontPage bulletin (see page 180).

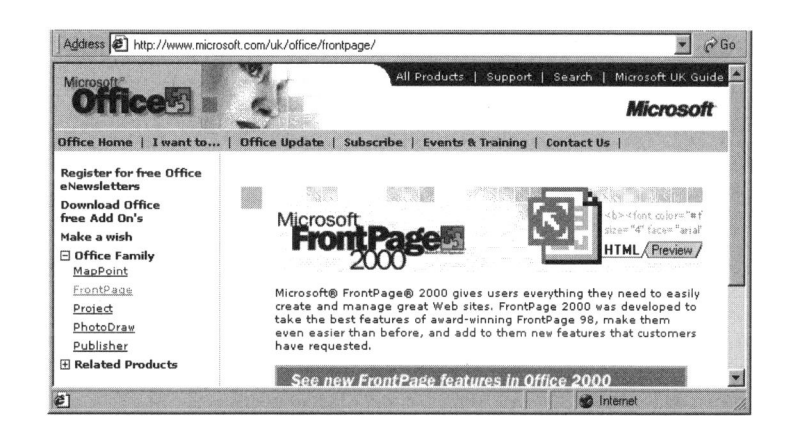

12. Sources of help | 179

FrontPage Bulletin

When you register for the monthly FrontPage Bulletin from Microsoft you can select a plain text or an HTML format. It will be sent as an e-mail message to the e-mail address that you specify.

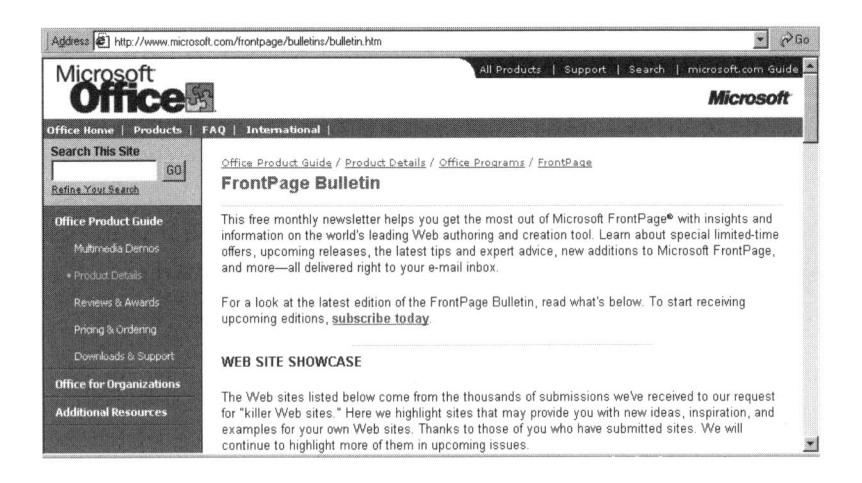

The bulletin covers a variety of information concerning FrontPage, such as:

1. News about additions, updates and fixes for FrontPage or related applications.

2. Special offers, demos and trials from Microsoft or from third party software suppliers.

3. Links to various FrontPage information sites and Web presence providers.

4. Tips, tricks and expert advice, in the form of articles, papers or tutorials.

There are similar regular newsletters for other Microsoft products or for special interest groups such as developers.

...cont'd

This is an example of a Web site that has been selected as one of the show case sites for FrontPage. Use them to identify practices that you admire (or ones that you would prefer to avoid).

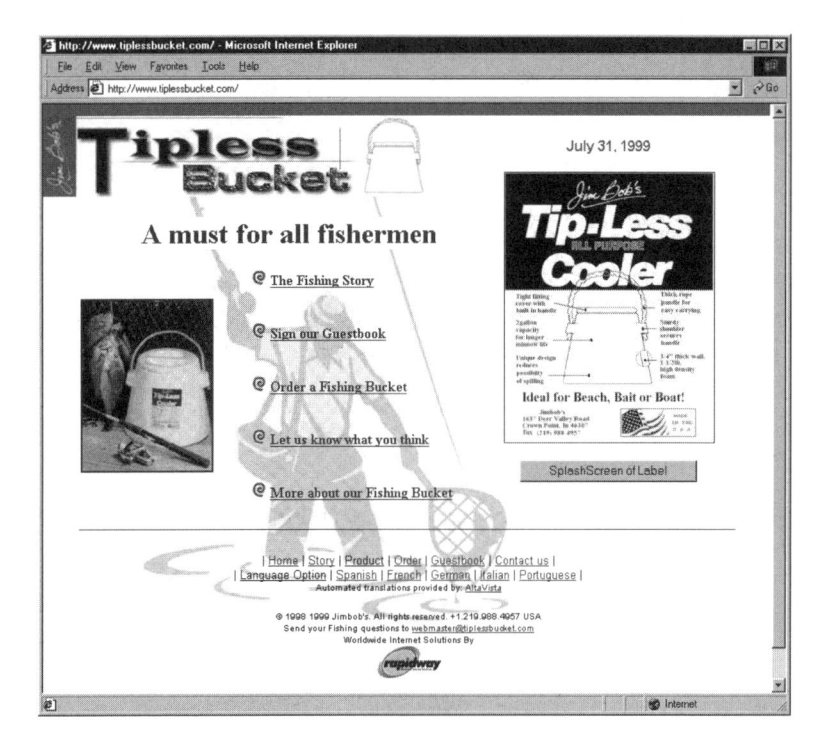

You can save parts of the example Web site to help you build or extend your own Web, though you should use hyperlinks rather than full copies to share another site with your visitors.

1. You won't be able to use FrontPage to Publish the Web site to your hard disk.

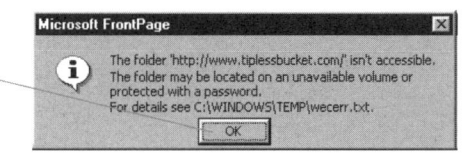

2. You can examine the HTML code in Notepad, if you select View, Source. You can File, Save the code to your hard disk.

3. Select File, Save As to save the Web page as an HTML document. This is particularly useful in IE5 (or higher) since it creates a subfolder with the image files.

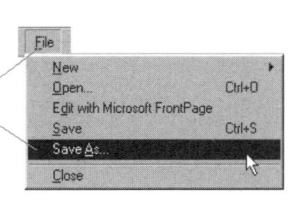

FrontPage Frenzy.

When you revisit this site, you should select Refresh or Reload in your browser, to make sure that you get the latest updates.

Among the many Web sites devoted to FrontPage there is one with the exotic title FrontPage Frenzy.

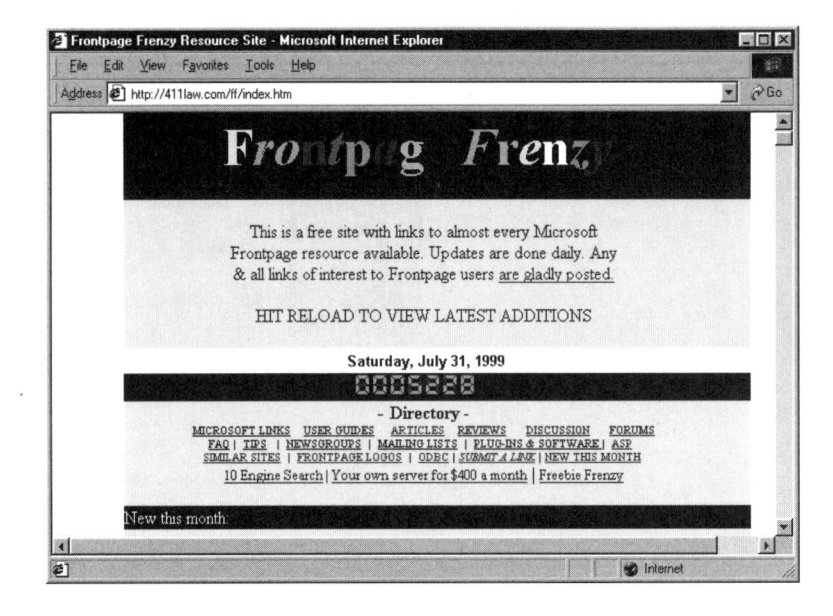

There are also other categories devoted to topics such as ASP and ODBC.

This is a free site which claims to have links to almost every Microsoft FrontPage resource available. Updates are done daily, and the site accepts suggestions to post other links of interest to FrontPage users. Categories include:

- Microsoft links.

- Online user guides.

- FrontPage articles and reviews.

- Discussion boards, newsgroups and forums.

- Frequently Asked Questions.

- Tips and how to's.

- Plug-Ins & other Software.

Design guides

When you view any design guides on the Internet, be sure to check the date created or last updated. You will find documents of all ages. The earlier guides are likely to be overtaken by the advances in Web or HTML features.

There are many Web sites that are provided to share information and experiences in designing Web sites. For example, Sun Microsystems have created a Guide to Web Style at http://wwweast2.sun.com/styleguide, that covers all the issues involved in making a site effective.

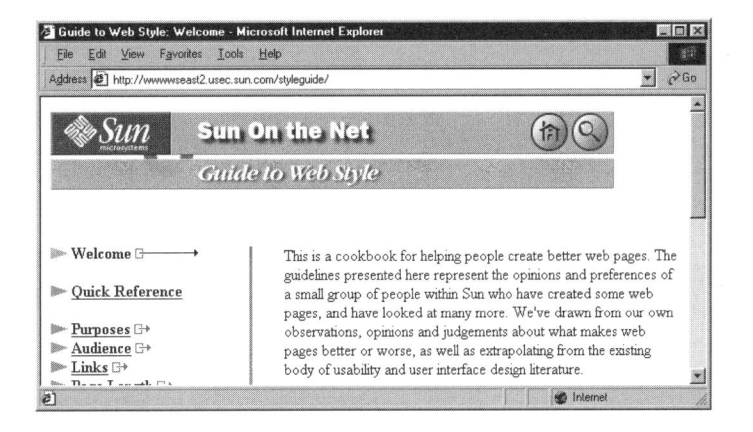

You'll find a comprehensive Web Style Guide from Yale University at http://info.med.yale.edu/caim/manual. You can also find advice on design elements, graphics and colour from (for example) the Web Design Group site at http://www.htmlhelp.com/design.

Other sites concentrate on the specifics of the HTML language, for example HTML Style House, with its collection of tutorials for all levels of experience.

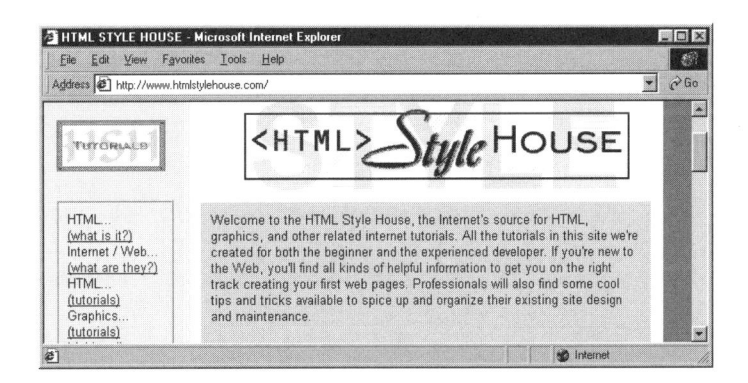

12. Sources of help | 183

VBA macros

HOT TIP — *With VBA Visual Basic for Applications you can create macros or programs to customise the FrontPage menus or toolbars.*

To add a new File menu command Save All:

1 Select Tools, Macro and Visual Basic Editor.

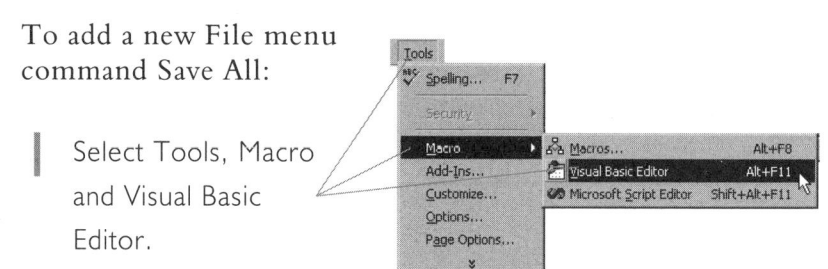

HOT TIP — *Save All will save all open pages in Page view, to capture all the outstanding edits and changes.*

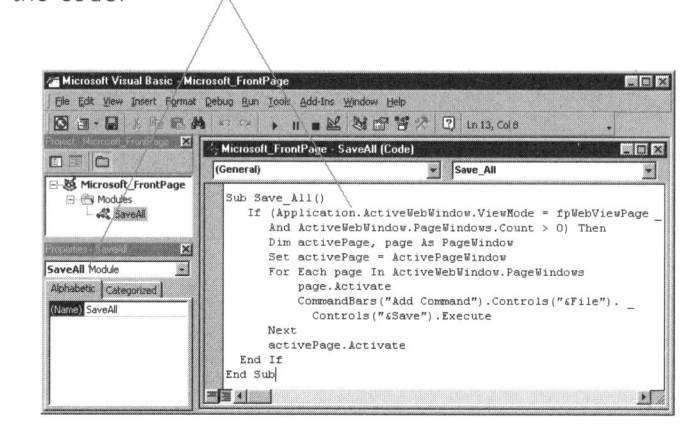

2 Select Insert, Module, enter the name SaveAll, and type in the code.

```
Sub Save_All()
    If (Application.ActiveWebWindow.ViewMode = fpWebViewPage _
        And ActiveWebWindow.PageWindows.Count > 0) Then
        Dim activePage, page As PageWindow
        Set activePage = ActivePageWindow
        For Each page In ActiveWebWindow.PageWindows
            page.Activate
            CommandBars("Add Command").Controls("&File"). _
                Controls("&Save").Execute
        Next
        activePage.Activate
    End If
End Sub
```

HOT TIP — *You can copy this code from the article entitled 'Extend FrontPage 2000 with Visual Basic for Applications' at:*

http://officeupdate. microsoft.com/2000/ articles/fpvba.htm

3 Do the following
- Name the macro SaveAll.
- Check for Page view with at least one page open.
- Save the name of the current active page.
- Loop through all open pages.
- File, Save each page.
- Restore the active page.

4 Select File, Close and Return to FrontPage 2000.

184 | FrontPage 2000 in easy steps

...cont'd

Hot tip: Add an entry to the File menu and assign the macro to it.

5 Select Tools, Customize, Commands and Category Macros.

6 Drag and drop the Custom Menu Item onto the File menu between Save and Save As commands.

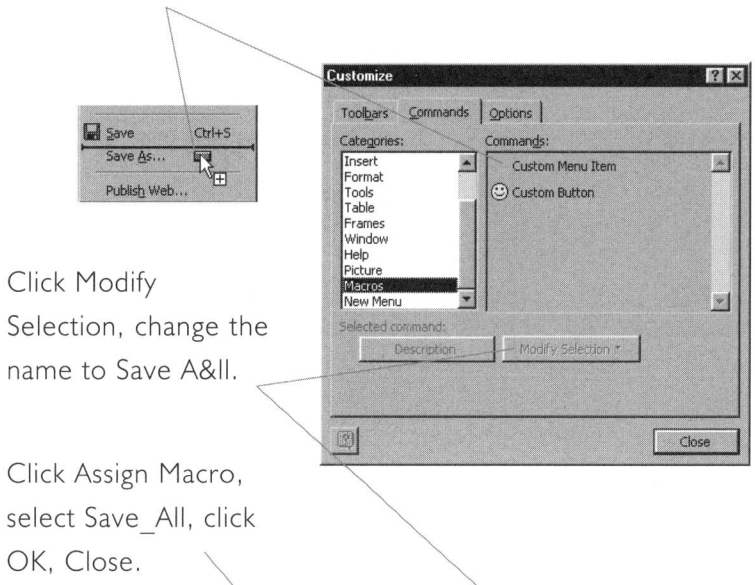

Hot tip: The ampersand makes Alt+L the keyboard shortcut for the Save All command.

7 Click Modify Selection, change the name to Save A&ll.

8 Click Assign Macro, select Save_All, click OK, Close.

Hot tip: You can drag the Custom Button onto the toolbar, and assign the macro to it, to create a Save All button.

The Save All command is added to the File menu.

When you next have several pages open, select the Save All command for a quick save.

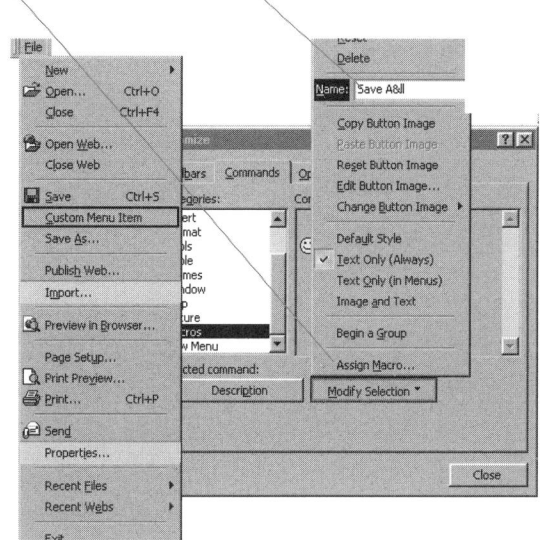

12. Sources of help | 185

Web Workshop

The MSDN site provides information at all levels, for the beginner and for the experienced professional developer.

The MSDN Online Web Workshop provides a vast amount of information about Internet technologies, with reference material and in-depth articles on all aspects of Web site design and development. You can select categories from the list on the left to view the site through content listings.

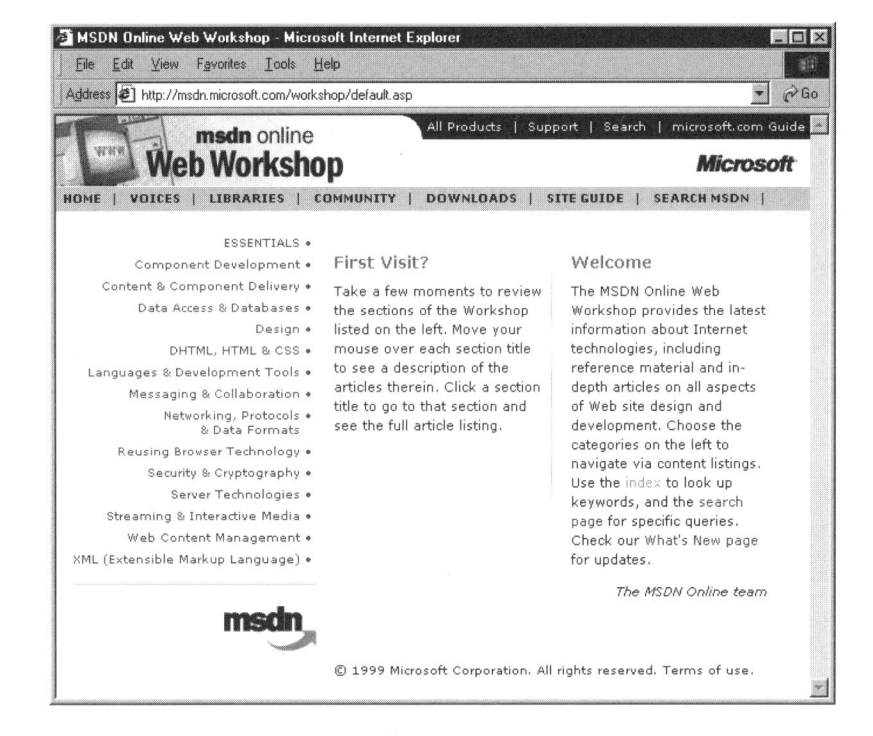

In Design, you find details of what constitutes good Web page design, with suggestions and tips from experienced designers.

1 Move the mouse over a section title to display a description of the articles contained there.

2 Click the section title to switch to that section and see the full article listing.

3 Use the index to look up keywords, and use the search page for specific queries.

186 | FrontPage 2000 in easy steps

Index

Add-ins
   El Scripto Lite   177
   J-Bots   178
   TagGen   177
Adverts   10, 95, 97–98
Alignment   34, 46
Animation   15, 36
   Animated picture   33
   Animation Shop   33
ASCII characters   29
AutoRun   21–22

Background sound   121
Backup   86
Bookmark   60, 158

Cable modem   15
Capacity   9
Cascading style sheets. *See* CSS
Clip gallery   46
Coding languages   17
Colour
   Transparent   127
   Web-friendly palette   126
Create Web page   19, 70
   Add Files   22, 44
   Add formatted text   42
   Arranging items   34
CSS   16

Design guides   19
   HTML Style House   183
   Sun Microsystems   183
   Web Design Group   183
   Yale University   183
DHTML. *See* Dynamic HTML
Digital camera   48
Digital images   48
Discussion group
   Conversation threads   171–172
   Format   169
   Maintaining   172
   Post messages   168
   Web   170
   Wizard   168, 170
Display timings   49
Domain name   12
Download times
   Estimated   24, 49
Dynamic HTML   16
   Effects   51

E-mail   8, 12
Embedded files   34, 50, 68
Exchanging mail   8
Expand menu   40

Feedback   94

Collate and interpret   72
Form   72
Submit   72
Visitor comments   72
File formats   41
File transfer program.   *See* FTP
Folder List   42, 45
Folders button   44
Folders view   20, 44, 46
   Arranging files and folders   68
   Create new folders   69
   Shared borders   69–70
   Sort by type   68
Font and text style   56
Format Painter   57
Formatting buttons   43
Formatting headings   56
Formatting toolbar   24, 43
Forms
   Feedback   95
   Form results   96, 124
   Registration   171
   Scrolling text box   73
   Text box   73
Frames
   Converting to   140
   Frames page   58, 138–139
   No frames   142
   Older browsers   141
   Table of Contents   139, 141
   Templates   138
FrontPage   13
   Bulletin   179–180
      Showcases sites   181
   Closing down   37
   Features   14, 16, 24
   Server extensions   93
   Tutorial   25
   Views   20
   Web site logo   31
FrontPage Frenzy   182
FrontPage Webs   18
FTP   19

Help   24, 173
   Local help   174
   Other sources   17
   Web help   175
Hit counter   10
   Number graphics   117
   Number of visits   116
   Reset the counter   117
Home page   8
   Example   10
Horizontal lines   120
Hotspots.   *See* Image maps
HTML   8, 41
   Code   13, 35, 97
   Display tags   35
   Edit   13, 17
   Graphical tags   35
   Heading styles   56
   Markup Language   51
Hyperlink view   20
Hyperlinks   32
   Active   53
   Automatic   53
   Broken   68, 88
   Create hyperlink   32, 54
   Create text hyperlink   52
   From favourites list   53
   From Web browser   54
   Hyperlink button   54
   Hyperlink text   53, 60
   Target   36, 52, 60
   Updating   69
   Validate   27, 54, 85
Hypertext markup language.   *See* HTML

Graphical image   31–32
Graphical themes.   *See* Themes
Guest book   10, 143
   Viewing   144

IE4.   *See* Web browsers
IE5.5.   *See* Web browsers
Image   8
Image maps
   Default hyperlink   165
   Hotspots

Shapes   166
Text   167
Import
  Files   44
  Import list   44–45
  Web   132
  Wizard   133
Insert a symbol   53
Insert plain text   40
Installing FrontPage   21
Internet
  Connection   8
  Image files   44
Internet Service Providers (ISP)   9, 11
  CIX   99
  Dial Pipex   12, 103
  EasyNet   99
  Freeserve   12, 103
  Hypermart   93–94, 97–98
  Tytek   98
Internet session   9
Intranet   18
Intranet site   13
ISDN   9

Bullets and numbers   43, 122
Bullets button   43
Collapsible lists   16, 123, 167

m

Markup language. *See* HTML
Menu bar   24
Message bar   24
Meta-variables   105, 116
  Meta-tags   108–109, 111
  System variables   108
  User variables   108
Microsoft
  Web sites   179
    Office Update   175, 179
    UK based   179
Modem   9
MSDN Online   186. *See also* Web Workshop

j

JavaScript   17

k

Keyboard shortcuts   43

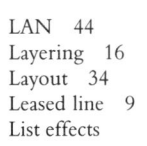

n

Navigation   9
Navigation bar   28, 55, 58
  Add new page   70
  Buttons   40
  New pages   63
  Preview in browser   63
  Qualifying pages   62
  Settings   62–63
Navigation mode   28
Navigation view   20, 28, 61
Network server   13
New Page   28
Normal paragraphs   41
Normal view   36

l

LAN   44
Layering   16
Layout   34
Leased line   9
List effects

o

Office 2000   13, 21

CD-ROM   22
   Editions   14
   Integration   16
Office Update
   Download Catalogue   175–176
   FrontPage 2000   175
Open last Web   38

Subwebs   153
Ways to publish   88
Web server   88

q

Qualifying product   14

r

p

Page display   24
Page element   16
Page properties   37
Page title   29, 37
Page view   20, 35–36, 40
   Tabs   24
Paint Shop Pro   33
Paragraph heading   56
Personalised menu   14
Photographs   48
Pictorial image   26
Picture button   32
Pictures toolbar   32, 50
Placeholder   28
Positioning   13
   Absolute and relative   16
   Images   48
   Pictures   47
   Pixel precise   16
   Relative   16
Potential audience   17
Preserve line ends   41
Preview   33, 46
Preview in Browser   51, 63, 74
   Set default   76
Printing
   From Web browser.   129
   HTML   128
   Navigation structure   129
   Print Preview   128, 129
Progress indicator   24
Protected Web   171
Publishing   8, 17, 19, 26, 45, 87, 92
   All pages   86, 100
   Backup   86
   Hyperlinks
      Broken   88
   Cancel part way through   86
   Changed pages   86, 100
   FrontPage Server Extensions   89
   FTP   88–89
   HTTP   88, 93–94

Ratings
   Apply the rating   114
   Filtering agents   114
   RSAC   113–114
   Voluntary, self-disclosure   113
Recent Webs   38
Recommendations   30
Register your site. *See* Web promotion
Rename   29
Repeat visits   30
Reports view   20, 84
Requirements   15
Reset the Format Painter   57
Reveal Tags   35
Rich Text Format   42

s

Save   34
   Button   37, 41, 46
Scanner   48
Screen
   Sizes and resolutions   47
Search sites
   AltaVista   105
   Directories   105
   Excite   106
   Forms   106–107
   Hybrids   105
   List of   112

Meta-variables   105
Snap   106–107
Useful links   112
Web robot   105
Yahoo   107
Self-repair   14
Server Extensions   17
Share documents   13
Shared borders
   Defaults   61
   Multiple pages   61
   Page banners   61
   Turning off a shared border   61
Simple list   43
Site Summary   84
Sketch   26
Snap-in tools   17
Source code   35
Specific paragraph   60
Spell checking   30
   Add term   81
   Background   80
   Change   81
   Completing task   82
   Entire Web site   80
   Ignore   81
   Special terms   81
Standard toolbar   24
Status   24
Style guides. *See* Design guides
Style of bullet   43
Subwebs   18
   Viewing   154–155

Tables   134
   Convert text to   163
   Creating tables   160
   Draw a table   162
   Toolbar   164
   Within tables   164
Target page   32
Tasks   17
   Assign task   81–83
   Change task name   81
   Create a reminder   85
   Create a task   82
   Perform tasks   81
   Priority   81
   Show task history   83
   Start task   81

Tasks view   20, 79
Temporary files   130
Themes   16, 43, 55
   Applying   41, 64, 67
   Background picture   65
   Bullets   64
   Buttons   64
   Colour   64
   Create new page   70
   Custom theme   66
   Customising   66
   Fonts   64
   Graphics   64
   Modify styles   66
   New name   67
   Override manual format   65
   Pictures   64
   Preview in browser   64
   Replace banner   67
   Replace graphics   66
Thumbnails   77
   AutoThumbnail   50
   Blue border   50
   Downloading images   50
   Images   48, 50
   versions   49
Time stamp
   Date last edited   119
   Refresh   119
   Time zone   118–119
Title bar   24
Toolbars
   Add or remove buttons   43
Tutorial   33
   Folder   25, 31, 40, 42, 66

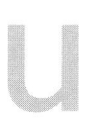

Undo button   59
Universal Resource Locator   8
Update the Web
   Modify text   78
   Save the changed files   79
Upgrade   14, 21
URL   8, 12
URL relative   45
URL shortcuts   53
Useful links   51

V

VBA
   Macros   184
      Save All button   185
      Save All command   184–185
Video   8, 15
View Bar   20
View, Hyperlinks   59
View page   74
View the Web   76
   Internet Explorer   76
   Netscape   76
   Other browsers   77
   Reload or Refresh   77
Viewing the page   35
Views bar   24, 40, 44
Virtual domain name   12
Visual Basic   17
Visual Basic for Applications. *See* VBA

W

Watermark   127
Web browsers   52, 54
   Add a new browser   75
   For Windows PCs   75
   Internet Explorer   9, 15–16, 36
   Netscape   9, 16
   Other platforms   75
Web design   25, 134
   Data for the Web   38
   Default page   30
   Define the requirements   19
   Frames   135
   Make and reverse changes   59
   Page size   146–147
      Default window size   147
      Scroll bars   146–147
   Positioning   135
   Shared borders   135
   Single page version   147
   Table structure   135
   Web structures   148
      Parent Web   148–149, 151

   Subwebs   148, 150–151
Web hosting   11
Web hosting service   92
Web management   13, 19
   Close page   24
   Close Web   38
   Delays   49
Web page   8
Web Presence Provider   11. *See also* Internet Service Providers
   Full function   99
   Supporting FrontPage 2000   92
   UK   92
   USA   92
   WPP button   92
Web programmers   35
Web promotion. *See also* Search sites
   Directory   102
   E-mail announcement   102, 104
   ISP or WPP   102–103
   Register your site   106
   Registration services   110
      Submit It   110–111
      WebPromote   110
   Search engines   102
   Search sites   105
Web reports
   Broken hyperlinks   85
   Default report   84
   Reset the default   84
   Site Summary   84
   Statistics   84
   Status and condition   84
Web server   8–9, 11, 18, 44
   Edit the Web   155–156
      Original copy   157
      Without server extensions   157
   Switching sites   158
Web site   7, 10–11, 18, 23, 26, 43
Web site address   12
Web site creation   13
Web site designers   35
Web site folders   46
Web site ratings. *See* Ratings
Web space   7, 10–11, 13
Web structure   28, 40, 70
   Home page   18, 29
Web template   27
Web Workshop   186
Welcome page   8
Which browser   75
Windows 2000   15
Windows Explorer   45, 68
Windows Installer   21
   First time of use   14, 22
Windows ME   15
Windows NT   15
Wrapping up images   46